*Produced in cooperation with
The Business Council of Alabama.*

Alabama

A STATE OF MIND

By *Wayne Greenhaw*
Special Introduction by *Dr. David Bronner*

Corporate profiles by Michael McKenzie and James D. Dunham

BlueCross BlueShield of Alabama

An Independent Licensee of the Blue Cross and Blue Shield Association.

Mercedes-Benz

The Business Council of Alabama and Community Communications, Inc.,
would like to express our gratitude to these companies for their leadership in the development of this book.

Photo by Robert Fouts.

• •

4

Alabama A STATE OF MIND

By Wayne Greenhaw
Special Introduction by Dr. David Bronner
Corporate profiles by Michael McKenzie and James D. Dunham
Featuring the photography of Pat McDonogh, Scott Wiseman, Robert Fouts, Paul Sumners,
Steve Goraum, Chip Cooper, Barry Fikes, and Elizabeth DeRamus
Contributing Writers: Mary Ann Neeley and Angela Mann

Produced in cooperation with The Business Council of Alabama

Ronald P. Beers, Publisher
Staff for *Alabama: A State of Mind*
Acquisitions: Henry S. Beers
Publisher's Sales Associates: Richard Tarrantino, Lori York, Bob Phillips and Marie Perdue
Managing Editors: Wendi L. Lewis and Angela C. Johnson
Profile Editors: Mary Catherine Richardson and Lenita Gilreath
Editorial Assistants: Heather Ann Edwards and Rebekah Monson
Design Director: Scott Phillips
Designer: Rebecca Hockman Carlisle
Photo Editors: Angela C. Johnson, Rebecca Hockman Carlisle and Wendi L. Lewis
Contract Manager: Christi Stevens
Sales Assistants: Annette Lozier and Sandra Akers
Acquisitions Coordinator: Angela P. White
Proofreaders: Angela Mann and Heather Ann Edwards
Accounting Services: Stephanie Perez
Print Production Manager: Jarrod Stiff
Pre-Press and Separations: Artcraft Graphic Productions

Community Communications, Inc.
Montgomery, Alabama

David M. Williamson, Chief Executive Officer
Ronald P. Beers, President
W. David Brown, Chief Operating Officer

Another truck leaves Mercedes-Benz U.S. International Inc., Alabama's largest exporter. In 1999, $300 million in parts and $700 million in vehicles were exported from the company's Vance plant, where some 350 Mercedes M-Class sports utility vehicles roll off the assembly line each day. Production and employment are expected to double by 2003 with the completion of the company's latest expansion. Photo by Chip Cooper.

Contents

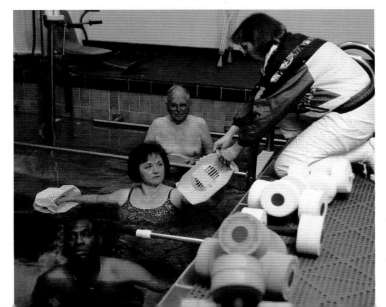

Foreword

FROM THE TENNESSEE VALLEY TO THE WHITE SANDY BEACHES OF THE GULF OF MEXICO AND EVERY-WHERE IN BETWEEN LIES THE MOST BEAUTIFUL LAND ON EARTH. GOD CREATED A SPECIAL PLACE, OUR HOME, ALABAMA.

We are blessed with vast stretches of wilderness from the Bankhead National Forest to the deepest gorge east of the Mississippi, located at Little River Canyon, and our unique Mobile Delta.

And from the state's highest peak, Cheaha Mountain, you can view majesty incomparable to that found anywhere else on earth. Our beautiful lakes and waterways, too, have given birth to rare and exotic wildlife and wildflowers.

The natural heritage, natural beauty, and natural wonders of Alabama are unparalleled among the 50 states, and it is with good reason that our state is known as "Alabama the Beautiful."

It is not nature alone, however, that forms the wonders of this state. It is the people who live here and call Alabama home.

This book celebrates the beauty and the fundamental strength of Alabama's unique combination of loyal, hardworking people and unparalleled natural beauty. The words and photographs contained in these pages will take you on a journey through our state's history, development, and growth, with insights into some of the keys to our future, including education, business, technology, tourism, and the arts. Readers also will be introduced to companies, organizations, entrepreneurs, and products that have helped Alabama stake its claim as a formidable force in the world of business.

Alabama is a unique place where the world's most advanced technological and industrial facilities share space with historic homes, buildings, and rich agricultural fields. From Alabama's emerging space, science, and technology sector to its growing automotive sector, to its agricultural base and early industries fundamental to the state's development, Alabama is a state on the move.

In today's fast-paced global market, Alabama has found a balance that allows us to compete successfully in a dynamic business environment while maintaining the charm and natural beauty of our great state. It is an interesting combination that lures more and more newcomers to Alabama every year.

Alabamians are proud of their history and even more excited about their future. In its natural beauty and cultural delights, its abundance of recreational attractions and nationally renowned educational institutions, Alabama provides a quality of life that is second to none.

Our roots reach deep into a rich soil, reminding us that our successful path to the future will be grounded always in a past secure in tradition and strong Alabama values. Exploring Alabama's history and the incredible strength of her people, one will understand why we say with confidence that Alabama has turned the corner and is headed in the right direction.

As Alabamians reach with confidence toward the promise of an exciting future, it is clear that "Alabama the Beautiful" is a state of being, as well as a state of mind.

With best regards, I am…

Sincerely,

Don Siegelman

Don Siegelman
Governor

This state has long been known as "Alabama the Beautiful." From the sugary beaches of the Gulf of Mexico to the vibrant canvases of the rural mountain roads, and whether natural scenery formed from the earth or colorful gardens shaped by people, the splendor of Alabama is spectacular.
Photos by Robert Fouts.

Alabama
A STATE OF MIND

Part I

The Gulf Coast region of the state is known for its white, sandy beaches. These beautiful beaches are a common vacation spot for natives and tourists alike. Photo courtesy of Alabama Bureau of Tourism and Travel/Karim Shamsi Basha.

Operations at the General Electric plastics plant in rural Lowndes County take place on only 350 of the almost 6,500 acres owned by GE. The rest of the property is covered with trees, streams and native wildlife and has been certified as a National Wildlife Habitat by the National Wildlife Habitat Council. The habitat is maintained by volunteers among the Burkville plant's more than 400 employees. Photo by Robert Fouts.

CHAPTER 1

Leadership

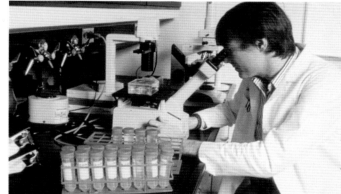

The UAB Health System is the heart of health care in Alabama. It is an innovative network of services that provides a complete continuum of care for patients from all over the world. The UAB Health System is internationally renowned for its expert physicians and groundbreaking medical research; but, more importantly, it stands out for its strong commitment to compassionate, personal care for every patient. Photo courtesy of UAB Photography and Instructional Graphics.

The International Space Station, or ISS, represents a global partnership of sixteen nations. This project is an engineering, scientific, and technological marvel ushering in a new era of human space exploration. The million-pound space station includes six laboratories and provides more space for research than any spacecraft ever built. Internal volume of the space station is roughly equal to the passenger cabin volume of a 747 jumbo jet. Alabama's Boeing Company played a key role in the construction of the space station. Photo by Paul Sumners.

SWEET HOME ALABAMA

by David G. Bronner, J.D, Ph.D.

WHEN THE RADIO BREAKS FORTH WITH THE FAMILIAR BARS OF LYNARD SKY-NARD'S "SWEET HOME ALABAMA," THE HEARTS OF MOST ALABAMIANS SWELL WITH PRIDE FOR THEIR HOME STATE. Although I was born in Iowa, and spent my youth in Minnesota, that song always brings to mind a reminiscence of my bygone youthful, carefree days spent in Alabama universities.

The aura of Alabama, however, is something much more—a distinct past incorporated into a future exploding with possibility and opportunity. It is this vibrant mix of past, present, and future that enables all her current, visionary individuals and corporations to sense, feel, and be a part of an exciting "history in the making" for decades to come.

The Past

Alabama has provided historians with a fertile field of knowledge for research. History teaches us that the early Georgian settlers homesteaded in the southern half of Alabama, while the early settlers from North Carolina mainly chose the northern half of the state for their new home. These hard-working, fiercely independent, agricultural families toiled from dusk to dawn seeking to support their families, while building a close family life squarely centered on God and their chosen religion.

Civil War, Civil Rights, and State's Rights have been issues that have dominated and, in far too many instances, held back a state that otherwise held the promise of unlimited potential. Politicians have all too often focused on maintaining the status quo, or a remote national issue, and simply forgotten about the basic essentials of attacking socio-economic issues that would improve the quality of life for their fellow citizens.

Some early leaders had the foresight to envision Alabama's unlimited potential—individuals like George Washington Carver, and his associate Booker T. Washington, with their keen interests in agriculture, education, and the dignity of labor and moral values. Add to that the intellectual fortitude and courage of a remarkable woman named Helen Keller, a Cum Laude graduate of Radcliffe College, despite being blind and deaf, and for years unable to speak. Looking at the lives of such people, it's easy to see that Alabama was awakening to an unfailing enthusiasm for life that made spectacular achievement against formidable odds possible for all Alabamians.

Dr. David Bronner, presently Chief Executive Officer of The Retirement Systems of Alabama, holds two degrees from the University of Alabama. Dr. Bronner has taught at various colleges and universities, and he has been featured in numerous business publications praising his investment strategies and market decisions. Photo by Robertson Photography, Inc.

The Present

The vigor and pride displayed in Alabama today has its roots in World War II, from a most unlikely source—German scientist Dr. Wernher von Braun. He and one hundred of his colleagues arrived and settled in a cotton field in North Alabama shortly after the war, at a site that was to become the home of the Marshall Space Flight Center and the Huntsville Space and Rocket Center. As director of the National Aeronautics and Space Administration (NASA), von Braun was named America's Man of the Year in 1958. Dr. von Braun brought to Alabama pride, expertise, and a level of achievement in the then-infant field of space exploration that many in America, much less Alabama, had never dreamed possible.

Shortly thereafter, a group of university and medical professors decided that if Alabama and the South were to prosper, a new medical university would have to lead the way. Together, they established the University of Alabama Birmingham (UAB) campus, which has grown to become Birmingham's largest employer and one of the top medical schools in America, as well as one of the great research hospitals in the world.

"World Class" was not a description usually associated with Alabama, certainly prior to the 1980s. However, excellence burst forth throughout Alabama in the '80s and '90s. One of the leaders in this movement was Montgomery businessman and philanthropist Winton "Red" Blount, who drew accolades from around the world with his creation of the Alabama Shakespeare Festival, located in the Wynton Blount Cultural Park in Montgomery. The Festival not only continues to prosper as an artistic beacon in the South, but the park itself boasts a world class museum and more than 100 acres currently under expansion to 300 acres.

The Retirement Systems of Alabama was a key contributor to downtown revitalization in Montgomery with several construction and development projects, including the RSA Tower, Alabama Activities Center, and others, with combined projects totaling an estimated $125 million. Photo by Robert Fouts.

Elsewhere in the state, Birmingham's McWane Center and the Mobile Emporium were established as centers of hands-on educational opportunities, intriguing the minds of young and old. Huntsville's Space and Rocket Center, too, is a learning adventure for all ages, and a "must-see" item included on the curriculum of fifth-graders and their teachers from throughout the country as they learn about man's journey into space.

But perhaps the state's biggest boom in the tourism industry—as well as providing a physical makeover - was sparked with the creation of the Robert Trent Jones Golf Trail in the late 1990s. Not only was it the largest golf course construction project in history, it generated what no other state was able to do on such a large scale—continuing waves of positive publicity for a state too long ignored by those passing out compliments. The axiom in journalism is that "bad news travels and good news stays at home." Clearly, no state in America's great history embarked on such a massive adventure and challenge in such a short time. Literally within five years, nearly five thousand positive articles about Alabama were being floated among the world press. From Singapore to Germany, and from small town newspapers and magazines, to such influential journalistic giants as *The Boston Globe, The Wall Street Journal, The Washington Post*, and *The New York Times*, articles were extolling the virtues of Alabama. Publications which had before been eager to point out Alabama's blemishes, now encouraged readers to experience the beauties and challenges of the state.

On the business side of the coin, great companies including Mercedes-Benz, Trico Steel, The Boeing Company, Briggs & Stratton, Ispco Steel, Navistar, Honda, and many others have begun to enjoy the "Alabama Experience." Community Newspaper Holdings, Inc., the nation's largest newspaper company in number of newspapers owned, has located in Birmingham. Raycom Media, the nation's fastest growing television group that reaches more than 11 percent of America's population, has located in Montgomery.

Alabama is clearly coming alive as the place to be to witness progress and growth. You need to be a part of Alabama, or risk losing the opportunity of a lifetime.

The Future

Alabama has certainly had its problems, as all states have. Very often I tell members of many leadership groups in Alabama that "Failure is not a crime. Aiming low is!" Alabama is on a roll and will eventually grow to lead the South in many areas as the new millennium begins.

Racism, once a cliched reality of the South, has been essentially replaced with a new and brighter way of life and a sense of growth and partnership. One can never completely destroy racism nor other forms of persecution, but the realization that certain people make a living keeping hate and fear alive is motivation for the rest of us to walk the walk and not merely talk the talk. Other than the normal one or two percent in society who live in ignorance and fear, Alabamians know that working together is what will significantly improve the lives of Alabamians and their children.

As is true with most states, problems and challenges still exist. In Alabama, we face a battle to improve education. Many Alabamians have rightfully concluded that they and their children must get involved in this fight, speaking out and lending their hands to improve education, making it possible for everyone to reach their potential for prosperity. We have a commitment from our governor and legislature to work for and support a stronger educational system for the future, and the promise of a new day for Alabama seems more possible than ever before. Likewise, the business community has united behind the cause of education, donating their time and money to special partnerships with schools in an effort to ensure a successful "work force of tomorrow."

The fundamental changes that took place in the 1990s will forever create an environment that will make Alabama a leader for business, intellectual, and capital expansion into the twenty-first century. Indeed, the intellectual capital of Alabama will be its greatest resource. Alabama's work force, and her business leaders, are the players in the future of the South.

There are numerous reasons why some of the most outstanding companies in the world's economy have chosen Alabama for their business home. Consider these reasons, discover your own, and you too will learn why a young man from Minnesota chooses to grow old in Alabama.

Alabama's people, its potential, and its natural beauty are unlimited to those who want to work for their success. We welcome old and new friends to come help us make this state a "Sweet Home Alabama" for people of all ages and backgrounds. ▪

Alabama proudly honors its place in the civil rights movement in museums, trails and other historic tourist attractions throughout the state. The Civil Rights Institute in Birmingham's Civil Rights District takes visitors on a journey through the trials, struggles, and triumphs of blacks in our state through modern day. Photo courtesy of Alabama Bureau of Tourism and Travel/Karim Shamsi Basha.

Alabama Farmers Federation and Alfa Insurance Companies

As president of the Alabama Farmers Federation and Alfa Insurance Companies, Jerry Newby relies on the same honesty, faith, and intense work ethic that made his family's Limestone County cotton farm one of the most successful in Alabama.

"God has blessed this organization with a loyal membership, dedicated employees, and wise leaders. Alfa is poised to provide its members and policyholders with a wider variety of financial security products and services while maintaining its commitment to improving the standard of living for all Alabamians," Newby said.

Since being elected president, Newby has focused on ways to help the farmer survive financially. He has been involved in intense and frequent meetings with government leaders to find ways to help farmers better manage risk, expand markets, and improve the prices they receive for their products. As president of the insurance company, he aims to cut costs, increase production, and provide the greatest return on investment for stockholders and policyholders. ▇

Birmingham-based Meadowcraft Inc. is the largest manufacturer of wrought iron furniture in the United States and a leading domestic producer of casual outdoor furniture. Here a welder fashions one of Meadowcraft's designs from heavy gauges of the highest quality U.S. manufactured hot rolled carbon steel solids. Photo by Paul Sumners.

Auburn University

Chartered in 1856, Auburn University's doors first opened in 1859 for 80 students. Today that number has risen to almost 22,000 students in attendance. *U.S. News and World Report* ranked AU 38th overall among the nation's top 50 public universities in its annual rankings for 1999-2000.

Auburn University has been widely acknowledged for its incredible success in many fields, including engineering, agriculture, veterinary medicine, and architecture. Likewise, the University's Fisheries Department has been recognized worldwide for its teaching, research, and extension programs.

Demonstrating that it has its sights set clearly on the future, Auburn University has earned its reputation as one of Alabama's most valuable institutions. ▪

Alabama isn't just about football anymore. Soccer is just one sport that has become increasingly popular in recent years. The Alabama Youth Soccer Association claims about 18,000 youth soccer players in Alabama, and offers soccer programs from the recreational level up to the elite player. Alabama has the highest growth rate of soccer in the United States, marking an increase of 122 percent in 1999. Seventy-five percent of that growth has come from female players. Photo by Paul Sumners.

Alabama boasts one of the nation's top producers of playground equipment for schools and public parks—GameTime Inc. in Fort Payne. The 70-year-old company has annual sales approaching $100 million. Its equipment can be found on playgrounds from New York City to Laguna Beach, Calif., as well as at schools and parks throughout Alabama. Photo by Paul Sumners.

Blue Cross and Blue Shield of Alabama

I n business over 63 years, Blue Cross and Blue Shield of Alabama now provides health coverage to more than 2.8 million people. The company's Preferred Care network is one of the largest and most successful PPOs in the nation.

Blue Cross utilizes the latest in computer technology to reduce costs and improve the quality of care for its customers. The company's medical information network, InfoSolutions, allows health care providers to share information and provide patients more effective care.

Known as "The Caring Company," Blue Cross has maintained a strong tradition of supporting efforts that promote the health and safety of Alabamians. Through unrivaled expertise and cutting edge technology, this company's goal is to treat each customer with the sense of urgency and compassion they deserve. ■

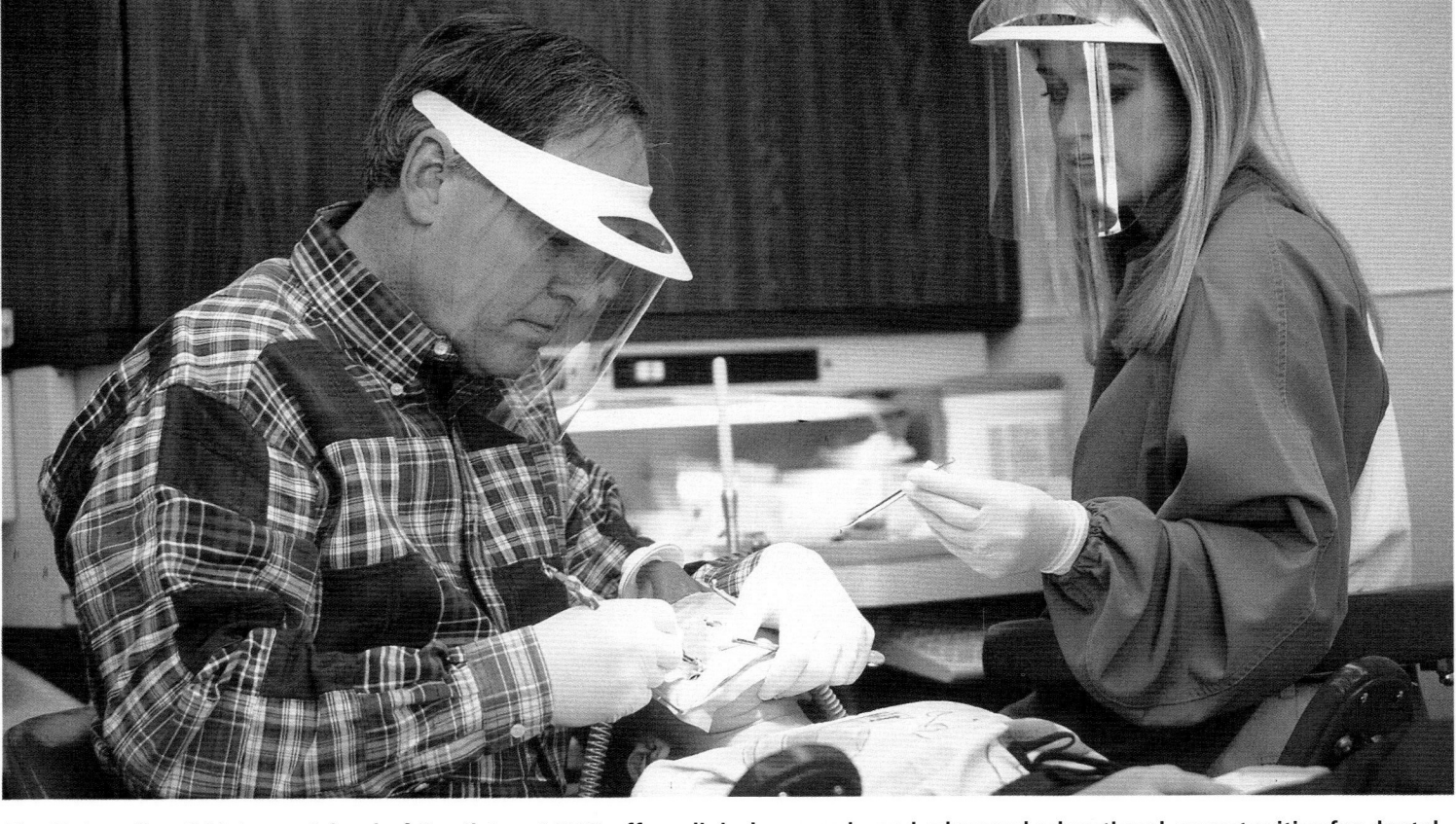

The University of Alabama School of Dentistry at UAB offers clinical, research, and advanced educational opportunities for dental professionals. Clinical training in specialties including endodontics, pediatric dentistry, periodontics, prosthetic dentistry, general dentistry, and orthodontics is available as part of the Dentist Scientist Program at UAB, with the clinical program individually tailored to meet the goals of the fellow's educational program. The Dentist Scientist Program at UAB is intended for the highly committed and qualified applicant who plans a career as a Dentist Scientist. In order to achieve this goal, advanced clinical training in a dental specialty and training in a basic science at the level of the Ph.D. are fully integrated so that the candidate will mature in each of the areas at a similar rate. Photo by Pat McDonogh.

Corus Tuscaloosa

Corus Tuscaloosa has carved a niche in the steel industry as a world-class producer of high quality hot rolled carbon coil, coil plate, and plate. Corus Tuscaloosa's annual capacity is 800,000 tons of carbon and high-strength low alloy coil and plate. A motivated, team-oriented work force steeped in tradition and ethics produces these products in a wide range of dimensions.

Built in 1985, the mill has consistently demonstrated product versatility, quality, and cost advantages readily translated to customer benefits and products that meet or exceed all AISI, ASTM, and ASME code specifications, customer specifications, and international requirements.

Corus Tuscaloosa's goal is to exceed customer expectations of quality and service by providing a cost-effective product produced and shipped on a timely basis. The company's efficient material handling facilities and accessible interstate, rail, and highway systems ensure on-time deliveries to customers.

Committed to being a welcomed, responsible neighbor to the Tuscaloosa community, Corus Tuscaloosa will continue to grow along with the city it depends on in the new millennium. ▪

Long Lewis, Inc.

From humble beginnings in the changing times following the Civil War, this company has traveled an amazing road. A background firmly rooted in hard work, ingenuity, and a willingness to accept new, and often feared, progress has proven to be the successful motivation which ensured the longevity of this company. To this day, these inherited traits enable Long Lewis, Inc. to remain a stable and profitable member of the Birmingham area community.

Long Lewis, Inc. has been a vital part of Alabama's economy for over a century, supplying the demands of retail and wholesale hardware customers and putting people behind the wheels of America's best automobiles. Long Lewis Ford is the largest volume Ford dealership in Alabama and the fourth largest in Ford's southeastern region. The company is still guided by the families that brought it to life and nurtured its growth, and it looks like their history of success won't change anytime soon. ▨

The latest technical equipment is used in modern printing and publishing, with products ranging from the manufacture of custom labels, tags, and bar codes to services such as graphic design, offset printing, and binding. Newspapers, magazines, books, and specialty publications are created using computer-aided technology, digital imaging, and other state-of-the-art techniques resulting in high-quality products that meet a wide range of consumer demands within the state and throughout the country. Photo by Pat McDonogh.

Mercedes-Benz U.S. International Inc.

T he goal for Mercedes-Benz U.S. International Inc. (MBUSI) was to create an evolution of the sport utility, a true off-roader, but with the passenger car attributes of a Mercedes-Benz, namely safety, performance, quality, and comfort—and priced in the mid-$30,000 range. Tuscaloosa was chosen as the home for the new Mercedes plant from an initial list of different areas all over the U.S. Tuscaloosa County represented the best combination of the criteria that Mercedes was looking for.

Since locating in Tuscaloosa County, MBUSI has worked diligently to create an American company that reflects the wealth of talent and diversity that exists within the U.S. and, more specifically, within the State of Alabama. In doing so, the company committed to responsible corporate citizenship and has tried to exercise this commitment in both its employment and business practices.

With skillful teamwork, state-of-the-art technology, and a commitment to be the best, Mercedes-Benz will continue to create its world-class product—made by Mercedes and the hands of Alabamians.

Family life is an integral part of southern heritage. With vision for a great future, city, county and state leaders make children a top priority by working together to improve education, the environment, and other qualities of life for their future. Photo by Elizabeth DeRamus.

Nature can be preserved in many ways, and one of those has become extremely popular with tourists. Gardens throughout the state such as Bellingrath Gardens, Jasmine Hill Gardens, and Shakespeare Gardens, have created havens of different varieties of plants and flowers for people to enjoy all year long. Photo courtesy of Alabama Bureau of Tourism and Travel/Karim Shamsi Basha.

Natural Decorations, Inc.

N atural Decorations, Inc. of Brewton, Alabama, has been helping people across the nation to bring the beauty of the outdoors into their homes for more than 35 years. Every NDI design is handcrafted by a dedicated staff, with the highest quality fabric foliages and flowers, made from a broad variety of materials.

NDI is well known for its exclusive use of natural flower forms and colors, as well as its award-winning collection of permanent florals and home fragrances marketed around the world. Realism is something of paramount importance to Joe and Carol Gordy, and it shows. Natural Decorations, Inc. has expanded tremendously during the past 10 years. Floral arrangements created at NDI have appeared on television soap operas, the Country Music Awards, and a number of home decorating magazines. As long as nature provides flora and fauna to inspire, Natural Decorations, Inc. will continue to share nature's beauty with customers around the world. ▣

Noland Health Services

D r. Lloyd Noland's vision was the establishment of a medical system which addressed the health needs of the communities it served. Today, Noland Health Services continues this ambitious legacy.

Noland Health Services sponsors various programs that focus on the improvement of services to meet the needs of elderly and other unique patient populations. One of these programs is The Oaks on Parkwood, a $50-million, 100-acre comprehensive retirement community. Other services include long-term acute care hospitals for patients who require extended or specialty-focused hospital care and The Noland Center at Carraway, a sub-acute program that provides care for patients who are medically ready to move out of traditional inpatient care but not yet ready to return home.

Continuing the dream that began in 1917, Noland Health Services is dedicated to providing high-quality health and educational services in a compassionate, efficient, and cost-effective manner. ■

Alabama is home to at least 25 daily and 97 non-daily newspapers. Alabama also serves as headquarters for Community Newspaper Holdings Inc., one of the nation's largest newspaper ownership groups. The company owns more than 200 daily and paid circulation weeklies or semiweeklies in 22 states with a combined circulation of more than one million. Photo by Scott Wiseman.

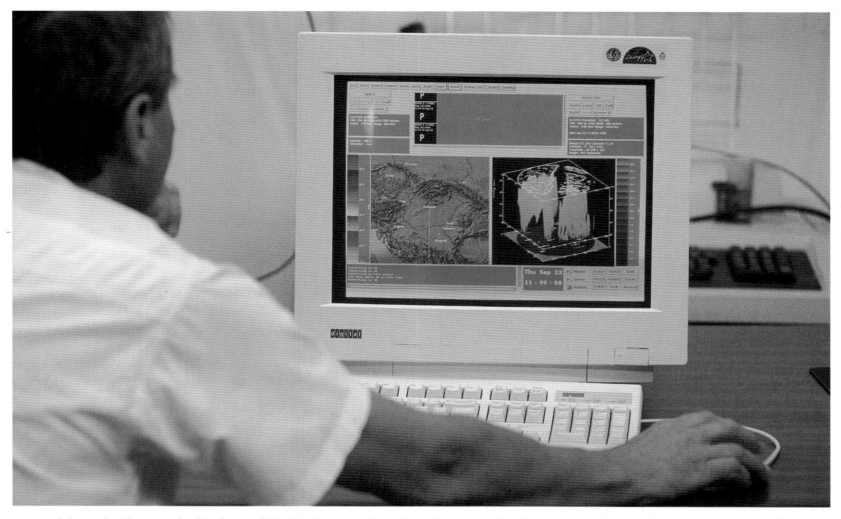

Alabama has been at the forefront of developing technology that allows weather forecasters to foresee changing weather conditions as soon as they develop. Enterprise Electronics Corp., based in Enterprise, Alabama, has held more than 80 percent of the world weather radar market for nearly a quarter century. The company developed the first commercially available Doppler radar and continues as the single source for the high performance radar system. Photo by Scott Wiseman.

Saks Incorporated

Quite successful, Saks Incorporated operates over 350 stores, with nearly 60,000 associates.

Customers count on the stores of Saks Incorporated for early indications of fashion trends as well as exceptional quality, attractive pricing, and the legendary service on which its reputation is built. Unlike other large retailing organizations, the key to the success of Saks' strategy is the careful handling and preservation of the valuable brand identities of the companies acquired.

A values driven company, Saks Incorporated is founded on four cornerstones of style, quality, service, and integrity. The growth prospects of its future are proving to be highly valued by investors, customers, employees, and the communities it serves. ▪

Forestry is Alabama's largest industry. From cutting timber to hauling trees to producing lumber, the industry directly employs some 70,000 people. Every county in Alabama has at least one forestry operation, from saw mills to veneer plants. Photo by Scott Wiseman.

Touchstone Energy®

• •

Touchstone Energy® cooperatives, including the Alabama Electric Cooperative and its member-owners, continuously seek ways to reduce costs as well as improve efficiency while providing for the high energy demands of their customers. Investing in increased application technologies to improve and preserve our natural resources and state-of-the-art operational systems has helped place Touchstone Energy® cooperatives and systems in the forefront of the utility industry.

Touchstone Energy® cooperatives and systems realize that success in the future lies in four basic values—integrity, accountability, innovation, and community spirit. ▪

The University of Alabama

W hat are the hallmarks of The University of Alabama? Students who excel, professors who increase the knowledge in their fields, outreach that transforms theory into practice, and the robust tradition of Crimson Tide sports. Alabama's business and law schools are ranked among the top 50 in the nation, including a number four ranking for UA's technology-based M.B.A. program. Numerous programs in UA's Colleges of Communication, Arts and Sciences, Engineering, and Social Work are also ranked among the nation's elite.

Community building and economic development are vital components of the relationship between The University of Alabama and the people she serves. Faculty researchers and students collaborate through 16 research centers, including the Center for Green Manufacturing, the Center for Freshwater Studies, the Center for Advanced Vehicle Technologies, and the UA System's University Transportation Center, working to improve the lives of Alabamians, on the job and in their communities. The University of Alabama is touching lives and making a difference, around the world and right next door. ■

Alabama's television markets have been growing steadily since the early 1950s until television became the leading media business in the year 2000. Many broadcasters who started their careers on Alabama television stations have gone on to earn national broadcasting visibility. Photos by Scott Wiseman.

Ample, adequate airports and airline accessibility are assets of which Alabama is most proud. Birmingham's airport reported a record 1.5 million passengers in the first six months of 2000, and Huntsville's airport recorded its third straight million-plus-passenger year in 1999. Airports in the state transport passengers, ship air freight, and provide runways and hangers for private planes and military aircraft. Photo by Scott Wiseman.

The University of Alabama in Huntsville

T he students and faculty of The University of Alabama in Huntsville help to define the future of our world by taking the strengths of its world-class research programs and bringing them into the classroom. Major research fields include propulsion, space physics and astrophysics, information technology, and biotechnology. In 1999, UAH received more than $44 million in revenues for active research projects.

The university also supports more than 100 clubs and organizations, as well as being home to 12 NCAA men's and women's sports programs. In both education and recreation, UAH encourages the development of opportunities for both students and the high-technology community that surrounds it. ■

Not even the sky is the limit in Alabama. Alabamians are reaching beyond the galaxy every day at the Marshall Flight Center and Space and Rocket Center in Huntsville. Photo by Robert Fouts.

Farmers would meet with cotton merchants at Court Square hoping for good offers for their crop before transporting the cotton to the river for shipping by steamboats including the *Alabama*. From the 1820s until the early twentieth century, these steamboats plied the Alabama River, carrying the cotton to Mobile for shipment to northern and European mills.

Cotton is synonymous with Alabama history. In the early days, plantations depended upon slaves to handpick the cotton and steamboats to transport the cotton. Then with the abolition of slavery and the progress of machinery, a new era in the cotton industry was born. Photos courtesy of Fouts Commercial Photography.

CHAPTER 2

Early Endeavors

Cotton is still an important part of Alabama's agricultural industry as well as a link to its past. Photo by Scott Wiseman.

Although the days of Southern Belles have long past, cities strive to preserve southern heritage through the restoration and maintenance of antebellum homes like Bragg Mitchell in Mobile. Photo by Steve Goraum.

FROM COTTON MILLS TO THE MOON

A History of Business in Alabama

by Wayne Greenhaw

WHEN MY GRANDFATHER, HIRAM D. ABLE, A FIRST-GENERATION IRISH-AMERICAN, RODE HIS BICYCLE BEHIND THE WAGON DRIVEN BY HIS FATHER FROM AIKEN, SOUTH CAROLINA, TO THE PINEY WOODS BETWEEN OPP AND FLORALA IN SOUTH ALABAMA, THE FAMILY WAS SEEKING OPPORTUNITIES IN A NEW COUNTRY. With the same pioneer spirit that motivated my great-grandparents to sail to the United States from Ireland, they moved south to Alabama. They settled among the virgin timber of the woodlands and started a turpentine mill to fuel the new-fangled machines of the Industrial Age that were being produced in the steel mills of Birmingham. Later, when Granddaddy grew up, he became a carpenter who specialized in building coffer-dams for utility companies constructing dams to harness hydropower and make electricity. And when he finally went to work for the Tennessee Valley Authority to help build Wheeler Dam on the Tennessee River, my mother met my father in nearby Town Creek. So, in the span of less than fifty years, my family connected from south Alabama to the northern border, and in the fifty years before and the fifty years since, Alabama's industrial growth leaped from a simple agricultural economy to a complex super-mega-computer-age society.

From the first construction of mills along the rivers and streams to turn corn into meal, cotton into cloth, timber into lumber, and agricultural products into usable consumer goods, Alabama has since become the home of efficient high-tech industry. From the days when cotton was picked by hand in the Black Belt and shipped by steamboat down the state's navigable waterways to the port of Mobile, Alabama has matured appropriately to accommodate its vigorous growth, expanding its horizons as well as its capabilities. ▪

The Saturn V rocket booster, a major contributor in America's journey to the moon, was built in Alabama by The Boeing Company. At the U.S. Space & Rocket Center in Huntsville, visitors can view this 363-foot rocket booster up close. Boeing is now building the Delta IV series of rockets at its Decatur plant. Photo courtesy of Alabama Bureau of Tourism and Travel/Karim Shamsi-Basha.

The impact of the early cotton industry cannot be forgotten as entire cities were founded because of it. Daniel Pratt relocated to central Alabama from Georgia in order to expand the cotton gin manufacturing operation he owned with partner Samuel Griswold. The two thousand acres he purchased in 1835 would become downtown Prattville, while the cotton gin he built still stands. Photo by Robert Fouts.

I N THE EARLY 1700S, THE FRENCH BECAME THE FIRST SETTLERS IN THE TERRITORY IN AND AROUND MOBILE. The French wanted to protect this new and valued land. French officials in Mobile sent soldiers as far north as Fort Toulouse at the confluence of the Coosa and Tallapoosa rivers to guard the northern border. Here, a wedge-shaped piece of high ground was visited by French traveler-and-writer Alexis de Tocqueville, who later predicted in his writings that this land, near where the town of Wetumpka was later founded, would become one of the two great industrial centers in America. The other location was on the southwestern shore of Lake Michigan where Chicago is now located.

In north Alabama, John Hunt made his home in the early Nineteenth Century near Big Spring, where clear water flowed from the hillside to feed streams that were used to transport goods from the rich farms of the Tennessee River Valley to the mills at the town of Huntsville — which soon became a financial center the same way Mobile prospered in its early years. Huntsville became Alabama's gateway to the population centers of the eastern seaboard.

In 1818, French Bonapartists colonized Demopolis on the Black Warrior River to build vineyards, cultivate grapes and make wines and to plant olive trees for oil. The same year, the first steamboat, the *Alabama*, was constructed at St. Stephens, the capital of the territory on the Tombigbee River. However, the *Alabama's* engines were not strong enough to push the boat against the river's currents, and more powerful steamboats were brought to the area. By the following year, steamboats appeared with regularity on the rivers as transportation for people and commerce.

The longest waterway system in the state was the Alabama River and its tributaries. After the Coosa and Tallapoosa joined eleven miles south of Wetumpka to form the Alabama, which flowed through the rich Black Belt farmland, it was joined by the Tombigbee to form the Mobile River forty-four miles north of the city on the bay. In its natural state, the low-water depths of the entire system varied from three to fifteen feet, making it navigable for light-draft boats most of the year. As such, the region soon caught the eye of entrepreneurs and speculators seeking a perfect home for commerce and industry. ■

Covered bridges were links between rural areas years ago when there were few roads that provided safe passage over creeks and streams. Travelers on horseback could easily maneuver the shallow waters, but wagons and buggies could not. Today, these wooden bridges are unique links to the past. Visitors can take tours and experience a time in history when these bridges were used not only for travel, but also for community events such as weddings and baptisms. Pictured is the Clarkson Covered Bridge in Cullman County.
Photo courtesy of Alabama Bureau of Tourism and Travel/Karim Shamsi Basha.

When the French settled in Alabama in the 1700s, they constructed forts to defend themselves from natives and others who would try to take the land from them. From Fort Gaines on Mobile Bay (pictured above) to Fort Toulouse outside of Wetumpka, the French fought for their established territory. Today these forts, which have been preserved and restored, offer tourists a true-to-life image of that period in history by presenting reenactments of real battles. **Photo above courtesy of Alabama Bureau of Tourism and Travel/Karim Shamsi Basha.**

Confederate Memorial Park, situated on 102 acres in central Alabama, is the site of two confederate cemeteries, as well as Alabama's only Confederate veterans' home, which operated from 1902-1939. Visitors can tour historic buildings found in the park or witness reenactments of Civil War battles. The park represents the state's desire to remember those who fought and died to protect their homeland. **Photo by Robert Fouts.**

Photo on facing page by Robert Fouts.

In Alabama, 87 percent of the communities are served exclusively by truck, according to the Alabama Trucking Association. There are about 10,000 corporate and family-owned trucking businesses in Alabama. Photo by Scott Wiseman.

CHAPTER 3

Transportation, Communications & Energy

In the 1960s, *Montgomery Advertiser* editor Harold Martin won a Pulitzer for uncovering corruption in the state's prison system. The staff of *The Alabama Journal* in Montgomery won a Pulitzer in 1988 for its articles on the high death rate among infants in the state. And in 1991, *The Birmingham News* won a Pulitzer for editorial writing. Photo by Scott Wiseman.

The Port of Alabama in Mobile is one of the busiest in the United States. The original federal project to improve the channels of Mobile Bay to the Gulf of Mexico was funded by Congress in 1826 with $10,000. Since then, millions have been spent to improve the harbor, build terminals and docks, and make other improvements. Photo by Steve Goraum.

ALABAMA'S FIRST GOVERNOR, WILLIAM WYATT BIBB, FORESAW THE TENNESSEE-TOMBIGBEE CANAL WHEN HE PROPOSED A MAN-MADE WATERWAY ACROSS NORTHWEST ALABAMA TO CONNECT THE TENNESSEE AND MOBILE RIVERS IN ORDER TO BYPASS NEW ORLEANS FOR RIVER TRANSPORTATION INTO THE MID-WEST. Although Bibb made the suggestion, the waterway did not become a reality until U.S. Congressman Tom Bevill engineered legislation through Congress midway into the Twentieth Century.

It was not until 1850 that the Alabama Legislature chartered the Alabama and Tennessee Railroad and the Tennessee and Coosa River Railway in an attempt to connect Selma with the iron-producing industrial centers of Montevallo and Gadsden as well as the Coosa with the Tennessee River at Gunter's Landing. However, the building of the railroads was a slow process, and by the time the Civil War broke out, Alabama still had very few miles of usable tracks.

In the southeastern part of the state, Mobile thrived. Steel made in the north was shipped worldwide through the Port of Alabama, with its thirty-two miles of deep channel to accommodate the largest ships. Bustling activity among stevedores working for shipping companies, cranes and conveyors moving commodities, and freighters from around the world soon became normal business at the huge sophisticated port. Later in the Twentieth Century, the Port completed its own terminal railroad with more than a dozen diesel locomotives operating on seventy-five miles of track, resulting in a savings of time and money for shippers doing business here. A series of inland ports, some with grain elevators to store cargoes between ship runs, were developed among the system of rivers through the state.

From the beginning of flight, Alabama was a ready and willing participant in this new venture. In 1911, a group of Montgomery businessmen persuaded Orville and Wilbur Wright to open the first school for pilots near the capital city where Maxwell Air Force Base would later house the War College and Air University. Today, hundreds of small private airplanes take off and land every day at airports and airstrips across Alabama. From single-strip private runways on plantations and farms to the multi-runway facilities in the large cities, air travel has become a way of life in the business world.

After World War II, during which the state played a key role when Fort Rucker in the Wiregrass and Fort McClellan near Anniston became U.S. Army training posts, the world of business grew with even more vigor. In the 1950s Redstone Arsenal near Huntsville became the centerpiece for space exploration, with German engineer Dr. Wernher von Braun directing the Marshall Space Flight Center. In the 1960s scientists there began work on the rocket that would launch man to the moon before the end of that decade. Satellite industries to the space program soared where a hundred years earlier cotton had been king. ▪

Although trucks carry merchandise from Alabama's manufacturing plants to all parts of the nation by means of the state's highway system, many industries still find rail and river routes to be economical means of transporting large loads of cargo. Photo by Robert Fouts.

Barge traffic is very important to industry locating in Alabama. The Tennessee-Tombigbee Waterway connects the Port of Alabama with the entire midwest through west Alabama to the Tennessee River, which eventually flows into the Ohio River and on into the Mississippi. Photo by Robert Fouts.

The aesthetic beauty of Perdido Pass Bridge at sunrise over the bay near South Alabama's beaches does not take away the practical necessity of bridging the gap between Alabama and Florida. Commerce between the two states is made easier by the access. Photo courtesy of Alabama Bureau of Tourism and Travel/Dan Brothers.

Many chemical companies use the rail system for safety and efficiency in transporting products including resins and plastics. Photo by Robert Fouts.

Alabama's interstate system will quickly get cars and trucks to where they are going, for both commercial and daily commuter travel. I-85 and I-65 lead to Atlanta, Birmingham, Mobile, Huntsville, and Nashville, and provide quick and easy interchange routes for connecting with other major highways. Photo by Robert Fouts.

Thousands of travelers arrive and depart from major airports in Birmingham, Huntsville, Montgomery, Mobile, Dothan, and Tuscaloosa every year. A $125-million expansion and renovation project at the Birmingham Airport was completed in 1992, making Alabama's largest airline terminal the most modern in the state. The modernization of the airport was praised by authorities throughout the South. After its modernization, the Birmingham Airport had 10 airlines operating from 21 gates in the revamped terminal. The airlines serve 60 cities, enhancing Alabama's air travel, making the Birmingham arrival/departure point service one of the most cost-effective in the nation. Photo by Scott Wiseman.

In 1910, Wilbur and Orville Wright established the first U.S. civilian flight school on the Kohn Plantation west of Montgomery. This school and their historic flight over the city, led to Montgomery becoming an important link in aerial mail service and the decision of the Army Corp Tactical School to locate at Maxwell. Photo courtesy of Fouts Commercial Photography.

Alabama is proud to be home to all branches of the Armed Forces. These divisions, both active and guard, are here to protect and serve whether locally or anywhere around the world. Museums such as the Aero Fighter Replica Museum (above) and Fort Rucker Vietnam War Display (left) commemorate the men and women of the forces who have bravely fought to protect our country. Photo above courtesy of Alabama Bureau of Tourism and Travel. Photo at left by Dan Brothers.

Alabama's communications industry, which has grown by leaps and bounds in the last quarter of the Twentieth Century, reaches out across the nation to relate what is happening today in the state. Radio networks span the countryside with the latest news and entertainment, and Alabama's public radio is one of the oldest in the United States. Photo courtesy of Auburn Network, Inc.

Alabama's newspapers flexed their muscles from the earliest days of the state's history. But perhaps the most productive time was the 1920s when Grover Cleveland Hall, the venerable editor of *The Montgomery Advertiser* won a Pulitzer Prize for a series of editorials attacking the Ku Klux Klan. He was cited for his bravery as a courageous journalist. Photo by Scott Wiseman.

The television broadcasting industry in Alabama encompasses local, regional, and national programming, ranging from award-winning Alabama Public Television to breaking news, and entertainment from around the world. Photos by Scott Wiseman.

Photo above courtesy of the Business Council of Alabama.

Natural gas is an important source of energy. Today, more than 470,000 homes, businesses and industries in central and north Alabama choose Alabama Gas Corporation, the natural gas utility for Birmingham-based Energen, to supply that energy. At right, Alagasco employees work to maintain the safety of the distribution system by inspecting and upgrading the pipes that bring this natural resource to the consumer. Energen's oil and gas subsidiary, Energen Resources, explores oil and gas properties in Alabama, New Mexico (shown in photo above), Texas and north Louisiana among other U.S. locations. Photo at right courtesy of Montgomery Area Chamber of Commerce.

Alabamians enjoy the latest in cellular phone technology, and with the recent growth in this new industry, customers have many choices in companies and features. Photos by Scott Wiseman.

When the Tennessee Valley Authority was first established by Congress in the 1930s as a part of President Franklin Delano Roosevelt's "New Deal", the Alabama Power Company challenged it in the courts, arguing that the TVA was a government agency in competition with free enterprise. After the two sides reached a compromise, dividing Alabama into TVA territory in the north and Alabama Power land in the south, Power Company President Thomas W. Margin helped to organize the Alabama State Chamber of Commerce. Photo by Pat McDonogh.

Industry requiring sufficient hydroelectric energy has found power in abundance from Alabama's river systems. The Alabama Power Company built its first hydroelectric power-generating dam in 1914. One of the largest was the Jordan Dam on the Coosa River in east central Alabama, built in 1937. Wilson Dam at Florence on the Tennessee River was begun in 1916 and became the cornerstone of the Tennessee Valley Authority that was established in 1933. From a modest beginning in the 1920s to the elaborate modern supplies of 2000, hydroelectric energy in Alabama has continued to grow to keep pace with the newest and most up-to-date industries relocating and building in the state. From the water that rushes over the dam through spillways, the power is harnessed within the power station and sent out to the residential and business clients who depend on it.

Photos by Pat McDonogh.

Alabama Power Company takes every opportunity to educate and encourage everyone who uses Alabama's waterways to appreciate, respect, and tread lightly on this valuable natural resource. The company's efforts have met with excellent results and have helped several endangered species such as the Red-Cockaded Woodpecker and Bald Eagle. Alabama Power is also active in helping provide habitat areas to encourage fish breeding. Photo by Robert Fouts.

Manufacturing & Distribution

The process of manufacturing and distribution depends on the transportation industry to carry products and goods to market. Although many companies depend on highway and rail systems, air transportation is also essential to businesses. Photo by Scott Wiseman.

For many years, steel has been the backbone of industrial growth in the state, especially the Birmingham area. Today, a welder, such as this one, becomes an artist for the steel industry when he puts his tools to work in the trade that he pursues. Alabama also is the third largest producer of iron and steel castings in the nation. Photo by Paul Sumners.

DURING THE YEARS PRIOR TO THE CIVIL WAR, SEVERAL INDUSTRIES THRIVED: Charles Cabiness built a cotton mill north of Huntsville, Daniel Scott employed more than a hundred workers at his mill at Scottsville on the Cahaba River, the Tuscaloosa Manufacturing Company operated a three-story mill around the clock seven days a week, and Daniel Pratt manufactured cotton gins at his plant in Prattville.

Gold was discovered in Tallapoosa County. A New York mining company hired several thousand employees who left Goldville and Gold Hill overnight when they heard that rich strikes had been made by individuals in California in 1849. Eventually interest was lost in Alabama's low-grade gold. But Alabama's coal was a different story.

Rich and plentiful veins of bituminous coal were found throughout much of north central Alabama. When iron ore was discovered in the same area, entrepreneurs from the North were led to look with speculative glee on Alabama. Several furnaces were started, but the most successful was one operated in Roupe Valley where the counties of Tuscaloosa, Bibb, Shelby, and Jefferson touched. A cotton planter, Ninion Tannehill, bought the facility and began to melt ore and pour it into what became known as "pig iron" because each piece was shaped like a small pig. In 1836, a Pennsylvania iron-maker named Moses Stroup bought the Tannehill Foundry and increased production overnight. A Massachusetts iron-maker named Horace Ware moved to Shelby County, built a furnace, and sold iron to Daniel Pratt to make his gins.

During the Civil War these plants became a part of the Confederate war effort, and by the end of the war were destroyed by Union troops when Wilson's raiders cut a violent swath through the state. Like the rest of the deep South, Alabama suffered greatly during the years of Reconstruction, but in the waning days of the Nineteenth Century, the state's future looked bright.

In the early 1870s, Elyton Land Company founded Birmingham, and its president, James R. Powell, "the Duke of Birmingham," sold the first lot on the corner of present-day First Avenue North and 19th Street for $100. It was said that the town grew like magic, and soon it was promoted as the Magic City. However, disaster struck: this time in the form of a cholera epidemic in the summer of 1873. Then came a national economic panic that reached near depression proportions that nearly wiped out the land company and the town.

In the years before the turn of the century, local businessmen Henry deBardeleben, William T. Underwood, J.W. Sloss, and Truman Aldrich revived the magic when they began making coke from Birmingham and Red Mountain coal. Blast furnaces began pouring pig iron, and the city's first steel was produced on Thanksgiving of 1899 by Tennessee Coal & Iron at its Ensley plant. Within a short time the city became the state's largest as its prosperity blossomed.

According to statistics gathered by the AFL-CIO, during the past century, women workers have grown steadily in number and as a proportion of the work force. The statistics indicate the number of working women has grown from 5.3 million in 1900 to 18.4 million in 1950 and to 63 million in 1997. Women made up 18.3 percent of the labor force in 1900, 29.6 percent in 1950 and 46.2 percent in 1997. Photo by Robert Fouts.

Alabama's many streams sometimes necessitated the use of ferries for both road and rail travel. Lumbering operations frequently put shortlines into service with ferries outfitted with rails. Photo courtesy Fouts Commercial Photography.

The lumber industry has been a leading employer in agriculture since before the Civil War, particularly in southwest Alabama's piney woods. Lumber is not only the backbone of the rural timber industry, it is used by builders to construct commercial and residential real estate. Photo by Scott Wiseman.

Other steel mills manufacturing pipe, steel slabs, fire extinguishers, and building materials opened at Fairfield, Avondale, and other locations around the "Pittsburgh of the South." Alabama Power Company, providing energy to the new industry as well as its increased residential base that swelled into cities and suburbs, began making plans to build lakes with dams to harness and produce hydroelectric power. And in 1937, Alabama Power President Thomas W. Martin brought together a group of state businessmen to organize the Alabama State Chamber of Commerce. In 1941, Martin was instrumental in founding the Southern Research Institute in Birmingham to further research for future expanding industry.

Today, Alabama's continued prominence in the field of manufacturing and distribution is evident. In the early fall of 1994, Governor Jim Folsom lured German manufacturers of the Mercedes-Benz luxury automobile to the Tuscaloosa area, where the company found a deep educational base at the University of Alabama and a work force capable of building their newly designed sport utility vehicle. Building on this success, Governor Don Siegelman approached the Japanese manufacturers of Honda in the spring of 1999 with a similar venture. The Governor and his team of industry-hunters at the Alabama Development Office, along with the Economic Development Partnership of Alabama and the Economic Development Association of Alabama, sold the Japanese industrialists on a site for their new plant near Talladega at Lincoln, about fifty miles east of Birmingham. Like much of Twentieth Century Alabama, the new Lincoln plant was carved from the geography that has proven rich with promise throughout its history. In 2000, both Mercedes and Honda announced plans to expand their Alabama-based operations. ■

Commercial ship yards dot the Alabama coastline. This boat belongs to Master Marine Inc. of Bayou La Batre, which has overseen an $18-million channel deepening project. Photo by Paul Sumners.

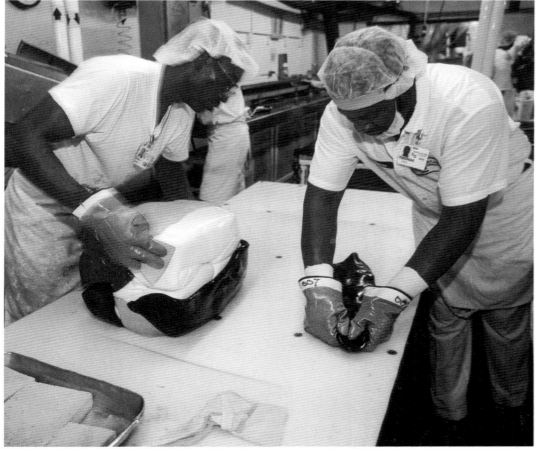

In the United States, American Candy Company is one of the leading manufacturers of flat lollipops and giant lollipops along with old-fashioned stick candy. It has had the license to produce candy for the Disney Company since 1975. Photos by Pat McDonogh.

The 101-year-old American Candy Company in Selma is one of the nation's leading exporters of non-chocolate candies. The company produces such sticky standards as candy canes and starlight mints as well as the more avant garde wax lips and fangs.

The Boeing Company, one of the largest manufacturers of airplanes in the United States, opened operations in Huntsville in 1962. While it did not make airplanes in Alabama, it did build and test the first stage of the giant Saturn V rocket booster, a major contributor to the journey to the moon, and is now building the International Space Station at its Huntsville plant. Photo by Paul Summers.

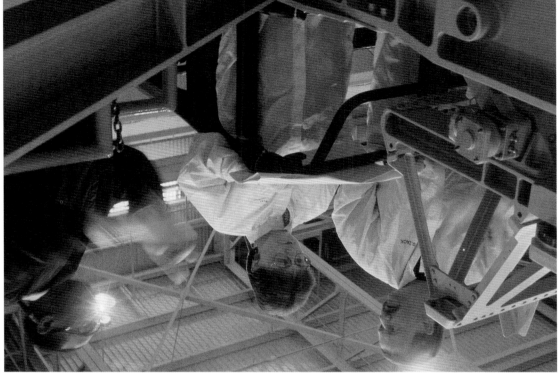

The Mercedes-Benz plant at Vance near Tuscaloosa not only makes luxurious sport utility vehicles, it has become a popular destination for tourists, offering a visitor's center and museum. Travelers along the interstate highway in west Alabama see the Mercedes-Benz star and know that a new star has fallen on Alabama. Photo by Barry Fikes.

Mining companies such as Shoal Creek Mine and Drummond Company have both underground and surface operations throughout several northern Alabama counties. Environmentally conscious, mining companies allow the land to be reclaimed and revegetated for future generations. Photo above by Charles Beck. Photo at left by Mike Rivers.

Alabama took its first steps toward today's modern cities and extensive industrial base with the discovery of bituminous coal in North Alabama in the mid-1800s. The mining industry was begun, and soon afterward iron ore was discovered in the same area. Birmingham quickly became a leader in the steel industry, even earning the nickname "Pittsburgh of the South." Today, both iron and mining operations are still foundations for Alabama industry.

Photo at right by Robert Fouts.

Oil refineries off the southern coast of Alabama use the best technology available to provide consumers with petroleum, natural gas, and other energy-related products while working to protect the environment by minimizing emissions and other wastes.

Alabama companies take advantage of advancements in computers and aerospace technology to produce and furnish parts for industries that manufacture airplanes and helicopters. Photos by Robert Fouts.

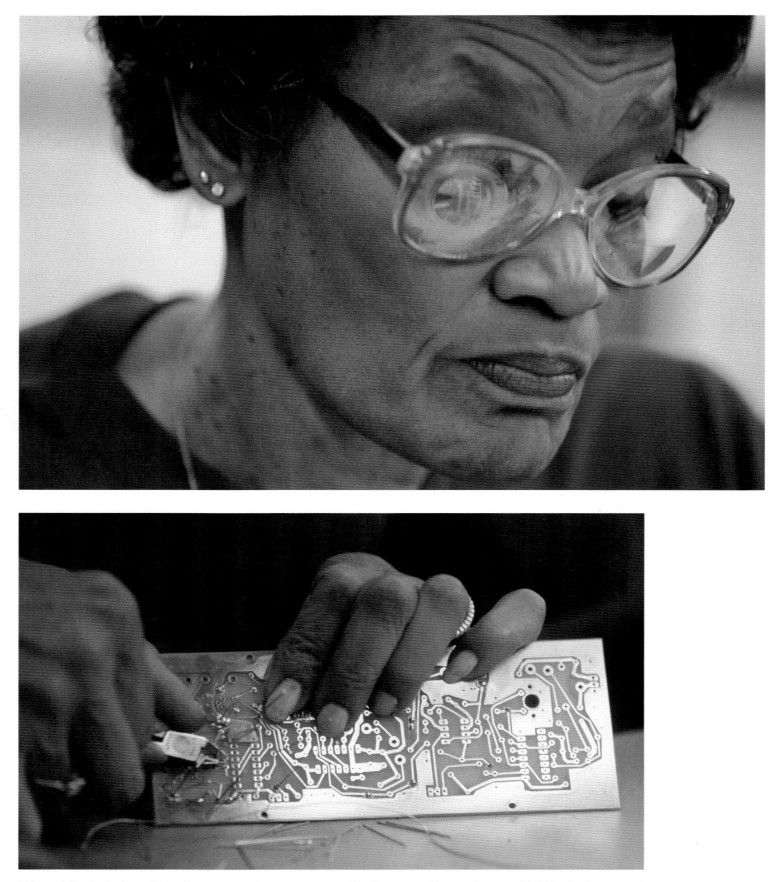

When skilled minds and hands are at work, they produce the finest quality products and intellectual components. Information technology companies have found Alabama to be a great source for those minds and hands. The state's more than 1,500 information technology companies employ 20,000 people. Photos by Scott Wiseman.

With 500 companies, operating 900 facilities, the textile industry continues to survive in Alabama, despite the exodus to foreign markets. While many modern machines make various types of clothing, hand stitching is still done at many establishments. This particular company, New Era Cap Company, makes baseball caps for teams from the West Coast to the East Coast including one that is a sign of the South, the Atlanta Braves.

New Era has two plants in Alabama, one in Demopolis in Marengo County and the other in Jackson, north of Mobile. In addition to Major League Baseball, New Era makes caps for minor league teams, professional football, hockey, and basketball leagues, colleges, and golf events. Photos by Pat McDonogh.

Large trucks are a common sight on Alabama interstates and highways because they transport almost ninety percent of consumer goods. Whether these tractor-trailer rigs transport clothing to retailers or produce for farmers, the trucking industry has an economic impact on a variety of industries in the state including manufacturing, retail, trade, agriculture, and forestry. Photo by Scott Wiseman.

National freight companies have headquarters and facilities throughout the state, fulfilling the various shipping requirements of businesses both large and small on a daily basis. These companies provide both ground and air transportation, as well as overnight delivery capabilities. Photo by Robert Fouts.

CHAPTER 5

Agriculture & Livestock

In 1919, the southern city of Enterprise erected a statue in honor of the boll weevil, the pest that forced farmers to diversify the state's agricultural economy when it devastated the cotton industry. Nearly 70 years later, the boll weevil still plagued the cotton crop so an eradication program began in 1987. Since then, boll weevils have been abolished from almost 600,000 acres. This has reduced the use of pesticides on cotton up to 80 percent and also has increased the yield per acre. Photo courtesy of Alabama Bureau of Tourism and Travel/Dan Brothers.

During the spring and summer growing seasons, fresh produce stands are a common sight along the two-lane highways and rural roads of Alabama. Additionally, large farmers markets like the State Farmers Market in Montgomery offer a central location drawing farmers from throughout the area to sell their wares. Photo courtesy of Alabama Bureau of Tourism and Travel.

AGRICULTURE DIVERSIFIED AND ADVANCED DURING THE TWENTIETH CENTURY. Farmers in the Wiregrass of the southeastern quarter of the state expanded on the revolutionary ideas of black scientist George Washington Carver, whom Dr. Booker T. Washington had brought to Tuskegee Institute, where he developed multitudes of ways to increase production and use of the peanut and the sweet potato, two of the area's primary crops.

Through the Black Belt, where cotton had filled steamboats that would ship the product out of Mobile, around the horn of Florida, and up the eastern seaboard to New England textile mills, cotton gave way to catfish and cattle. Farmers discovered catfish production was much more effective economically than previous crops, and cattle could graze on the rich grasses that grew around the many ponds near Uniontown, Greensboro, and Demopolis.

Soybeans replaced cotton for a while, but cotton remained a stable crop for much of north Alabama and throughout the Tennessee River Valley. In many small towns of northeast Alabama, like Roanoke, textile mills were built to turn cotton to cloth locally without having the exorbitant expense of shipping the product hundreds of miles.

For generations, seasonal crops sustained the agricultural industry, but, economically, the industry has become the largest in the state from the revenues of forestry, poultry, and cattle. Those involved in these particular components of agriculture have developed systems through research and technology to increase the growth and production needed to sustain their markets. These major agricultural industries are ensuring a stable, successful future not only for themselves, but also for the state's economy.

Today, not only does the agricultural industry account for more than one-third of the state's exports, which exceed $4 billion annually, but it also contributes to almost one-third of Alabama's annual payroll. ■

Cotton farmers in the state have increased their cotton acreage two-fold in the past decade ranking Alabama ninth in the country in cotton acreage by 1996. Today, cotton is the largest row crop grown in Alabama making it the fifth largest commodity in the industry. Using the most modern equipment, farmers efficiently harvest and clean their crop, preparing it for the marketplace. Photo above by Pat McDonogh.

Photo by Scott Wiseman.

Peanuts replaced cotton as the mainstay of the market, and the man that led the way in this new agricultural industry was George Washington Carver. Born a slave in Missouri, Carver grew up to become the director of the Department of Agricultural Research at Tuskegee University. Here he began extensive research into the uses of peanuts, pecans, sweet potatoes, and soybeans, while also producing a new type of cotton. Carver's experiments and discoveries greatly advanced the agricultural industry. Photo above courtesy of Alabama Bureau of Tourism and Travel/Karim Shamsi Basha.

Peanuts and their by-products are the third largest agricultural export in Alabama, and the sixth largest component of the state's agricultural industry. Peanut receipts place Alabama third after Georgia and Texas in peanut production in the nation. Photos at left courtesy of Alabama Farmers Federation.

The increasing uses of soybeans over the years have boosted the yearly production of the crop, as well as its contribution to Alabama's economy by making it fourth among the state's agricultural exports. Producing more than $50 million per year, soybeans are used not only in food products, but also in every-day items such as cosmetics. Almost 80 percent of the oil used in food manufacturing and food service is derived from soy-beans. Photos above courtesy of Alabama Farmers Federation.

When the need came for Alabama farmers to diversify their crops, pecans became a new product for the agricultural industry. Pecans are harvested from full-grown trees, maturing during the early fall months. Even though pecans are not planted in the ground each season, the pecan crop is just as susceptible as row crops are to changing weather conditions. Photo by Robert Fouts.

The Alabama Forestry Association works with its members by addressing their concerns about government regulations, ensuring the renewal of forest resources by replanting more than 3,000 trees for each child born in the state every year, and by maintaining clean water and a suitable wildlife habitat for the more than one million white-tailed deer and other creatures of the forests. Photo courtesy of Alabama Forestry Association.

The forestry industry has been a leading source of capital for the state of Alabama for ten years. Encompassing 22 million acres, every county in Alabama has at least one forestry operation including sawmills, pulp and paper mills, veneer and panel plants, and several hundred related wood processing businesses. When combined with timber receipts, the by-products boost this industry's economic value above all other commodities in the state of Alabama. Photo by Robert Fouts.

Although fish is not the largest component of the agricultural industry in Alabama, the state harvests both freshwater and saltwater fish. Sports-fish hatcheries raise fish to stock private ponds, as well as public lakes and rivers, while commercial hatcheries produce catfish and other common fish to supply demand from restaurants and food service distributors. In three decades of producing catfish, Alabama ranks second only to Mississippi in the aquaculture industry. With approximately 25,000 commercial ponds, the state is also home to the second largest processing plant in the U.S. Photo by Wade Collins/Courtesy of Alabama Catfish Producers.

The gulf waters provide ample quantities of seafood including crawfish, shrimp, crabs, and oysters, and fish such as mullet and snapper. Mobile Bay traffics fishing vessels that deliver the seafood for processing at local canneries and for shipping to markets further inland. Photo courtesy of Alabama Bureau of Tourism and Travel/Karim Shamsi Basha.

The fishing fleet at Bayou la Batre has become one of the most famous shrimping areas of the world. After the movie *Forrest Gump*, written by Mobile novelist Winston Groom, portrayed the title character making a fortune with his shrimping boat, the area has attracted tourists, as well as seafood lovers. Photo courtesy of Alabama Bureau of Tourism.

The poultry industry has flourished in recent years, becoming the largest commodity in the agricultural industry in Alabama. One of the most technologically advanced manufacturers in the world, the poultry industry uses genetic research and line automation. The Alabama Poultry and Egg Association promotes the poultry industry and serves farmers, processors, and other industry components. It is also the largest poultry and egg association in the nation. Photo above by Wade Collins/Alabama Farmers Federation. Photo at left courtesy of Alabama Farmers Federation. Photo below by Robert Fouts.

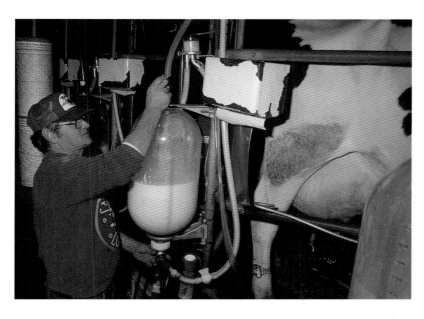

Dairy farming not only involves the milk produced by select herds of dairy cattle, but also milk by-products such as cheese, butter, and ice cream. With the introduction of cooperative associations, dairy farmers have seen many improvements in their industry including marketing conditions, and the standardization and grading of dairy products. In turn, modern machinery and transportation have contributed to greater efficiency and distribution. As with other industries, today's advanced research has helped expand the dairy economy by developing more uses for milk and milk by-products.

Even though pork producers only contribute a small portion to the state's agricultural industry, in 1996 pork receipts totaled over $70 million dollars. Pork also is consumed more than any other meat in the world including beef, but pork has more value than just as a food product. The by-products of pigs are used for medical advancements such as heart valve replacements and medical treatments like insulin. Photos courtesy of Alabama Farmers Federation.

Hay production is a crtitical aspect of cattle farming as ranchers depend on hay as a feed supplement for their livestock especially during long winter months. Photo by Robert Fouts.

Beef cattle farmers continue to be large contributors to the agricultural industry in Alabama with 30,000 farms owning one or more head of beef cows that represent all major breeds of cattle. By-products of beef, which include candles, paint, and perfume, allow 99 percent use of each beef cow. And though trucks and SUV's have replaced the cowboy's horse on most farms, some ranchers find there is no substitution for the quickness and agility of a well-trained cowhorse. Photos courtesy of Alabama Farmers Federation.

The agricultural industry continues to be a strong factor in the state's economy, and the advancements in technology only serve to ensure the future of this industry. Organizations such as FFA, Future Farmers of America, provide opportunities for school children to learn about agriculture, its future, and how to improve that future. Of course, the tradition of parents teaching their children the family business at a young age also reinforces the impact agriculture will have on the state from generation to generation. Photo by Wade Collins/Courtesy of Alabama Farmers Federation.

Horticulture may not naturally be thought of as an agricultural product, but it contributes almost $200 million dollars annually to the state. Nurseries across Alabama grow plants, shrubs, and trees to sell commercially—50 percent of which is exported. When fruit-tree crops, such as peaches, are added into the yearly total, horticulture accounts for almost $300 million of the state's revenue.

Bees are known for their sweet-tasting honey, but they also play another important role in the agricultural industry. Farmers depend on these insects to pollinate their crops, but there are laws prohibiting the interstate travel of bees. The U.S. Department of Agriculture must carefully monitor the bee population to ensure that bees from other states, which could be transporting diseases foreign to Alabama, do not contaminate local hives. Photo above by Wade Collins/Courtesy of Alabama Farmers Federation. Photos at left courtesy of Alabama Farmers Federation.

The cattle industry in Alabama ranks third in the state in farm and forestry cash receipts following broiler and forestry. In 1999, the cattle industry generated $414.5 million. As of January 2000, the inventory of cattle and calves on Alabama farms totaled 1.46 million head, ranking the state 24th nationally. Of the total cattle inventory, beef cows numbered 793,000 head, ranking the state 16th nationwide in that category. Photo by Robert Fouts.

CHAPTER 6

Health Care & Business Professionals

Every day in Alabama, scientists and other specialists are striving to improve and enhance the quality of life through experiments and research. Products from tires to textiles are affected by chemical research. Every year the chemical industry alone generates more than $60 billion in foreign sales as Alabama's largest exporter. Medical research breaks new ground in the treatment of disease and the search for cures. Photo courtesy of UAB Photography and Instructional Graphics.

The fountain in front of the Retirement Systems of Alabama Tower in downtown Montgomery symbolizes not only the beauty of the area but the enormous contribution the RSA has made to the state. Photo by Robert Fouts.

The Capitol of Alabama is located in Montgomery, and is one of only a few state capitol buildings that has been designated a National Historic Landmark. Built in 1850-51, the building was renovated and restored in the late 1990s to preserve its original design. Situated at the end of Dexter Avenue downtown, the Capitol is a popular tourist attraction, as well as government facility.
Photo courtesy of Alabama Bureau of Tourism and Travel.

I N BIRMINGHAM, THE GROWTH OF HEALTH CARE AS A BUSINESS REPLACED THE STEEL INDUSTRY IN THE LAST QUARTER OF THE TWENTIETH CENTURY. What had started as an extension of the University of Alabama grew so rapidly that by the last years of the century UAB was the leading employer among the city's industries. With classes, hospitals, clinics, labs, and other health care services, UAB provided education, research, and treatment centers that soon expanded into private hospitals, clinics, and foundations that specialize in virtually every medical problem. Just as Huntsville developed satellite industries founded on technology developed at the Marshall Space Flight Center, Birmingham began to draw other health-related businesses which gained quick and profound success. An example is Dr. Richard Scrushy's HealthSouth which tended to the medical problems of professional and amateur athletes before it expanded to include other everyday problems and soon spread across the South. By the beginning of the new millennium, Birmingham was one of the finest medical centers in the world.

While Alabama has nurtured and helped build many mega-companies, it also has great appeal for the small businessperson. According to the *Small Business Survival Index 2000*, Alabama ranks eighth in the nation, between Florida and Michigan, in friendliness to the development of small businesses and entrepreneurship. Alabama is home to more than 200,000 full-time businesses, 60 percent of which are operated by sole proprietors and one in four that have fewer than 10 employees. ■

Small and minority-owned businesses have been on the increase in the past few years in Alabama due in part to advanced technology that cultivates qualified workers and manufactures innovative products. Items such as laptop computers allow workers to have mobile offices, thus their businesses can operate more efficiently and economically. Alabama boasts about 20,000 minority-owned businesses, according to the U.S. Small Business Administration and has been named by Dun & Bradstreet as one of the best places in America to start a new business. Photo by Robert Fouts.

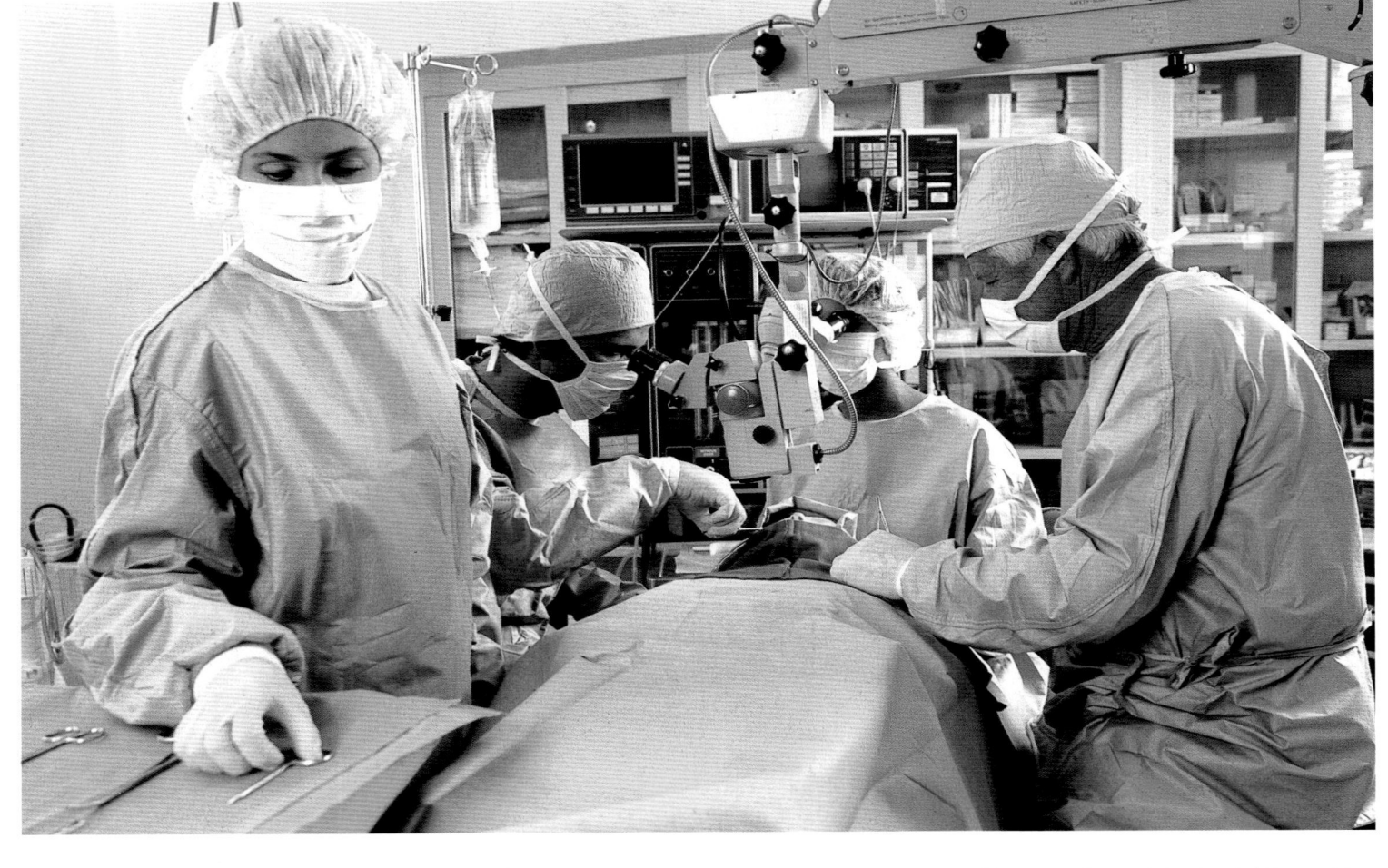

Alabama's extensive network of comprehensive medical facilities offers quality care for those seeking treatment. Using the latest advancements in medical research and treatments, hospitals are able to provide specialized services especially in the surgical field where laser surgery has vastly improved the types and techniques of procedures performed.

Eye exams and optical surgery are a part of the daily routine at hospitals, clinics, and private practices throughout the state that specialize in treating injuries and diseases of the eye. In recent years, laser surgery to correct vision problems has become a refined procedure that can be performed cost-efficiently on an out-patient basis. Photos by Robert Fouts.

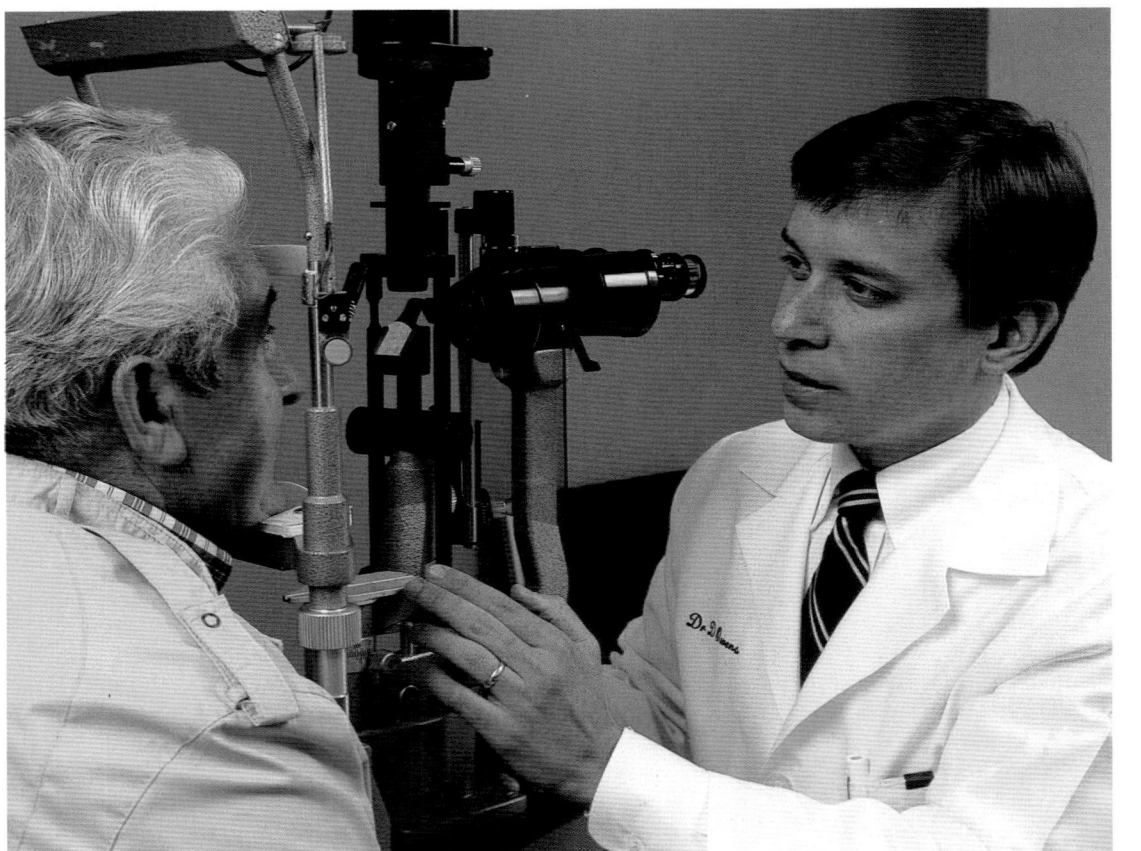

Maxwell Ambulatory Health Care Center, located on Maxwell Air Force Base, features a new state-of-the-art building. Inpatient care is accomplished at local off-base facilities as part of resource sharing agreements. On base, the facility offers a myriad of out-patient medical services. Photo by Robert Fouts.

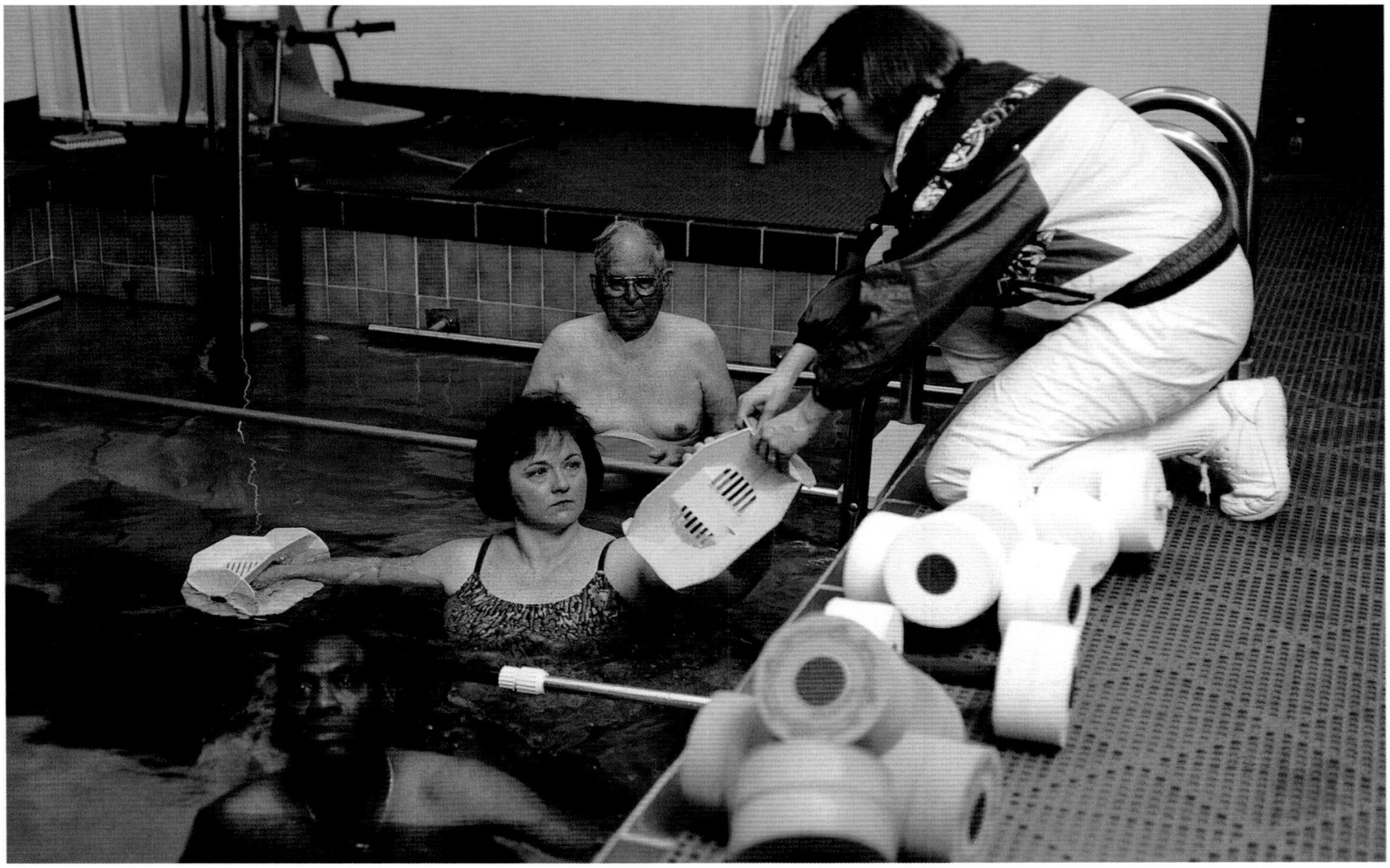

Rehabilitative medical services are available across Alabama through hospitals or private facilities and can be provided on an inpatient or an outpatient basis. Patients are referred to rehabilitation clinics after injury or disease has left them with lost mobility or a disability. Through rehabilitation, they can regain partial or full mobility or learn to cope with their disability. Photo by Robert Fouts.

No matter what the ailment—whether sports related or bones broken in accidents—physicians work with the most up-to-date technology in order to ensure a patient receives the best medical care possible. Photo by Robert Fouts.

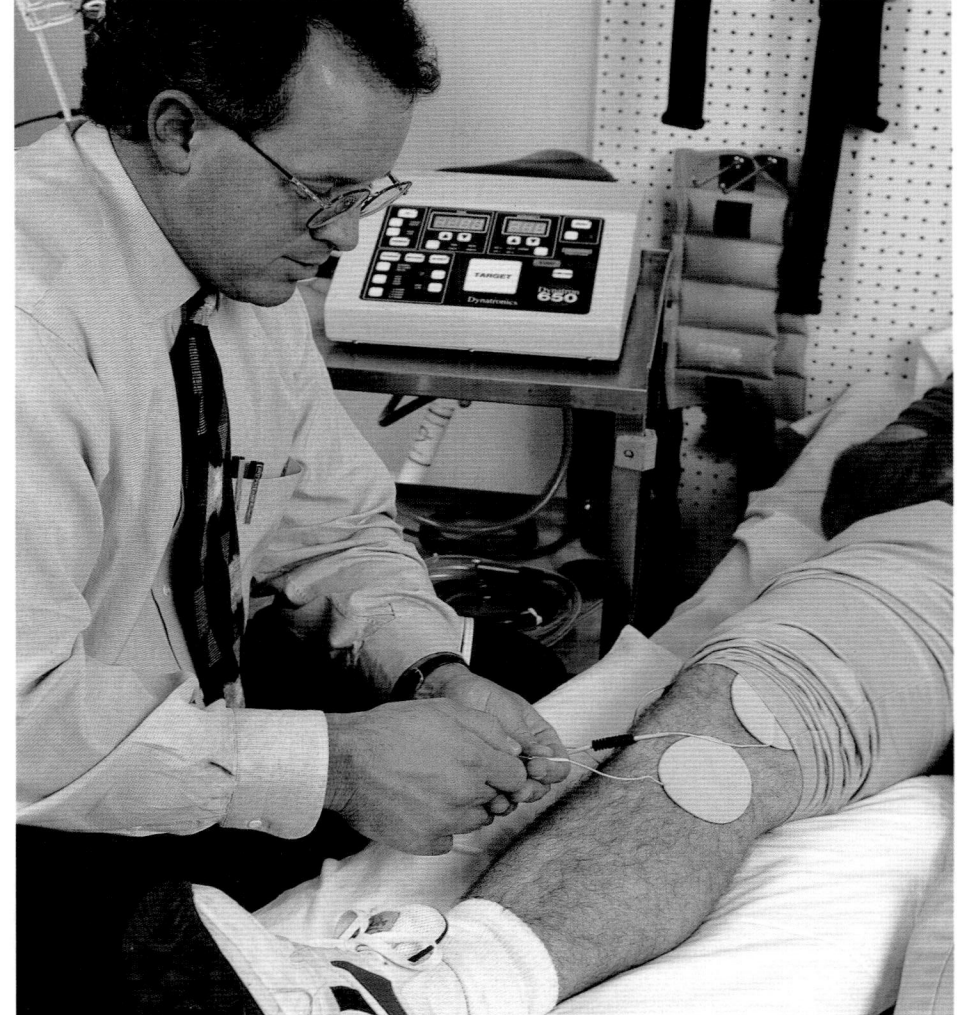

Modern office buildings incorporating state-of-the-art amenities and features supporting new technologies provide attractive settings where work is pleasurable as well as efficient. Alabama boasts a diverse economy that supports a range of professional service providers and industries. Photo by Robert Fouts.

Many branches of the armed services have a strong presence in Alabama. Key among these are Maxwell Air Force Base and Gunter Annex in Montgomery, home of Air University. Air University plays a vital role in fulfilling the mission of the United States Air Force as the center for advanced education in the Air Force, and also offers specialized military instruction for all branches of the services and to international officers as well. Gunter Annex is home to the Standard Systems Group, which plays a crucial role in the development of information systems used throughout the military. Photo by Robert Fouts.

Alabama has more than 11,000 licensed lawyers who live and work in our state. Many of those in smaller firms spend hours in law libraries like this one doing research and court preparation. Photo by Robert Fouts.

Business in Alabama reaches around the world. Many foreign businesses have chosen Alabama to locate offices and industrial centers, while Alabama businesses stay home to perform services and produce top-quality products for customers throughout the world. Photo by Robert Fouts.

Today's business meetings can include participants from throughout the world. By utilizing modern communications technology as basic as a conference call or as advanced as satellite networking, Alabama businesses truly work a global marketplace.

Despite high-tech advances, customer service and personal attention will always be the most important components of any successful business. Photos by Robert Fouts.

Facing page: Alabama's banking industry has responded to the growing and changing needs of its customers by offering new and expanded conveniences such as the latest in online banking services. Alabama's strong financial industry, with major holding company headquarters in Birmingham, ranks among the top in the nation. Photo by Robert Fouts.

CHAPTER 7

Real Estate

A thriving job market and low unemployment rate draws new residents to Alabama each year. As a result, the real estate market is flourishing in both the residential and commercial markets. The current trend in residential development is toward planned communities that offer single-family homes, town homes or apartments, and amenities such as clubhouses, pools, and golf courses. Some planned communities also offer shopping and schools within the property. Photos by Robert Fouts.

Many cities are working to revitalize their downtown areas by erecting new commercial structures to encourage economic growth. But, at the same time, developers are careful to preserve the natural beauty and history of existing buildings. Photo by Pat McDonagh.

Habitat for Humanity International, which has helped more than 100,000 families in need build homes, was founded and continues to be led by Alabama native Millard Fuller. Fuller, a graduate of Auburn University and the University of Alabama School of Law, began a marketing firm while still in school and by the age of 29 was a millionaire. However, he has generously shared his wealth with others and has dedicated himself to what he calls the "economics of Jesus." Habitat for Humanity International now is one of the top 20 house builders in the United States and among the nation's largest non-profit organizations. Although based in Georgia, the organization has many Alabama affiliates. Those who receive Habitat homes work side-by-side with volunteers to construct their home and realize the dream of home ownership. Photos by Paul Sumners.

The Retirement System of Alabama's Robert Trent Jones Golf Trail has opened opportunities for residential and recreational development. The Robert Trent Jones Golf Trail is a world-class development that has been praised by golf authorities around the world.

Photos by Pat McDonogh.

Renovation and restoration are the flip side of home ownership in Alabama. In addition to the construction of new homes, many people choose to preserve the unique architecture and design of homes and buildings from the state's past, breathing new life into well-loved neighborhoods. Photo by Pat McDonogh.

Photo at left courtesy of Montgomery Area Chamber of Commerce.

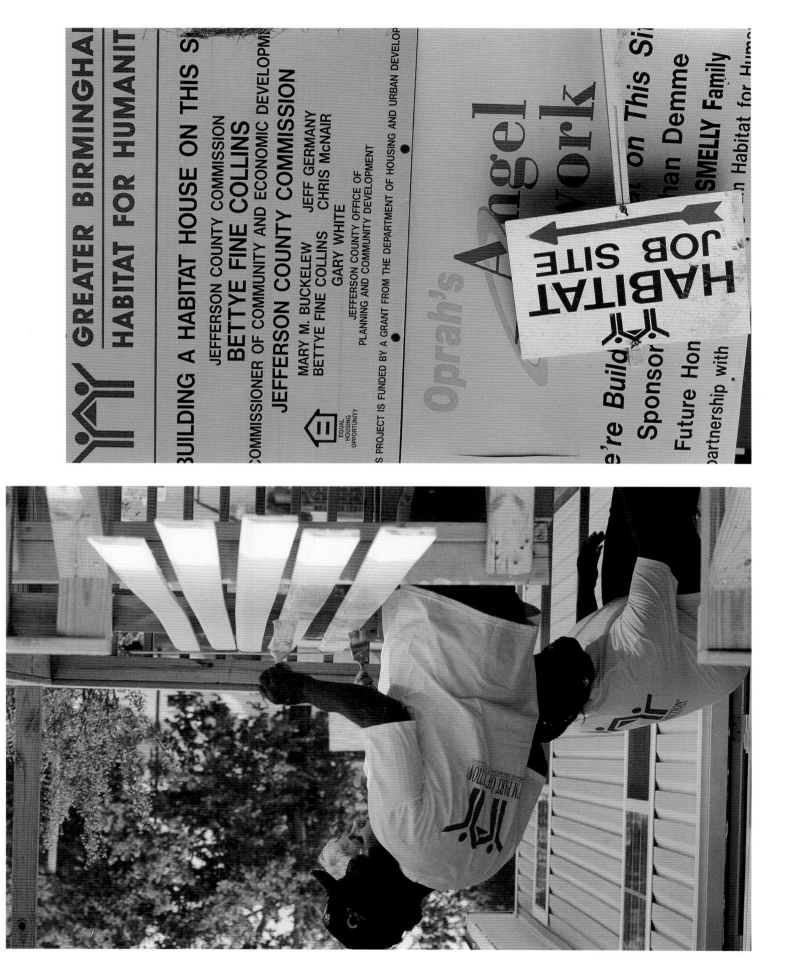

(Above) Alabama-based contractors work throughout the country and around the world managing a broad scope of projects, including the construction of medical complexes, office buildings, hotels, casinos, industrial plants and military airstrips. Alabama leaders in the industry include Brasfield & Gorrie, Vulcan Materials (the nation's largest producer of construction aggregates), Bill Harbert International Construction and BE&K, which was selected as one of the Best l00 companies to work for in America. Photo by Pat McDonogh.

(Above and right) New single-family homes are being built in residential subdivisions across Alabama to meet not only the influx of new citizens, but also the continuing prosperity of current residents. A key player in Alabama's economy, construction has an annual in-state impact of $3.3 billion. There are more than 3,000 licensed general contractors in the state, many of whom build single-family homes in residential subdivisions across Alabama. Photos by Pat McDonogh.

Multi-family homes—such as apartments, duplexes, and townhomes—provide a desirable option for those busy professionals who need low-maintenance and less time-consuming housing. Photo by Robert Fouts.

Luxury housing is a market that has recently come into its own throughout the state with builders working to construct new homes without destroying the natural surroundings that homeowners desire. Photo by Robert Fouts.

Families and builders work together to design a home that meets the needs of the buyer as well as fitting his particular tastes and budget. Photo by Pat McDonogh.

B Y 1819, WHEN ALABAMA BECAME A STATE, MONTGOMERY, ON THE SOUTHERN BANKS OF THE ALABAMA RIVER, WHERE HERNANDO DE SOTO AND HIS BAND OF SPANISH CONQUISTADORS SEARCHED FOR GOLD IN 1540 IN THE LAND OF THE ALABAMU INDIANS, HAD BEEN DEVELOPED BY REAL ESTATE PROMOTERS JOHN SCOTT AND ANDREW DEXTER. Two years later, a stagecoach line between Milledgeville, Georgia, where the federal land office for the southeast was located, and Montgomery was opened, bringing more settlers from the east into the frontier. By 1830, stage travel was offered from Montgomery to Tuscaloosa. At the same time, public transportation across north Alabama, from Huntsville to Russellville, made the area more accessible to travelers from the east, and the area around the tri-cities—Florence, Sheffield, and Tuscumbia—on the Tennessee River, began to grow and prosper.

In the north, among the first enterprises to open its doors was the tavern at Mooresville built by Llewelyn Jones, a veteran of the Revolutionary War. Travelers found the hospitality of a warm fire in the main room, a clock on the mantel, wine or liquor with dinner, ice chiseled from the ice house only a few feet from the back door—all for the cost of one-half dollar. For another fifty cents his horse would be fed a bushel of corn or, for six-and-one-half cents, three bundles of fodder.

In the late Nineteenth Century, rich residential areas of Spring Hill in Mobile, Cloverdale in Montgomery, mountainous streets near Huntsville, and other small tree-lined neighborhoods began to flourish. In the 1920s, the Jemison Company laid out the streets and shopping vistas of Mountain Brook Village, one of the first planned communities of the state.

By the mid-1950s, the Aronov brothers of Montgomery had built the state's first shopping mall at Cloverdale, anchored by Loveman's of Birmingham. And by the end of the Twentieth Century, the Retirement Systems of Alabama's grand Robert Trent Jones Golf Trail, with championship courses dotting the state from Mobile to Huntsville, created a real estate mecca, the likes of which few developers had ever dreamed. ■

The first brick structure in Montgomery, Freeney's Tavern, at the corner of Commerce and Tallapoosa streets, was the scene of the grand ball for the Marquis de LaFayette on April 4, 1825. Photo courtesy of Fouts Commercial Photography.

Education & Quality of Life

Sara Bopp Strange, an American Visual Arts Teacher of the Year, makes art come alive for her students at Montgomery's Booker T. Washington Magnet High School. School systems throughout Alabama have added "magnet" programs that offer options beyond the standard curriculum that are taught by award-winning instructors. Photo courtesy of Montgomery Public Schools.

Although Alabama is known for a large population of Southern Baptists, the state welcomes those of all religious faiths from Christian to Jewish to Islamic and any another religious sect. And while some prefer to attend a small, quiet country church, others participate in large metropolitan houses of worship. Photo by Robert Fouts.

EDUCATION IS A TOP PRIORITY IN ALABAMA, WITH LEARNING OPPORTUNITIES AVAILABLE TO PEOPLE OF ALL AGES. Formal educational institutions throughout the state include public and private preschools, K-12 programs, colleges and universities, vocational training programs, and special education facilities and programs for those with unique needs and challenges.

Alabama's students have the highest Stanford Achievement Test scores than at any time in the state's history, with students consistently scoring at or above national averages. In fact, for the past two years Alabama has ranked second in the nation among the states that give the Stanford Achievement Test. Currently, Alabama high school seniors averaged 20.2 on the ACT test—the highest ever—and above the Southeast regional average. Additionally, Scholastic Assessment Test scores (used for college admission) of Alabama students have increased every year since 1972 and are consistently above the national average.

Secondary education continues to build on that foundation of academic excellence, with some of the nation's premier educational institutions located in Alabama. These include The University of Alabama, with campuses in Tuscaloosa, Birmingham, and Huntsville; Auburn University, in Auburn and Montgomery; Troy State University in Troy and Montgomery; University of South Alabama, University of North Alabama, and Alabama State University, along with many other colleges and universities throughout the state. Secondary educational opportunities also include community colleges and schools offering intensive training in the arts or hands-on career training programs.

And Alabama's educational opportunities continue for a lifetime. Residents enjoy access to a variety of continuing education programs for personal or career enrichment, through such programs as the Alabama Adult Literacy Resource Center or the Alabama Institute for Education in the Arts, to touch just the tip of the iceberg.

Obviously, education is in itself a resource that enriches a community and a state. In Alabama, there is a wealth of people, programs, and opportunities that add life and quality to daily life. Volunteerism thrives. The arts are strong and vibrant. People reach out to one another with a true concern for making the state a better place to live, work, and raise a family.

Often, individuals make an indelible difference. When he returned from World War II, Montgomery Businessman Winton "Red" Blount expanded Blount Brothers Construction Company with projects that inlcuded domed sports complexes and entire foreign universities, as well as bridges, dams, airports, and the Cape Canaveral Rocket Launch Station. Blount, himself, became a U.S. Postmaster General in President Richard Nixon's administration. Back home in Montgomery, he gave $21.5 million to build a permanent home for the Alabama Shakespeare Festival and later tripled that amount with expansion of facilities at the Wynton M. Blount Cultural Park, which also included a

Alabama students are fortunate to have a wealth of options for higher education. Two-year and four-year institutions can be found throughout the state, offering both traditional daytime courses as well as evening and weekend course schedules. Photo by Robert Fouts.

Many talented artists have been proud to call Alabama home. Not only has this state produced nationally recognized songwriters, singers, playwrights, novelists, actors, and artists, but it has also provided the setting for a number of motion pictures. Photo by Robert Fouts.

museum of fine arts and an outdoor amphitheater. Today, ASF and the cultural park draw hundreds of thousands of visitors each year from throughout the world.

The state's culture also has been elevated to new heights by individual artists who have displayed their work for national and international audiences, sharing a bit of the state's creative finery with the world. These artists include painters such as David Parrish in Huntsville, Dick Jemison in Birmingham, and Barbara Gallagher, Clark Walker, and Mose T. in Montgomery; writers such as Vickie and Dennis Covington and Charles Gaines in Birmingham, Madison Jones and Judy Troy in Auburn, Winston Groom in Point Clear, W.E.B. Griffin in Fairhope, Kathryn Tucker Windham in Selma, Tom Franklin in Mobile, Pulitzer Prize-winning author of *All Over But the Shoutin'*, Rick Bragg; and the great Pulitzer Prize-winning author of *To Kill a Mockingbird*, Harper Lee in Monroeville. Playwrights showcase their work in venues ranging from the small community theater to the stage of the Alabama Shakespeare Festival through ASF's Southern Writers Project. Musical artists include Lionel Ritchie of Tuskegee, founder of the group The Commodores; Randy Owens and Teddy Wayne Gentry of Fort Payne, who formed the Group Alabama, and Jimmy Buffett of Mobile. All have kept alive a rich heritage begun by artists like

Although educating students in the basic courses of study and the new-age of technology is a priority for Alabama schools, it is still important for students to exercise their bodies as well as their minds. Whether participating in physical education classes or swinging from playground equipment, children still need to test their strength and develop skills of coordination in order to perform at their best levels. Photo by Paul Sumners.

Kelly Fitzpatrick and Charles Shannon, writers like Truman Capote and Walker Percy, and musicians like Hank Williams and Nat King Cole. Alabama also has provided the inspiration and the backdrop for numerous motion pictures including *The Long Walk Home*, *The Grass Harp*, *Stay Hungry*, and even parts of *Close Encounters of the Third Kind*.

A wealth of educational opportunities. A rich arts community. A wealth of opportunity for involvement and enrichment. Alabama truly is a state of mind. ◼

Technology is an important part of the work force, as well as everyday life, and educators believe it is important to introduce students to computers at a young age. In May of 2000, Alabama school systems received $6.4 million in grants from the federal government to provide the state's 106 public school systems with Internet access in each of their 70,000 classrooms. This money will be used to complete network systems, purchase one multimedia computer per classroom along with any necessary software and hardware, and to provide technology training for teachers. Photo by Robert Fouts.

Students of all ages can take advantage of a wide range of traditional and alternative education opportunities in Alabama, with choices including nightime class schedules, internships, cooperative education, and work-study programs. Photo courtesy of Huntingdon College.

Post-secondary education has long been important to the people of Alabama. Colleges and universities established more than a century ago are stronger than ever today, building on the foundation of academic excellence while reaching to meet and exceed the demands of the future. Photo at right by Barry Fikes. Photo below by Chip Cooper.

Photo above courtesy of Auburn University Relations.

Many colleges and universities now also offer distance-learning programs, allowing students to take classes through televised broadcasts, email, and the Internet. Photo by Chip Cooper.

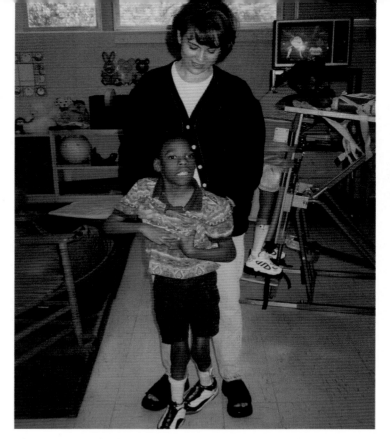

The purpose of education is to meet the needs of all children in the state. During the 1998-99 school year, special education services, which include rehabilitation and occupational therapy, were afforded to almost 100,000 children and youth ages three to 21. At that same time, more than 20,000 gifted students participated in special education classes. Photo courtesy of Montgomery Public Schools.

Both public and private schools in the state continuously strive to improve the quality and diversity of education within their systems. By emphasizing individual strengths in not only academics, but also the arts, students are able to excel at their own pace and in their own way. Photo by Robert Fouts.

As of the year 2000, there were approximately 1,445 public schools in the state of Alabama with more schools under construction or in the planning stages for the coming years. The public school system serves more than 732,000 students and more growth is expected. The public school system constructs new buildings to accommodate the children in the growing neighborhoods and expanding city limits that are a direct result of the state's continuous population increase. Photo by Robert Fouts.

The state's technical and vocational schools prepare students for the world of work with hands-on instruction. Students may choose from culinary arts, medical training, automotive repair, cosmetology, electrical, and a host of other courses of study. These schools provide training for students in order to meet the constant demand of the business community to fill jobs for specialized fields. Photos by Robert Fouts.

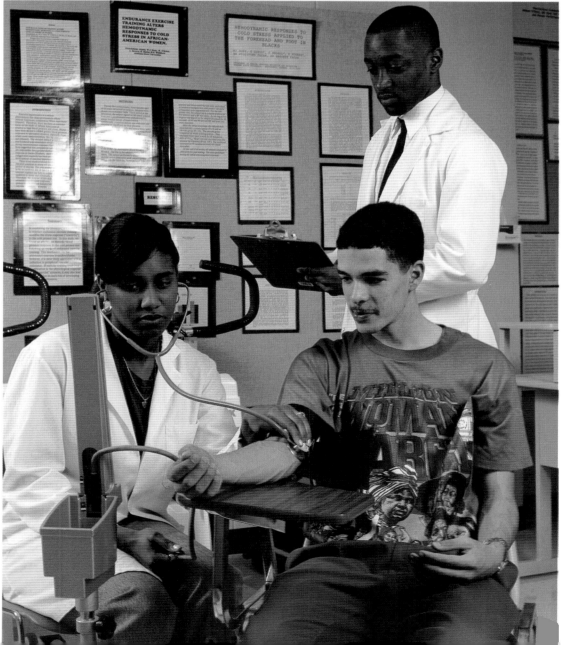

In the early 1900s, horses continued to provide common, convenient transportation. Families traveled around town in style with their horsedrawn buggies, just as the children of Mr. and Mrs. John P. Kohn enjoyed riding in a cart pulled by their pony, Belle. Photo courtesy of Fouts Commercial Photography.

Times may change, but the simple pleasures in life rarely do. Children can still wile away hot summer days with cool treats while enjoying the innocence of their youth. Photo courtesy of Alabama Bureau of Tourism and Travel.

Not only are friendships cherished, but also the family bond is strong in Alabama. Traditional values remain close to the heart and are passed down through the generations. Family time is a priority even if it only involves a leisurely breakfast in the backyard. Photos by Paul Sumners.

The temperate climate makes Alabama a playground for gardeners. No matter the season, flowering fauna thrive in the state. Photo courtesy of Alabama Bureau of Tourism and Travel.

Alabama is a wonderful and popular place to retire. The state offers a moderate climate, scenic state parks and beaches, the nationally acclaimed Robert Trent Jones Golf trail, and a variety of affordable housing options. Photo by Annette Bitto.

Alabama folk artist Mose T. had humble roots as a house painter before he turned his brush to simple wooden canvases to create the fanciful people and animals of his imagination. His work has been recognized worldwide by art critics and fans alike as among the finest of the genre. Photo by Robert Fouts.

Although Alabama has kept pace with the new age of technology in the areas of farming and transportation, sometimes it is hard to resist the less hectic times of days long gone. Whether it is a farmer indulging his hard-working plow mules, or visitors relaxing in a nostalgic carriage ride, pieces of history are easily recaptured throughout the state. Photos courtesy of Alabama Bureau of Tourism and Travel.

Police departments work diligently to let the public know that police officers are there to help, no matter the situation. Using a variety of communication methods, officers are able to share and receive information in order to keep communities safe. Photos by Robert Fouts.

State law enforcement officers cooperate with local police departments in protecting and serving the citizens of Alabama.

By using McGruff the Crime Dog, police officers share with children the message that police officers are friends. This police mascot demonstrates to children important rules regarding safety and strangers. Photo by Robert Fouts.

This state is known as "Alabama the Beautiful" and its residents work to keep it that way. As the need to preserve the environment continues to increase, many communities offer curbside pick-up of recycling as part of the regular sanitation routes, and citizens help to preserve the environment and natural resources by recycling paper, plastic, and glass items. Photo above by Pat McDonogh.

Communities in Alabama strive to ensure the future of their citizens by conducting safety courses and enforcing state safety laws. The residents also take great pride in the achievements of all individuals through local community programs. Photos at left by Robert Fouts.

Alabama's churches are some of the oldest structures in the state. Beautiful hand-made stained glass windows, intricate stonework, and carved wood can be found in the sanctuaries of these buildings that are architectural marvels as much as places of worship. Photo by Robert Fouts.

Religion in Alabama dates back to the state's formation. Churches, synagogues, and temples can be found throughout the state to suit anyone's religious preference. Photo by Robert Fouts.

Football is a favorite pastime in Alabama, and the most talked-about athletic event of the year is the annual "Iron Bowl" showdown between Auburn University and the University of Alabama. Rivalries run strong on game day between the two teams and also families and friends as fans choose sides. Photo courtesy of Auburn University Relations.

Athletics have long been an integral part of Alabama's culture. High schools, colleges, and universities offer track and field, football, baseball, basketball, swimming, gymnastics, and a host of other sports where Alabama's teams excel. Photo by Robert Fouts.

Baseball, the American pastime, is popular in Alabama. Fans can watch minor league action in such cities as Birmingham, Huntsville, and Mobile. Photo by Robert Fouts.

The Talladega Super-speedway has grown to be one of the most popular NASCAR venues among drivers and fans alike. The track hosts two major NASCAR events each year and boasts the fastest 500-mile automobile race ever recorded. Photo courtesy of Alabama Bureau of Tourism and Travel.

While Alabama is fully into the digital age, its residents remember the state's roots and deep musical tradition. Bluegrass music helps define Alabama's musical heritage and serves as the backbone to many other types of music. Photo courtesy of Alabama Bureau of Tourism and Travel.

The "Rattlesnake Rodeo" is sponsored by the Opp Jaycees on the first weekend in March. The annual event has been enjoyed for almost forty years and grows more popular each year. It features arts and crafts, food and, of course, rattlesnakes! Photo courtesy of Alabama Bureau of Tourism and Travel.

New Orleans may be famous for its Mardi Gras, but this nation's birthplace for the celebration is Alabama's very own Mobile. Lavish parades and magical balls are highlights of the pre-Lent festival. Photo courtesy of Alabama Bureau of Tourism and Travel.

Fall is the season for small community and large state fairs. People of all ages enjoy the sights, smells, and sounds found there, while children enjoy the exciting attractions and thrilling rides. Photo by Robert Fouts.

CHAPTER 9

Marketplace, Hospitality & Tourism

The charm of an old general store cannot be diminished by the changing world. Stop lights and streetlights are anachronistic elements among the collection of classic metal signs and old-fashioned gas pumps. Photo courtesy of Alabama Bureau of Tourism and Travel/Karim Shamsi Basha.

Water parks are popular attractions in the south that provide a fun and exciting diversion from the summer heat. Photo courtesy of Alabama Bureau of Tourism and Travel.

Alabama's capital city, Montgomery, is also known as the birthplace of the Civil War and of Civil Rights. The Civil War Memorial is located on the grounds of the State Capitol building and honors the confederate soldiers who gave their lives in the War Between the States. Photo by Robert Fouts.

A T HUNTSVILLE, A SPIN-OFF OF THE SPACE INDUSTRY WAS THE DEVELOPMENT OF THE SPACE AND ROCK-ET CENTER THAT SKYROCKETED RAPIDLY TO THE TOP OF THE STATE'S TOURISM BUSINESS. On Mobile Bay, the World War II battleship, USS *Alabama*, became the centerpiece of a 75-acre memorial park including the submarine USS *Drum* and a vintage B-52 bomber called the *Calamity Jane*. By the end of the Twentieth Century, the pristine white beaches along Orange Beach and Gulf Shores had found world fame as a tourist destination. Meanwhile, the Robert Trent Jones Golf Trail, with its fascinating and challenging terrain ranging from a links-style course at Huntsville to the hills and hollows of Greenville and the subtle twists and turns at Mobile, has become the most talked-about new golfing adventure by sports enthusiasts and sports professionals from Japan to Alaska to Scandinavia.

In Birmingham, the McWane Center science and industry museum restored an old downtown department store that had gone out of business when suburban malls took over the retail market in the 1960s. With the new influx of tourists to the center's IMAX theater, more businesses are springing up downtown. And when VisionLand Theme Park in Bessemer opened and was an instant success, it proved that tourism could be a big-money business.

What had once been a detriment to the growth of business and industry—the battle for Civil Rights by the black population of Alaba-ma - became a highlight of tourism for the Twentieth Century. In Montgomery, which boosted itself as the home of Civil War and Civil Rights, a Civil Rights Memorial to those killed in the struggle was designed by famed artist Maya Lin and constructed at the Southern Poverty Law Center. In Selma, local citizens formed the National Voting Rights Museum on Water Street overlooking the Edmund Pettus

The Robert Trent Jones Golf Trail is the largest golf course construction project ever attempted anywhere in the world, with 378 holes and more than 100 miles of golf. These are not "manufactured" courses though—all partake of the natural topography. Each was extracted from the land, not imposed on it. The "Trail" offers genuine championship layouts that will stand the test of time and pose major tests of golf for years to come. Tee markers on the Trail are pegged to ability level, not age or gender. The courses were designed to measure as short as 4,700 yards and as long as about 7,700 yards from the tournament tees, with as many as twelve tee boxes in-between, offering a tremendous amount of flexibility in play. The Trail has won rave reviews and numerous awards, and more than 3,000 articles have been written about it world-wide to date. Photo courtesy of Alabama Bureau of Tourism and Travel.

Pivotal leaders in the Civil Rights movement are honored throughout Alabama. Pictured above is a statue honoring Rosa L. Parks, who established herself as one of the most important figures in the civil rights movement when she refused to give up her seat on a Montgomery bus to a white passenger in 1955. Her action sparked the Montgomery Bus Boycott, which gave momentum to the Civil Rights movement. The above monument is located in the Selma Voting Rights Museum. Additionally, Troy State University at Montgomery recently has completed construction of the Rosa L. Parks Museum and Library, located at its downtown campus on the very spot where Rosa Parks waited for the bus.

The founders of the National Voting Rights Museum and Institute envisioned a space that captured the essence of struggles to empower America's people through the ballot box. Most of the founders were participants or supporters of the Voting Rights Movement of the 1960s, which culminated in Selma, Alabama, on the Edmund Pettus Bridge. There, people were brutally attacked by officers of the law as they marched to protest the death of Jimmy Lee Jackson and to demand the right to vote. Following this tragic event and the momumental Selma to Montgomery march, the Voting Rights Act was passed. The National Voting Rights Museum is located in Selma near the Edmund Pettus Bridge, the cornerstone of the contemporary struggle for human dignity. Today, an annual commemorative bridge crossing is held each spring. The event was attended by President Bill Clinton in 2000.

This marker honors Viola Liuzzo, a civil rights worker who came to Alabama to help with voter registration. She was murdered in 1965 en route to a civil rights meeting. Her murder was allegedly committed by KKK members Eugene Thomas, Collie Leroy Wilkins, Jr., and William Orville Eaton. Thomas and Wilkins were found not guilty of first degree murder in state court. However, all three suspects were found guilty of civil rights violations in U.S. District Court in Montgomery and sentenced to ten years in a federal prison. Eaton died on March 9, 1966, from natural causes, before serving his sentence. Photos courtesy of Alabama Bureau of Tourism and Travel.

Bridge where marchers were attacked by Dallas County deputies and state troopers with tear-gas and billyclubs at the height of Civil Rights tension. It, along with Selma's Civil War history and its antebellum mansions, are today among the Black Belt's leading tourist attractions. The route of the Selma-to-Montgomery March was designated a national monument with sites signified along U.S. 80, including the place where Detroit housewife Viola Liuzzo was shot and killed by Klansmen. In Birmingham, the Civil Rights Institute was built near the 16th Street Baptist Church, where four little black girls were killed in a bombing in 1963. And at Tuskegee, the entire campus of

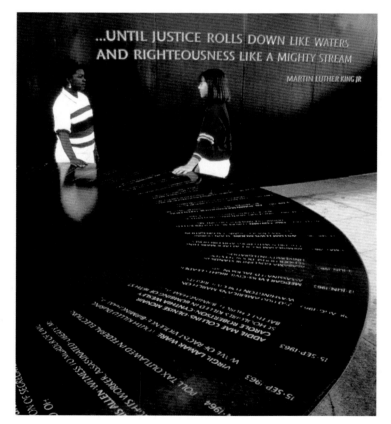

The Civil Rights Memorial, located in Montgomery on the site of the Southern Poverty Law Center, lists the names of those who gave their lives in the struggle for equality. Photos courtesy of Alabama Bureau of Tourism and Travel.

Tuskegee University was made a National Historic Site, including the home of the great black educator Booker T. Washington and the laboratory-office of scientist George Washington Carver.

A place called Alabama, known to the early Indians as "a clearing in the thicket," was first valued by settlers for its geographical diversity — hills and canyons, wide rivers and broad lakes, crystal white beaches and the clear blue-green Gulf waters. Alabama offered abundant natural resources as well, including herds of buffalo, plentiful deer, bears, thousands of acres of thick forest, and, later, layer upon layer of minerals beneath the soil.

Through all of the changes, discoveries, and challenges, Alabama's people remain its richest asset: people who learn quickly, have vivid imaginations, and meet the world with warm smiles and pleasant words.

Alabama people—whether native to the state or newcomers—glory in its exuberant history and look forward to fulfilling expectations of a grand global future. Our business boundaries are expanding into a limitless vision of tomorrow, when our goals will reach new, previously unexplored vistas. ■

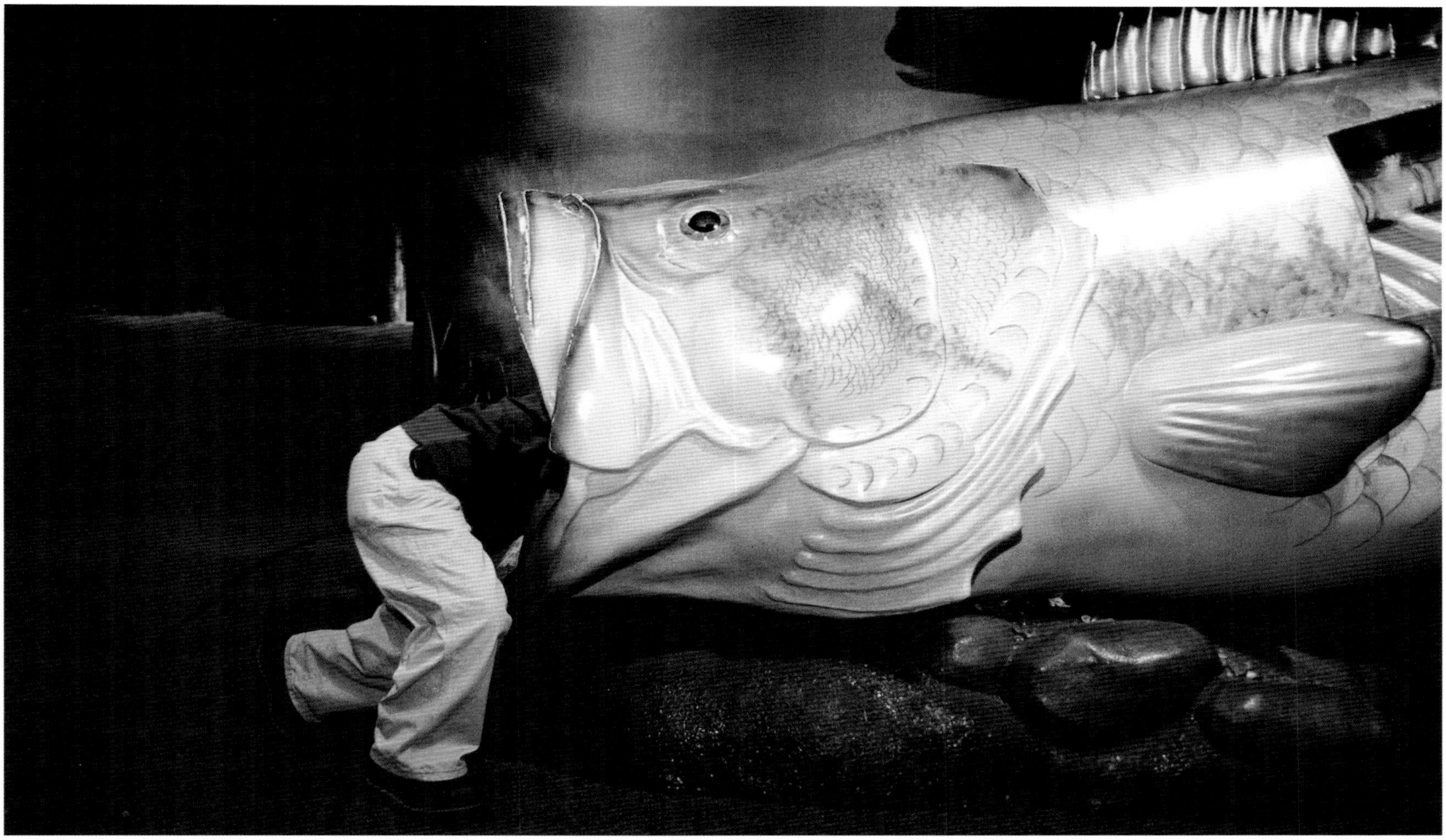

The McWane Center, located in Birmingham, is an interactive, hands-on activity center that allows visitors of all ages to explore the realms of science and nature through a variety of interesting exhibits and galleries. Additionally, the McWane Center boasts an IMAX theater that shows a selection of entertaining and educational features on a stunning domed theater screen. Photos courtesy of Alabama Bureau of Tourism and Travel.

The Estuarium at the Dauphin Island Sea Lab presents an unforgettable educational experience to visitors. Attractions include the beautiful Living Marsh Boardwalk, a 10,000-square-foot Exhibit Hall, and the Weather Station. Dauphin Island, which is located 33 miles from Mobile, is Alabama's marine education and research center and site of the Marine Environmental Sciences Consortium. Also located on Dauphin Island is Discovery Hall Programs, which allows secondary school students to learn through hands-on field and lab experience.

Alabama's zoological parks and aquariums utilize the latest information to create natural habitats, educational programs, and conservation efforts that are the cornerstone of modern zoo facilities and programs. Photos courtesy of Alabama Bureau of Tourism and Travel.

The retail sector in Alabama generates almost $40 billion in revenue annually, with restaurants alone accounting for $3.5 billion of those sales. Restaurants in Alabama employ about 100,000. The total retail and wholesale trade sector employs slightly more than 434,000. The University of Alabama Center for Business and Economic Research had predicted about 7,000 new retail and wholesale trade jobs would be added by the end of the year 2000. The retail sector pays in excess of $1 billion in wages each year. Photo by Paul Sumners.

Photo by Robert Fouts.

Shopping malls and open-air centers in cities throughout Alabama provide residents with diverse selection, dining venues, and recreational opportunities. Photo by Robert Fouts.

Photos above and at left by Scott Wiseman.

Alabama's Gulf Coast offers miles of beautiful white-sand beaches and a whole host of recreational, lodging, and dining choices. Thousands of visitors flock to Orange Beach, Gulf Shores, and Perdido each year, among other coastal destinations, for family, recreational, or romantic getaways. The coast is not only for pleasure—the area is host to local, state, regional, and national conferences and conventions every year. Photos courtesy of Alabama Bureau of Tourism and Travel.

Experience a day of first-class fun for the whole family at the world's largest space travel attraction—The U.S. Space & Rocket Center, located in Huntsville. From incredible displays of artifacts from our nation's space program, to space travel simulators, the U.S. Space & Rocket Center experience is unlike any other. The Center is the Official NASA Visitor Center and home of U.S. SPACE CAMP® and AVIATION CHALLENGE®. The U.S. Space & Rocket Center features more than 1,500 artifacts representing the nation's achievements in space exploration.

The USS *Alabama* Battleship Memorial Park is located in Mobile. Visitors to the park can tour the USS *Alabama* Battleship, which was transferred to the State of Alabama after being decommissioned in 1947. The ship was towed 5,600 miles from Bremerton, Washington, to USS *Alabama* Battleship Memorial Park in Mobile, still the longest non-military ton/mile tow in history, and opened for tours on January 9, 1965. Today, the Memorial park also features a submarine open for tours, an historic aircraft collection, and an historic military equipment collection, among other attractions. Photos courtesy of Alabama Bureau of Tourism and Travel.

A unique alternative to staying in a large hotel is the charm of a "Bed & Breakfast" establishment. Usually located in an historic home, the Bed & Breakfast experience is always one-of-a-kind, with hosts knowledgeable about their home's history and the area's attractions, and often featuring home-cooked breakfasts and individually decorated rooms and suites. Visitors should check with local tourism and travel agencies to find out about Bed & Breakfast establishments located throughout Alabama. Photos courtesy of Alabama Bureau of Tourism and Travel.

The Legends at Capitol Hill Conference and Golf Resort, a $12.5 million complex a mile off Interstate 65 in Prattville, was built by the Economic Development Partnership of Alabama for the state of Alabama. The resort offers state-of-the-art meeting accommodations and access to 54 holes of golf designed by Robert Trent Jones. Photo by Rich Michaelson.

Situated on 550 secluded acres, Marriott's Grand Hotel Resort and Golf Club is a spectacular location for a business convention, company retreat, private respite, or family vacation. With a championship golf course, tennis courts, horseback riding, and water activities, there is something to keep everyone entertained. Located in Point Clear on Mobile Bay, the hotel offers deluxe suites and fine dining with a scenic view of the beautiful Mobile Bay. Photo courtesy of Marriott's Grand Hotel Resort & Golf Club.

Conventions and trade shows are hosted throughout cities at civic centers and similar multi-purpose facilities. This allows companies the opportunity to showcase their businesses to local consumers and potential customers through exhibits and demonstrations. Photo by Robert Fouts.

The Galleria Mall is a popular attraction located in Birmingham, offering some of the finest stores in Central Alabama. Additionally, the property offers four-star lodging and dining at the Wynfrey Hotel and its adjoining restaurants. The hotel is connected to the mall, and visitors often can take advantage of special packages offering discounts on lodging, dining, and shopping. Photo courtesy of Alabama Bureau of Tourism and Travel.

Alabama is a sportsman's paradise, with miles of lakes and rivers throughout the state, and the Gulf of Mexico close at hand.
Photo by Pat McDonogh.

DeSoto Caverns Park, located in Childersburg, was developed in 1965 by Fred Layton of Munford, Alabama, as a show cave named Kymulga Onyx Cave. In 1975, land owner Ida Mathis' great grandson, the present owner and manager, Allen W. Mathis, III, took over operation of the cave from the retired Fred Layton. He changed the name of the cave to DeSoto Caverns, believing it should be renamed in honor of the famous Spanish Explorer who discovered it in 1540 — Hernando DeSoto. Today, the Park offers a variety of activities in addition to cave tours.

Alabama's terrain offers wide variety, including mountains, beaches, pastures, rivers and lakes, and woods. Photos courtesy of Alabama Bureau of Tourism and Travel.

One of Dekalb County's most famous scenic spots is the magnificent DeSoto Falls, tumbling 104 feet down a rock cliff about twelve miles from Fort Payne and about five miles beyond the entrance to DeSoto State Park. The canyon, representing one of the deepest gorges east of the Mississippi River, runs sixteen miles within DeSoto State Park. Photo courtesy of Alabama Bureau of Tourism and Travel/Dan Brothers.

Alabama's many State Parks offer camp sites, cabins and other lodging, hiking and bike trails, and other amenities attracting visitors to spend the day—or even longer. Photo courtesy of Alabama Bureau of Tourism and Travel.

Hank Williams, Sr. began his short, but legendary singing career when he was a teenager. Today, Hank is remembered throughout his home state of Alabama for his contributions to country music. Museums in his honor have been established in his home in Georgianna, and in Montgomery, where he was laid to rest. These museums house personal and professional memorabilia, and the Montgomery location displays the 1952 Cadillac in which Hank made his final journey. Thousands of people make the annual trip to these museums and to his gravesite.

Helen Keller, a renowned figure of strength and courage for overcoming both blindness and deafness to learn to speak, was born in Tuscumbia, Alabama, in 1880. Many people are familiar with the story of how her teacher, Anne Sullivan, helped Keller to learn to speak, and this story is often re-enacted at a museum at Helen Keller's birthplace. Photos courtesy of Alabama Bureau of Tourism and Travel.

The original sixty acres that are now Bellingrath Gardens and Home were purchased by Walter Bellingrath in 1917 upon the advice of his physician. Dr. P.D. McGehee advised his patient to learn how to play and told him to buy the fishing camp he had been admiring. In the following years, he and his wife, Bessie Morse Bellingrath, turned the land into a garden. They opened the garden for one day to the public during the Depression, and were overwhelmed by the response. In the years since, Bellingrath Gardens and Home has grown into a favorite destination for thousands of visitors each year. Photo by Robert Fouts.

The Alabama Shakespeare Festival (ASF) is located in Wynton M. Blount Cultural Park in Montgomery. ASF is currently the fifth largest Shakespeare Festival in the world and attracts more than 300,000 visitors to Montgomery from all 50 states and more than 60 foreign countries. The Alabama Shakespeare Festival offers the only fulltime, resident professional acting company in the Southeast and produces more than 14 productions each year.

Also situated within the Park is the Montgomery Museum of Fine Arts, which displays a fine collection of Old Master Prints, as well as local and traveling exhibits. Relatively new to the Park is the Shakespeare Gardens, one of only seven Shakespeare Gardens in the United States. The secluded 56,700-square-foot garden complex includes various plants and Elizabethan herbs mentioned in William Shakespeare's poems and plays. Photo by Robert Fouts.

With 24 state parks in Alabama, there is an activity for anyone who enjoys outdoor recreation from hiking scenic mountain trails to playing challenging golf courses to skiing on placid lakes. Alabama State Parks have facilities available including campgrounds, cabins, and resorts with amenities such as conference rooms and meeting spaces.

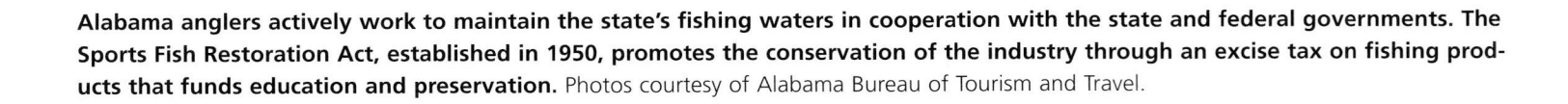

Alabama anglers actively work to maintain the state's fishing waters in cooperation with the state and federal governments. The Sports Fish Restoration Act, established in 1950, promotes the conservation of the industry through an excise tax on fishing products that funds education and preservation. Photos courtesy of Alabama Bureau of Tourism and Travel.

When looking for someone to design eighteen golf courses, start at the top. Enter legendary architect Robert Trent Jones, Sr., arguably the premier golf-course architect in the world. In his unparalleled career, Jones designed more than five hundred golf courses around the world, many of which are listed among *Golf Digest's* "America's 100 Greatest Golf Courses." Jones emerged from semi-retirement to tackle the project of designing what became Alabama's award-winning Robert Trent Jones Golf Trail. Photo by Robert Fouts.

Exploring the history of Alabama, the strength of her people, and the depth of her resources, one will understand why the state today has emerged as a leader in global economy. As Alabamians reach toward the promise of tomorrow, it is clear that Alabama will always be a state of being, as well as a state of mind. *Photo courtesy of Alabama Bureau of Tourism and Travel. Photo on facing page by Robert Fouts.*

Part II

Photo by Robert Fouts.

Photo by Robert Fouts.

CHAPTER 10

Communications
Transportation
& Energy

Photo by Pat McDonogh.

Touchstone Energy®

As electric utility restructuring unfolds, a growing alliance of electric cooperatives has united under the Touchstone Energy® brand to help identify Touchstone Energy as preferred providers of energy services. With the launch of Touchstone Energy in 1998, the brand quickly became the third largest energy brand in the country.

Touchstone Energy promotes cooperative strengths and the benefits of cooperative membership. Touchstone Energy symbolizes the basic values on which cooperatives were founded more than 60 years ago—integrity, accountability, innovation, and community spirit.

Cooperatives nationwide have not changed their names. Addition of the Touchstone Energy name and logo underscores a promise to provide customer and community service unsurpassed in the electric utility industry. The Touchstone Energy brand is built on a foundation that leverages the community relationships that the Alabama Electric Cooperative (AEC) member system has built and nurtured for decades.

Touchstone Energy cooperatives are delivering energy and energy solutions to more than 15 million customers each day. Touchstone Energy cooperatives are local, active members of their communities. For business and residential customers, Touchstone Energy offers the advantages of a strong local presence, plus the expertise and resources of a nationwide network of energy services. As participants in Touchstone Energy, they are beneficiaries of extensive consumer and market research at the national, regional, and state levels.

Under AEC's regional federation, 22 consumer-owned utilities are Touchstone Energy marketing allies: City of Andalusia, Alabama; Baldwin EMC, Summerdale, Alabama; City of Brundidge, Alabama; Central Alabama EC, Prattville, Alabama; CHELCO, DeFuniak Springs, Florida; Clarke-Washington EMC, Jackson, Alabama; Coosa Valley EC, Talladega, Alabama; Covington EC, Andalusia, Alabama; Dixie EC, Union Springs, Alabama; City of Elba, Alabama (Water Works and Electric Board); Escambia River EC, Jay, Florida; Gulf Coast EC, Wewahitchka, Florida; Pea River EC, Ozark, Alabama; Pioneer EC, Greenville, Alabama; South Alabama EC, Troy, Alabama; Southern Pine EC, Brewton, Alabama; West Florida EC, Graceville, Florida; and Wiregrass EC, Hartford, Alabama. Cullman EC, a Tennessee Valley Authority-supplied cooperative located in Cullman, Alabama, participates in Touchstone Energy through AEC's regional license. In addition, Delta EPA, Greenwood, Mississippi; Coast EPA, Bay St. Louis, Mississippi; Yazoo Valley EPA, Yazoo City, Mississippi; and Twin County EPA, Hollandale, Mississippi, participate in Touchstone Energy under AEC's regional license.

Touchstone Energy took the spotlight at the Touchstone Energy 300, a NASCAR Busch Grand National race at the Talladega Superspeedway.

The electric utility industry is experiencing the effects of legislative and regulatory actions at the state and federal levels that are leading to a restructuring of utility operations. As a national alliance of local, cooperatively owned utilities, Touchstone Energy ensures high standards of service to customers, both large and small, and their communities. Touchstone Energy allows AEC and Touchstone Energy to build upon a firm foundation that emphasizes its greatest strength—"the power of human connections".

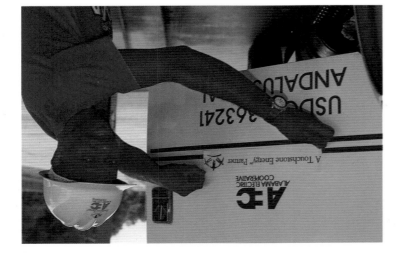

Touchstone Energy promotes cooperative strengths and the benefits of cooperative membership. It symbolizes the basic values on which cooperatives were founded—integrity, accountability, innovation, and community spirit.

The continued prosperity of AEC's member-owners is the result of implementing innovative maintenance programs to ensure reliable and efficient service while containing costs.

More than half a century ago, residents in rural areas were left in the dark because profit-driven utilities considered these areas unprofitable. Electric cooperatives were organized to provide the convenience and benefits of electricity to their farms and homes. The last 60 years of electric cooperative history is full of firsts and inspiring success stories, but it's the commitment to improving the quality of life in rural America that has withstood the test of time. That commitment is the cornerstone that founded Alabama Electric Cooperative (AEC) and its 21 consumer-owned member distributors: Baldwin EMC, Summerdale, Alabama; Central Alabama EC, Prattville, Alabama; CHELCO, DeFuniak Springs, Florida; Clarke-Washington EMC, Jackson, Alabama; Coosa Valley EC, Talladega, Alabama; Covington EC, Andalusia, Alabama; Dixie EC, Union Springs, Alabama; Escambia River EC, Jay, Florida; Gulf Coast EC, Wewahitchka, Florida; Pea River EC, Ozark, Alabama; Pioneer EC, Greenville, Alabama; South Alabama EC, Troy, Alabama; Southern Pine EC, Brewton, Alabama; Tallapoosa River EC, LaFayette, Alabama; West Florida ECA, Graceville, Florida; Wiregrass EC, Hartford, Alabama; city of Andalusia, Alabama; city of Brundidge, Alabama; Water Works & Electric Board of the City of Elba, Alabama; Utilities Board of the City of Opp, Alabama; and Opp & Micolas Mills, Opp, Alabama. Collectively, these member-owners serve the energy needs of more than 800,000 residents,

from the beaches of northwest Florida to the foothills of the Appalachian Mountains in northeast Alabama.

Today, these electric cooperatives provide not only reliable electric power at the lowest possible cost, but they also provide numerous value-added services like energy audits and other services like advanced home security systems. Electric cooperatives have overcome a number of obstacles since the early days of stringing wire. State-of-the-art equipment and technology ensure reliable electric service unmatched by competitors.

As electric utility restructuring accelerates, electric cooperatives remain focused on low-cost, service-oriented relationships with their customers. A light-year exists between the philosophy of providing only electricity to rural consumers and the philosophy of enhancing life in rural communities. Realizing that service-oriented relationships are critical to meeting customers' evolving expectations has led to the development of services such as digital satellite television, Internet access, rural water systems, and area job recruitment.

Electric cooperatives are active in a number of industrial and community development projects directed to revitalize America. Recognizing that new and expanding industry not only stimulates economic growth, but also attracts additional businesses and creates new employment opportunities, cooperatives serve as catalysts for job creation. Working with state agencies, community leaders, and economic development authorities, cooperatives are making a difference by opening doors to new job opportunities.

Development of rural infrastructure through technical assistance

Recognizing that new and expanding industry not only stimulates economic growth, but also attracts additional businesses and creates new employment opportunities, cooperatives serve as catalysts for job creation.

and funding is directly related to business start-ups and expansion. In addition, consumer-owned electric systems are uniquely positioned to develop additional services through use of available federal and state loan grant programs.

As customer expectations change, residential programs are changing to provide additional amenities for comfortable living. In addition to energy services, consumer-owned electric systems offer a variety of marketing services, including energy efficiency programs, home security systems, appliances, surge protection equipment, electric water heaters, rural television programming, and power quality consulting.

Several electric cooperatives in AEC's service area are located near metropolitan areas and progressive urban centers. These cooperatives are experiencing rapid growth and power system development due to residential, commercial, and industrial expansion.

The continued prosperity of AEC's member-owners is the result of implementing innovative maintenance programs to ensure reliable and efficient service while containing costs. Improved technology, progressive engineering services, and prudent materials and equipment procurement have also led to cost-effectiveness.

Quality education is essential to area growth and development, and electric cooperatives are engaged in various partnerships with schools to provide educational support. Consumer-owned electric systems' involvement in educational programs, including Writing

Electric cooperatives provide not only reliable electric power at the lowest possible cost, but they also provide numerous value-added services like energy audits and home security systems.

to Read and computer technology, ensures students are grounded in their educational curriculum. In addition, cooperative employees teach classes on electricity use and safety.

A strong and empowered workforce and employee incentive programs encourage creative thinking throughout each level of the cooperative structure. Staffed with professional and educated employees, cooperatives offer assistance in a variety of energy-related matters. Consumer-owned electric cooperatives are committed to spurring economic growth and improving the quality of life for people in rural areas. Different from their competitors in that the employees are local and the boards of directors are elected locally by those whom they serve, consumer-owned electric cooperatives have a vested interest in seeing their communities grow and prosper.

Unity has served as the foundation for electric cooperatives since the early days of the rural electric program. That unity, combined with integrity, innovation, accountability, and community service, is synonymous with consumer-owned electric cooperatives and the power of human connections.

Electric cooperatives continue adapting to the evolutionary changes of the electric utility industry. Heightened competition mandated by industry restructuring has put added pressure on electric utilities to work smarter. As a result, rural America is flourishing. Electric cooperatives are using their unique strengths to embrace change, and they lead America into a future far different from the past.

In the electric utility industry, quality is measured by reliable service and customer satisfaction. In 1941, when most of rural

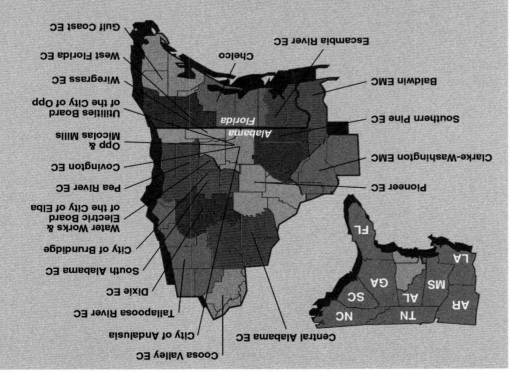

AEC Member-Owner Map

Gulf Coast EC
Escambia River EC
Chelco
West Florida EC
Wiregrass EC
Utilities Board of the City of Opp
Baldwin EMC
Opp & Micolas Mills
Southern Pine EC
Covington EC
Clarke-Washington EMC
Pea River EC
Pioneer EC
Water Works & Electric Board of the City of Elba
City of Brundidge
South Alabama EC
Dixie EC
Tallapoosa River EC
City of Andalusia
Central Alabama EC
Coosa Valley EC

Alabama
Florida

FL LA MS AL GA SC AR TN NC

An aggressive maintenance program ensures AEC and the member-owners are equipped to offer reliable electric service at the lowest possible cost.

America was without electricity, 11 electric cooperatives joined forces to demonstrate their commitment to providing reliable service at the lowest possible price. That unity has served as Alabama Electric Cooperative's (AEC) foundation from its early days until today, when it is recognized as a leader among generation and transmission cooperatives nationwide.

Headquartered in Andalusia, Alabama, AEC provides wholesale power to 12 Alabama distribution cooperatives, four Florida distribution cooperatives, four Alabama municipal systems, and one industrial member-owner. The 21 member-owners meet the energy needs of more than 800,000 consumers in 39 counties in Alabama and 10 counties in northwest Florida.

In 1998, AEC joined an alliance of cooperatives in a nationwide branding initiative promoting electric cooperatives as preferred energy providers. Under Touchstone Energy®, *the power of human connections*, AEC has a national image that is easily recognized and underscores its promise to provide customer and community service unsurpassed in the electric utility industry.

AEC is distinguished in its progressive and visionary implementation of strategic business decisions. Investing in the latest operational systems and processes—ranging from state-of-the-art generation and transmission technology to increased application technologies to improve and preserve our natural resources—has helped place AEC in the forefront of the utility industry.

Recognizing economic development benefits not only AEC and its consumer-owned member systems, but local communities as well, AEC emphasizes local and regional development by promoting employment opportunities through industry and business recruitment. AEC's membership realizes the economic benefits of industrial development oftentimes outweigh the benefits as the power supplier of industrial customers who seek to expand their

Recognizing economic development benefits not only AEC and its consumer-owned member systems, but local communities as well, AEC emphasizes local and regional development by promoting employment opportunities through industry and business recruitment.

operations. As competitive energy providers to prominent United States and international corporations and industries, AEC and its member-owners are providing more than electricity—they are spurring economic growth and marketing a way of life for area residents.

Active in a number of industrial and community projects directed to revitalize rural America, AEC helps access funding for rural infrastructure available through state and federal programs. Focusing on specific projects promoting customer density and sales volume, AEC is committed to working with its distribution systems to develop more efficient and economic business opportunities.

An aggressive maintenance program ensures AEC is equipped to offer reliable electric service at the lowest possible cost. A strong generation system is dependent on a strong transmission system; therefore, AEC gives priority to implementing prudent operational strategies and continuously seeks ways to reduce costs while improving efficiency.

AEC's service area encompasses approximately 24,500 square miles in Alabama and 7,500 square miles in Florida. District service centers strategically located in south Alabama and northwest Florida enable AEC to efficiently respond to the energy needs of its member-owners.

AEC's generating capacity totals 1,713 megawatts. The generating plants are the Charles R. Lowman Power Plant in Leroy, Alabama; the McIntosh units 1, 2, and 3 in McIntosh, Alabama; the McWilliams Power Plant near Andalusia, Alabama; an ownership interest in the James H. Miller Electric Generating Plant near Birmingham, Alabama; two hydroelectric plants on the Conecuh River in Covington County, Alabama; and the Portland Gas Turbine in Walton County, Florida.

AEC's ongoing success is the result of making the right decisions at the right time, and those decisions are grounded upon meeting the member-owners' needs and providing the most reliable service at the lowest reasonable price. As one of the strongest generation and transmission cooperatives in the nation, AEC realizes that success in the future lies in four basic values—integrity, accountability, innovation, and community spirit. These values will augment its strength in the future. ■

BellSouth

Three years after Alexander Graham Bell invented the original telephone in 1876, a group of investors founded the first telephone company in the Southeast. Later in 1880, Southern Bell Telephone and Telegraph Company opened for business in 11 cities. By the end of its first year, Southern Bell was serving 1,653 customers and it had 1,200 miles of wire. By the end of the century, Southern Bell was serving 29,369 telephones in 80 exchanges. Cumberland Telephone and Telegraph opened in 1883 and merged with Southern Bell in 1912 creating a company with 338,000 telephones in service and 10,000 employees. Those were the humble beginnings of what is today the largest telecommunications company in Alabama, BellSouth. Since then, the company has continued to grow—moving from the dirt roads of the late 1800s to today's Information Superhighway.

BellSouth is Birmingham's connection to a worldwide telecommunications network.

Through the company's constant network upgrades and investments, BellSouth customers have access to the world's foremost information resources through advanced digital switching and signaling systems, fiber optic cable and high-speed Internet access. Today, BellSouth provides the backbone for communications throughout the region and Alabama's connection to worldwide telecommunications networks. The company provides telecommunications, wireless communications, directory advertising and publishing, video, Internet, and information services to more than 37 million customers in 20 countries worldwide. BellSouth currently serves 24 million telephone lines.

BellSouth not only excels with its technical expertise, it has also been a leader in community involvement throughout the state. The company contributes to many community endeavors through financial support, expertise, and through employees and retirees who volunteer their time. Some of the contributions go toward charities, the arts, research of diseases, education, local chambers of commerce, wiring schools to connect to the Internet, or any one of many other community efforts in which BellSouth has a role. BellSouth commits additional resources on an ongoing basis to the BellSouth Pioneers, the volunteer service group made up of active and retired employees who focus their efforts on community

projects. BellSouth strongly supports the state's economic development initiatives and provides expertise that helps bring businesses to the state. Through the BellSouth Foundation, millions of dollars are allocated throughout the South to improve education.

In addition to BellSouth's expansive role in the community, the company's place among service providers is excellent. Dedication to customer service has earned BellSouth top honors nationally in the 1996 and 1997 Yankee Group surveys. In addition, the company also received the highest customer satisfaction ranking in local telephone companies from J. D. Power and Associates in 1996, 1997 and 1998.* Plus, BellSouth scored highest in both the 1995 and 1996 American Customer Satisfaction Index, a national survey conducted by the University of Michigan Business School and the American Society for Quality Control, published in *Fortune* magazine each spring.

BellSouth has many organizations that specialize in various services to meet specific customer needs. For instance, for directory listings and advertising, customers rely on BellSouth Advertising and Publishing Company. For Internet services, there is BellSouth® Internet Service. Wireless services, phones, pagers, and accessories come from BellSouth Mobility or from the BellSouth Telecommunications' business offices.

The Customer Operations Units of BellSouth Telecommunications handle your home and business telephone needs. Each unit is dedicated to serve specific customer groups. Small Business and BellSouth Business work with all types of business customers. Consumer Services helps residential customers with their home telecommunications services. Consumer Services

The Alabama Operations Center, an award-winning building for its design and environmental consciousness, is the headquarters for BellSouth—Alabama and is located along the Highway 280 Corridor in Birmingham.

The Real Yellow Pages Online gives users quick access to the most current and accurate online directories available. Photo Copyright Edward Badham 1998.

also offers special services for customers who are speech- or hearing-impaired through the Telecommunications Center for Customers with Disabilities.

To remain well postured in an era of aggressive competition and rapidly evolving technology, BellSouth serves its customers through customer operations units and separate subsidiaries dedicated to specific customer segments.

BellSouth Advertising and Publishing Corporation

Innovation is the signal word at BellSouth Advertising and Publishing Corporation (BAPCO) which is recognized as one of the largest and most progressive publishers of telephone and classified advertising directories in the world. In addition to its traditional line of paper products, the company is also a pioneer in the areas of audiotext services, online listings and the development of niche directories that literally span the globe.

As publisher of The Real White Pages® and The Real Yellow Pages® from BellSouth, the company publishes more than 500 directories for the Southeast United States. These directories list the products and services of local, national and foreign advertisers. In addition, BAPCO publishes several well-known niche directories, including the internationally-acclaimed BellSouth Guia Directory, which links American manufacturers with the international and Latin American trade industry, and the Real Yellow Pages® Homebook.

Many of these directories include voice information services. These audio offerings include Consumer Tips, Health Tips and a Restaurant and Entertainment Guide. Advertisers can take advantage of Real Talking Ads, a service that allows a business to frequently update information, like specific product details, promotional programs or operating hours. The Real Talk section of a directory enables the user to access free audio information on various topics of interest by dialing a specific telephone number and a four-digit code.

In 1997, BAPCO put The Real Yellow Pages® online for its major markets. Accessed at http://www.realpages.com, this online resource is updated regularly and gives users quick and easy access to the most current and comprehensive online directories available. The search results for a business include a detailed map a user can print

out. The Real Yellow Pages Online also takes the guesswork out of seat selection at stadiums and theaters. Users can talk on the phone with local ticket services and check out the location of available seats on one of The Real Yellow Pages® Online seating charts.

BellSouth Customer Units

BellSouth has trained specialists who are experts at providing efficient solutions for customers. They work with businesses in helping them determine the best options for their specific telecommunications needs. Others specialize in residential services, wireless services and Internet connection services.

BellSouth Small Business Services

BellSouth Small Business Services, the division of BellSouth Telecommunications that specializes in telecommunications products and services for small and mid-sized businesses, serves customers in a consultative role, providing insight and solutions specific to the needs of each customer's business.

Every small business has access to a BellSouth Small Business Specialist who is dedicated to determining the most appropriate communications products and services for making businesses run more smoothly and efficiently. Specialists can design a comprehensive communications package of services that meets the individual needs of a small or mid-sized business. Such communications packages may include local service, wireless service, Internet access, web hosting in markets where it is available, and a variety of telephone service features like Caller ID, Preferred Call Forwarding, BellSouth® MemoryCall® service, and others.

Beyond the specialists' expertise, small business owners may take advantage of a number of free services available through the BellSouth Small Business Services web site at http://www.smlbiz.bellsouth.com. At that site on the Internet, customers can access articles for small business owners, order products and services, take a look at their current bill and pay it over the Internet, ask for a list of products and services available in the small business's location, and many other options.

BellSouth Business

New management strategies are altering the faces of decades-old corporate philosophies. Competitive forces are waging full-scale assaults on every industry, on every front. Large businesses need to stay ahead of the game with communications and information transmission technology that positions them to make the right moves. BellSouth Business (www.bellsouth.com/bbs) was created to help companies meet the challenges of the present and the future.

A substantial commitment has been made to customers in the

The BellSouth Mobility's hot air balloon is the company's airborne "ambassador of goodwill." The balloon flies at major community happenings and company events such as groundbreakings and retail store openings. Photo by Neil Dent.

Southeast, demonstrating a willingness to do what it takes to design and deploy a network that can stand up to everything—from cable cuts to hurricanes. To better serve business customers in this exciting era of innovation and change, BellSouth Business provides a variety of enhanced services and business tools, including local area network (LAN) interconnections, video and voice conferencing, voice messaging and facsimile transmission, electronic commerce tools and high capacity data services. BellSouth Business solves communications challenges with strategies that put companies in a competitive situation to win.

BellSouth Consumer Services

BellSouth offers an array of services for residential customers including local phone service and a number of calling features. BellSouth Consumer Services also offers voice mail service, Internet access service, wireless service, pagers, and maintenance plans for your telephone equipment and telephone wiring inside your home. In addition, several calling plans are available to help customers manage their monthly phone bills. BellSouth is a one-stop source for telecommunications needs in the home.

Another part of BellSouth's Consumer Services is the Telecommunications Center for Customers with Disabilities that serves customers with visual, hearing, speech and physical disabilities. Special equipment, such as the TTY/TDD (teletypewriter/telecommunications device for the deaf), allows BellSouth service representatives to communicate with hearing-impaired and speech-impaired customers. These customers can order special products that make it easy for them to use the telephone. In addition, BellSouth publishes a telephone directory of all TTY customers in its territory and makes it available through this center.

Information about BellSouth's products and services for residential customers is available from service representatives, through the Internet at www.bellsouth.com and through BellSouth®

RightTouch® service, an automated customer service system via the telephone which is available to customers 24 hours a day.

BellSouth® Internet Service

BellSouth offers fast, reliable access to the Internet for residential and business customers through BellSouth® Internet Service. The Bellsouth® Internet Service homepage focuses on extensive local news and links to local cities and their surrounding communities. Local movie listings, restaurants, sports events and the World Wide Web are never more than a click away.

BellSouth offers faster connection options like ADSL and ISDN access, personal Web pages, additional Web accounts, and 24-hour/7-days-a-week, toll-free expert help. The service has received an "A" rating from top industry analysts.

BellSouth® Internet Service offers businesses a full range of options that allows them to customize a networking solution tailored specifically to their needs. This includes dial-up Internet and Intranet access that can serve a company's work-at-home employees or mobile work force. The company also provides businesses with customized, secure Web hosting and manages customers' routers and networks, including IP address assignment and domain name services. Around-the-clock network monitoring and trouble-shooting are also provided.

BellSouth Mobility

Wireless phones were first marketed in 1983 and came to Alabama as BellSouth Mobility in 1985. BellSouth Mobility continues its dedication to serving its customers with cutting-edge technology, advanced calling features, and the highest quality technical support for customers. The company also is focused on being a good corporate neighbor by sponsoring things like the Bruno's Memorial Golf Classic, NASCAR, 911 services and by assigning "star" numbers for special events. The company also loans cellular phones and provides free service to officials during crisis situations such as natural disasters.

BellSouth Pledges Quality and Service to Customers

As a leader in telecommunications, BellSouth pledges to provide the highest quality service, continued technology research, and product and service development to meet both the wired and wireless needs of Alabama customers now and into the 21st century. ▪

*J.D. Power and Associates 1996-1998 Residential Local Telephone Customer Satisfaction Studies.sm 1998 Study conducted among 14,260 residential users of local telephone services.

Photo by Robert Fouts.

Management and Advisors gather at the statue of Ervin S. Cooper at Cooper Riverside Park.

Cooper/T. Smith Corporation

Cooper/T. Smith is one of America's oldest and largest stevedoring and maritime related firms. Headquartered in Mobile, Cooper/T. Smith has operations on all three U.S. coasts encompassing 38 ports, and has foreign operations in Venezuela, Brazil, Colombia, and Mexico. The company also maintains ownership in numerous satellite companies, complementing the multi-faceted maritime objectives.

The story of the Cooper family is as interesting as a saga out of the Old West. It begins right after the Civil War when Henry Harrison Cooper and his two brothers came to the New World from Scotland and settled in South Carolina. They soon immigrated

to Alabama and settled in Baldwin County in an area later appropriately named Rosinton. They were rosin farmers securing rosin for naval stores from the plentiful Baldwin County pine trees. Each of the three brothers married one of the McKenzie sisters, homesteaded 160 acres each, and put their roots down to establish ties which would link their descendents firmly to Alabama over the next century and more. Henry Harrison Cooper and his wife, Matilda McKenzie Cooper, had 14 children; the next to the youngest was named Angus Royal Cooper. It was this son who established the waterfront tradition which the family would follow for generations. Angus was born in 1877, and at an early age he

Ervin S. Cooper (1911-1982) Dedicated to the maritime industry throughout the world, the city of Mobile built a riverside park to honor the accomplishments of Cooper/T. Smith.

went to work on the Mobile docks as a tally man (one who counts the ships' cargoes). His early days on the docks prepared him to build a strong stevedoring company in America. It was on February 5, 1905, that he established what has now become Cooper/T. Smith Corporation through various name changes and acquisitions over the years. In 1925, Angus Cooper and his family moved to New Orleans where he would expand his stevedoring business and manage the Munson Line's gulf-wide operations. The Munson Line prospered so well that Munson built one of the first true skyscrapers in New York City. However, hard times hit when the bottom fell out of the economy in 1929, and Munson Line fell into financial difficulty. Angus Cooper continued handling stevedoring for one of Munson's allies, Alcoa Steamship Company, and as a result, the Munson Line surrendered all of their equipment to him in lieu of pay. This was the next big step in building a significant family-owned stevedoring company.

Meanwhile, Angus Cooper's youngest son, Ervin, who was born in 1911, graduated from Tulane University in 1933 and joined Alcoa Steamship in New Orleans and in New York, then later joined his family business. After he married Margaret Folmar of Troy, Alabama, had two sons (Angus II and David), he went on to personally direct the firm's expansion to ports throughout the U.S. Both sons, Angus II and David, graduated from the University of Alabama, joined their family's company, and set out on a seemingly impossible mission. This mission was to grow the business worldwide and compete internationally in the global market with the biggest maritime firms in the world.

Today's Cooper/T. Smith is a progressive and innovative organization employing thousands worldwide. Its subsidiaries include warehousing, insurance, terminal operations, tugboats, push boats, barging, barge fleeting, floating terminals, and the most recent acquisition of Kimberly Clark's Marine and Timberlands Division, now renamed Cooper Marine and Timberlands Corporation. In fact, the company impacts an astonishing array of industries throughout the country, from agriculture and energy to chemicals and construction.

Stevedoring is still a central part of Cooper's business. The company's state of the art equipment and automation provide customers with fast and cost-effective movement of cargo to and from ships at port. Cooper/T. Smith prides itself on its ability to operate globally. "We have huge barge-mounted cranes that can be transported anywhere a customer needs the service," says David Cooper. "The company's barge-mounted cranes can be sent virtually anywhere in the world in 45 days or less. Our people can also help clients adapt or modify their own equipment and facilities to significantly enhance their performance."

One hundred years earlier in Rosinton, Alabama, the Coopers were drawn to the waterfront by producing rosin for naval stores. Each generation had made their contribution, and the legacy was left in the hands of the younger Coopers with a dream. Today, at the foot of Government Street in Mobile, Cooper Riverside Park honors the memory of Ervin S. Cooper (1911-1982). There, a bronze statue of Ervin Cooper presides over the area. Within, he is immortalized sitting on a Waterman Steamship Company bench gazing over the Mobile River which has meant so much to the Cooper family. Cooper/T. Smith has grown from a modest beginning to a complex, multifaceted maritime giant in the last one hundred years. Earning a worldwide reputation for lasting partnerships and high quality service, Angus Cooper II and David Cooper plan to make the next century of the business just as exciting. ▪

Alabama Power Company

Alabama Power's low prices, reliable service, and community development make Alabama a better place to live. As a Southern Company subsidiary, Alabama Power is part of one of the most successful, fastest-growing, and exciting companies in the electric-utility industry.

You name it; electricity makes it work. Lights, air-conditioning, computers . . . Alabama Power is the power source for so many things Alabama residents and businesses use every day. And the prices the company's customers pay for that energy are among the lowest in the nation.

Best of all for the state's communities, low prices and world-class customer service are bolstered with a sense of community as old as the company itself.

Development from the start

Alabama Power was founded in 1906 by William Patrick Lay, a steamboat captain. In 1907, Congress gave Lay approval to build a dam and power plant on the Coosa River. To raise the necessary money for the project, Lay teamed up with hydroelectric pioneer James Mitchell and Montgomery attorney Thomas Martin.

With the help of English and American investors, the three men underwrote an ambitious 20-year plan for hydroelectric development in Alabama. The original plan also called for extensive efforts to bring new businesses and residents to Alabama.

"Company founders such as William Patrick Lay and Thomas Martin knew that community and economic development for this state would have a profound and positive effect on the company's business success," says Alabama Power President and CEO Elmer Harris. "We continue to focus on their vision because thriving communities and growing businesses improve the state's economy. And a strong economy helps education, culture, and the overall quality of life in Alabama."

The company established its corporate headquarters in Birmingham in 1912. Since then, the company has developed a reputation as the state's leading corporate citizen. Alabama Power's long-running commitment to economic development and community enhancement adds value to the reliable electric service it provides.

Economic growth

Alabama Power was the first electric utility in the United States to establish its own economic-development department. If you

Lay Dam is one of Alabama Power's 14 hydroelectric facilities that produce electricity for their customers and create recreational waterways and wildlife habitats.

Alabama Power employees collect water samples to help gather data to further environmental research studies.

Community

Because strong communities are sure-fire business incubators, Alabama Power puts a lot of time, energy, and resources into community activities.

"Through programs related to education, the environment, and social involvement, Alabama Power and its employees continually work to strengthen our communities," Harris says.

The company, the Alabama Power Foundation, and the Alabama Power Service Organization contribute millions annually to community programs, education initiatives, and environmental programs throughout the state. And the company annually contributes sponsorships and employee time to numerous cultural events across the state such as the City Stages music festival in Birmingham and Bay Fest in Mobile.

Environmental stewardship

Alabama Power is safe, responsible, and committed when it comes to the environment. They either meet or do better than the standards set by state and federal agencies for protecting human health and the environment. Over the last several years the company has made major reductions in their air emissions and continue to support initiatives that help address air quality issues. One of every 50 employees at Alabama Power has direct, full-time environmental responsibilities. Alabama Power ranks in the top 10 of all investor-owned utilities for its investment in equipment and technology to improve the environment, according to the U.S. Energy Information Agency. Their commitment to the environment goes beyond their business. By sponsoring, supporting, and running a variety of programs, they're helping to teach the public, student, and teachers about environmental responsibility.

think about it, Alabama Power's commitment to economic and community development makes a lot of business sense. New and growing businesses locating in the company's service territory mean new customers and more profits.

But company leaders say that there are other, more broad-based, motives at work.

"Our company recognizes the importance of vibrant, growing communities," says Alan Martin, an executive vice president at Alabama Power. "We believe that the health of our company and society depends on helping all citizens share in the nation's economic growth. To this end, we must encourage and support the growth of all business—large and small."

A true corporate citizen

Alabama Power offers affordable electricity to customers, superior customer service, and is a leader in the community. Those are the hallmarks of being the state's leading corporate citizen.

"We've been doing business this way for 90 years now, and our business keeps getting stronger," Harris says. "And as our business gets stronger, we'll continue to invest in the overall health and success of the community and our state." ▪

CHAPTER 11

Manufacturing & Distribution

Photo by Robert Fouts.

Corus Tuscaloosa

● ●

C orus Tuscaloosa has carved a niche in the steel industry as a world-class producer of high quality hot rolled carbon coil, coil plate, and plate. These products are produced in a wide range of dimensions by a motivated, team-oriented work-force steeped in tradition and ethics.

The company originally known as Tuscaloosa Steel Corporation became a subsidiary of British Steel plc in 1991, and recently adopted the name of the new parent company, Corus Group plc, formed by the merger of British Steel plc and Koninklijke Hoogovens.

Located on the banks of the Black Warrior River, Corus Tuscaloosa has direct water access to all international ports and U.S. waterways for economical transportation of raw material and finished product. The company's efficient material handling facilities and accessible interstate rail and highway systems ensure on-time deliveries to customers.

Corus Tuscaloosa was the first steel mill in the country to employ Steckel mill technology for producing high-quality wide plate from coil. Built in 1985, the mill has consistently demonstrated product versatility, quality, and cost advantages readily translated to customer benefits and products that meet or exceed all AISI, ASTM, and ASME code specifications, customer specifications, and international requirements.

Corus Tuscaloosa started from humble beginnings. Opened in November 1985 as a steel slab converter, the company has grown to become a world-class producer of flat rolled steel products operating in a global economy. Corus Tuscaloosa's goal is to exceed customer expectations of quality and service by providing a cost-effective product shipped on a timely basis.

Corus Tuscaloosa's annual capacity is 800,000 tons of carbon and high-strength low alloy coil and plate. Coils weighing 40 tons can be produced in thickness from .170 inches to 1.000 inches and widths from 36 inches to 100 inches. Coils can be further processed to plate on a .750 x 102 inch wide cut-to-length line. Discrete plate can be also be produced in thicknesses to 2.500 inches and widths to 100 inches.

The production process begins with the accumulation of raw materials for melting in Corus Tuscaloosa's 150-ton twin shell D.C. electric arc furnaces. The feed stock consists of recycled steel scrap and processed iron ore from Corus Tuscaloosa's direct reduced iron ore facility in Mobile, Alabama.

Once melted, the steel is further refined to specification and then continuously cast in the company's unique mid-thickness (5 inch) variable width slab caster. As the steel exits the caster, slabs are cut to specified lengths and moved through a temperature

Continuous cast slabs weighing up to 40 tons are heated to precise temperatures and rolled to customers specifications on Corus Tuscaloosa's 4-high reversing Steckel mill.

controlled equalizing furnace before being rolled to finished coil or plate. The entire process from melt to finished product requires just over three hours of production time. This unique computerized hot-connect process has been developed with world class facilities and capital investments of more than $250 million.

Corus Tuscaloosa's products are used in numerous market segments. Manufacturers of truck components, railcars, barges, ships, bridges, and storage tanks for LPG gas and other liquids—both above—and below-ground—represent a large share of Corus Tuscaloosa's business. Pipe and tube products ranging from petro-

Corus Tuscaloosa's state-of-the-art 150 Ton Twin Shell DC electric arc furnaces are equipped with DRI continuous feed systems to insure efficient quality production of hot metal.

Located on the Black Warrior River, Corus Tuscaloosa has direct water access to all international ports and U.S. waterways for economical transportation of raw materials and finished product.

chemical transmission pipelines to structural tubing represent another significant market for Corus Tuscaloosa products. Distribution of the plant's products is further proliferated by national service center chains to a vast array of end-users. A world-class facility, Corus Tuscaloosa can export product worldwide for consumption.

Quality is an important ingredient in world-class operations. Corus Tuscaloosa employs a team-working concept with continuous quality improvement and performance. This attitude has earned the company certification to the highest quality standards in the industry including Japanese Industrial Standards, American Bureau of Shipbuilding, and ISO 9001 certifications.

Employees at Corus Tuscaloosa are fully committed to steadfast customer service, productivity, and quality improvements. These standards are key elements in providing and maintaining a quality work environment for everyone. Corus Tuscaloosa employees are highly trained professionals. As leaders in the carbon coil and plate markets, the company routinely invests in new equipment, training, and technology to ensure the highest quality products, delivered on time with total customer satisfaction. Professional sales service teams provide excellent communications and total customer satisfaction. Innovative vendor-managed inventory systems and rapid delivery programs are available to customers.

At the heart of Corus Tuscaloosa is the quality and caliber of the workforce. A non-union facility, the work place is a prime example of a cohesive effort focused on building a world-class facility with state of-the-art equipment and a skilled, well-trained staff to operate at peak performance.

Corus Tuscaloosa's philosophy of empowering employees with decision-making capability is the company's key to success. This management style holds true in manufacturing as well as customer support through customer value teams and customer partnering programs. The result is high morale for the company's 400 employees and a satisfied customer base.

By the use of new and emerging technologies, Corus Tuscaloosa can maintain world market competitiveness and long-term relationships while providing profits for company growth and stockholders equity. Enhanced productivity and intense dedication ensures that Corus Tuscaloosa's customers and steel consumers are getting the very best in quality.

Corus Tuscaloosa is proud to be located in the heart of West Alabama. Corus Tuscaloosa's proximity to environmentally sensitive wildlife areas, waterways, and residential communities requires strictly enforced operational procedures that ensures compliance with all environmental regulations.

Corus Tuscaloosa is committed to being a welcomed, responsible neighbor to the Tuscaloosa community. It will continue to grow along with the city in the new millennium. ■

Corus Tuscaloosa's efficient warehouse is designed to ensure on-time delivery of our high quality, precision cut, coded plate.

Mercedes-Benz U.S. International Inc.

I n early 1993, when Daimler-Benz AG (now DaimlerChrysler) decided to embark on the M-Class project as part of its globalization strategy, the task was enormous: develop and produce a new vehicle, at a new plant, in a new country, with new people. And, of course, it had to be competitively priced and a true Mercedes-Benz.

Faced with this challenge, the company started with a clean slate, in terms of vehicle concept, in the way it would produce the M-Class, in the design of the factory, and in the establishment of a new corporate culture. The result was the M-Class All Activity Vehicle, which set a new standard in the sport utility market.

Since locating in Tuscaloosa County, Mercedes-Benz U. S. International Inc. (MBUSI) has worked diligently to create a company that reflects the wealth of talent and diversity that exists within the U.S. and, more specifically, within the State of Alabama. In doing so, the company committed to responsible corporate citizenship and has tried to exercise this commitment in both its employment and business practices.

In less than 10 years in Alabama, Mercedes-Benz has already demonstrated significant progress in these areas. Approximately 1,900 team members, mostly Alabamians, are currently employed

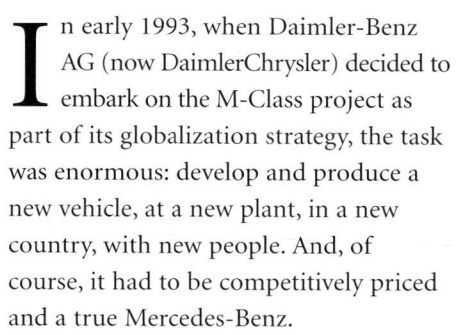

With the combination of Germans and Americans, and team members with experience from U.S. and Japanese automakers, as well as from Mercedes-Benz, the MBUSI corporate culture is truly a "melting pot" of experience and skills.

at the plant. As part of its commitment to Alabama, Mercedes-Benz has established a cooperative training program that will provide citizens in Alabama with the latest skills in automotive and manufacturing technology. Located on its site near Vance, the Mercedes-Benz Institute is a state-of-the art training facility that will help enhance the skill base in Alabama.

Located 12 miles east of Tuscaloosa and 32 miles west of Birmingham, the contemporary one-million-square-foot facility sits on a 966-acre site and includes a Training Institute and a Visitor Center, in addition to the plant. The major sections of the plant include a body shop, an environmentally safe paint shop that is pressurized to keep out the fine red-clay soil of Alabama, and an assembly shop, where the chassis is married to the body. The plant configuration breaks the typical automotive paradigm. All shops—body, paint, and assembly— as well as the administrative areas, are located under one roof, with the administrative office running through the heart of the manufacturing area. This helps foster a team approach and open communication, aids in the process and material flow, and enables the full system of manufacturing to function efficiently.

The public can learn about the history of the world's oldest automaker at the 24,000-square-foot Mercedes-Benz Visitor Center, which offers an entertaining presentation of DaimlerChrysler's history, its vehicles from the late 1800s to the present.

The development process of the Mercedes-Benz M-Class began in early 1993 with an unprecedented amount of market research, which enabled the company to develop a product tailored to customer needs. Tuscaloosa was chosen as the home for the new Mercedes plant from an initial list of different sites all over the U.S. Tuscaloosa County represented the best combination of the criteria Mercedes was looking for.

The goal was to create an evolution of the sport utility, a true off-roader, but with the passenger car attributes of a Mercedes-Benz, namely safety, performance, quality, and comfort—and priced in the mid-$30,000 range.

The Mercedes-Benz U.S. International, Inc. one-million-square-foot manufacturing plant, located 12 miles east of Tuscaloosa, Alabama and 32 miles west of Birmingham, Alabama, sits on a 966-acre site that includes a Training Institute and a Visitor Center.

MBUSI selected approximately 65 major suppliers to work as its partners in the development and production of the M-Class, a small number compared to other auto manufacturers that may have well over 500 suppliers for a particular vehicle. Of the 65 system suppliers, seven are located in Alabama—suppliers that produce everything from the M-Class' interior trim, to cockpits, to body stampings. Meanwhile, the engines and transmissions for the M-Class come from DaimlerChrysler plants in Germany, and are shipped to the U.S. out of the port of Bremerhaven.

For an order of 5,000 vehicles and nearly 2,500 requirements for basic parts, it only takes MBUSI's customized software approximately 90 seconds to organize all the requirements for all the vehicles, which is one of the fastest MRP times in the world. DaimlerChrysler is studying this technique as one of many possible innovations it can incorporate into its worldwide operations. Response to the M-Class has been positive, as demonstrated by the vehicle achieving a spot as one of the most popular vehicles on the market today. In response to high demand for the M-Class, a decision was made to increase production of the sport-utility vehicle through the Eurostar plant production lines in Graz, Austria. With this supplemental production, MBUSI projects it will produce in excess of 80,000 vehicles each year.

Training is a vital component of the MBUSI corporate strategy. It begins even before a team member joins the organization, during their interview and screening process. Production team members underwent extensive training in Germany, some living and working there for more than six months.

Following the DaimlerChrysler tradition of being an environmentally conscious company, MBUSI has integrated sweeping environmental policies throughout its vehicle development, production process, and plant engineering. Part of the company's mission statement includes its commitment to meet and, in many cases, exceed environmental standards.

Since its location to Tuscaloosa County, MBUSI has increased its initial $300,000-million investment by another $8 million to open a parts consolidation warehouse in Bessemer, Alabama, where supplies are received, separated for two destinations—for the Tuscaloosa plant and for Graz, Austria. Economic development surveys show that MBUSI shipped $1.3 billion in parts and M-Class vehicles from Alabama to overseas destinations this year. Based upon those numbers, MBUSI is the state's largest exporter—with 14 percent of the state's total export dollars.

MBUSI also has served as an active leader in our community. To introduce aspects of German culture in Alabama, the company has sponsored cultural festivals in Birmingham and Tuscaloosa featuring food, beverages, and music native to Germany. These festivals also serve as a platform to support charity initiatives in the local community. In recent years, the company has contributed to organizations such as the American Red Cross, Salvation Army, United Negro College Fund (UNCF), and United Way.

With skillful teamwork, state-of-the-art technology, and a commitment to be the best, Mercedes-Benz will continue to create its world-class product—made by Mercedes and the hands of Alabamians. ∎

The commitment to excellence—a quality for which all Mercedes-Benz products are known—will always be the foundation upon which Mercedes-Benz U.S. International operates.

Since its launch in 1997, the M-class has won more than 40 awards including the 1998 North American Truck of the Year, Motor Trend Truck of the Year, and Consumers Digest "Best Buy."

Rheem Manufacturing

Montgomery, Alabama is home for Rheem Water Heater Division, America's largest water heater manufacturer. The Rheem brand is widely recognized by consumers and has long been the brand of preference for installing contractors. Through consistent attention to quality, product innovation, and customer service Rheem has grown steadily through the decades. Today, Rheem makes approximately one out of every three water heaters sold in the U.S. and Canada.

Rheem Water Heater Division designs, builds, and markets a broad range of gas and electric water heaters for residential and commercial applications. Rheem is unique in that they enjoy market leadership in both the wholesale (traditional plumber installations) and retail markets. Much of the recent growth in the water heater industry has been in the so-called DIY or do-it-yourself market made possible by "big box" retailers such as Home Depot. Rheem also sells products for use in manufactured homes and has a growing base of international customers. The company is poised to capture growth in any or all of several key-marketing channels.

Rheem has manufacturing plants in Montgomery, Alabama; Eagan Minnesota; Nuevo Laredo, Mexico; and Hamilton, Ontario. The Montgomery plant, the company's largest, has been expanded several times since it was built in 1972.

Scanning products before shipment is part of a comprehensive supply chain management system at Rheem. Rheem and Ruud distributors can find the exact status of product orders via the internet. Over half of all water heater orders are handled through direct EDI transactions, helping reduce transaction costs for both Rheem and its customers.

This 700,000-square-foot-plant located in Montgomery, Alabama is one of four North American Rheem Water Heater manufacturing facilities. Products produced here are distributed throughout North America, as well as international markets including Europe, Asia, and the Middle East.

Oxford Manufacturing Facility.

Hager has developed new operations in its Oxford and Montgomery plants in recent years and moved other key operations to Alabama from other parts of the country. Trim and Auxiliary product manufacturing was begun in Montgomery in 1990. Manufacturing operations for Threshold and Weatherstripping were relocated to Oxford in 1992. Hager moved its Roton continuous geared hinge production to the Oxford plant from Chicago in 1996. Each of these new divisions has added significant growth to the company's product line.

In addition to its manufacturing operation, Hager has its main distribution center in Montgomery. Products from all three manufacturing plants are shipped to Montgomery before delivery to customers throughout the United States and around the world. Architectural hinges and related products are marketed and warehoused in Central and South America, Mexico, Saudi Arabia, and other Middle Eastern nations and in parts of Europe.

The employees, owners, and executives of Hager take an active part in the life of their communities. The company has won numerous participation awards in United Way fund-raising in both Montgomery and Oxford, and employees take part in Red Cross blood drives in both cities. Executives of the company participate in various councils and committees of their local chambers of commerce. At Christmas time, each facility adopts families in need within their community. In Oxford, Hager plays a highly visible role in the annual Cancer Walk-a-Thon.

Oxford Manufacturing Facility.

The hardware business has changed a lot in 150 years. But some things never change. In 1849, founder Charles Hager said that success could only result from making a quality product competitively priced and producing it on time. That has been the company's mission statement ever since. Through five generations, family members have made decisions that expanded Hager Companies and positioned it for future growth. A sixth generation is waiting to continue that legacy. ■

Thompson Tractor Company, Inc.

Thompson Tractor Company, Inc. is the full-line Caterpillar dealer for Alabama and northwest Florida and the Caterpillar forklift dealer for central and northern Georgia. The company specializes in the sale and service of Caterpillar products, including earthmoving, construction and material handling equipment, and diesel and natural gas engines and gas turbines. Founded by Hall W. Thompson in 1957, the company is headquartered in Birmingham and employs more than 1,000 people. The company's history has been distinguished by a dedication to excellence and a commitment to service.

"We'd like to be recognized as a business partner by our customers," says Michael D. Thompson, President and CEO of the company.

Thompson Caterpillar provides a diverse array of services to customers in its region through four divisions: Thompson Tractor Company, Thompson Power Systems, Thompson Lift Truck Company, and the new Thompson Cat Rental Store. Thompson has full-service facilities in Birmingham, Montgomery, Mobile, Anniston/Oxford, Tuscaloosa, Decatur, and Dothan in Alabama and in Panama City, Florida. The company has "mini-branches" in Tuscumbia, Opelika, Grove Hill, and Attalla in Alabama and Crestview and Marianna in Florida. Future plans call for the construction of another facility in Pensacola, Florida.

Thompson Tractor Company is best known for sales and support of Caterpillar earthmoving, general construction, forestry, and industrial equipment. Thompson provides customers with one-stop shopping for equipment sales, parts, service, rentals, and leasing. The company offers options on used parts and used equipment as well.

Thompson Lift Truck Company offers a complete line of material handling products and product support from Caterpillar, Mitsubishi, Crown, Teledyne-Princeton, KD Manitou, Shuttlewagon, Royal, and Atlet. This division is a full-service supplier of in-plant offices, material storage, and rack and shelving from Steel King. Thompson also carries a line of floor sweepers and scrubbers from Quadra, and recently began distributing the line of EZ-GO utility vehicles. Thompson Lift Truck Company also serves the Cat lift truck needs of the central and north Georgia markets with stores in Atlanta, Augusta, and Macon which were acquired in 1999.

Thompson Power Systems is ready to supply the energy for customers in its territory. Thompson carries all Caterpillar diesel engines and power systems for prime and standby power for any electric power generation application as well as engines, parts, and service for on-highway trucks and for marine propulsion applications.

The Thompson Cat Rental Store is the newest addition to Thompson, serving industrial and contractor customers with short-term equipment rentals. The Cat Rental Stores were opened in Birmingham and Montgomery initially, and have since expanded into Axis, just north of Mobile and Lincoln near the site of the Honda plant. Future plans call for further expansion throughout Thompson's territory.

Thompson Tractor Company is always looking for new ways to serve its customers. Thompson was a leader among Cat dealers in applying quality control techniques to reduce costs and increase uptime. The company has developed preventive maintenance programs that help customers extend the life of their equipment and avoid extensive downtime due to component failures. Thompson pioneered a Rapid Rebuild assembly line for Caterpillar equipment at the dealership level.

In the future, customers of Thompson Tractor Company can look forward to new and more diverse products from Caterpillar, more services from Thompson, equipment that is easier to acquire for short- and long-term rentals, more use of information systems and information technology, and better communications. Thompson will continue to innovate and adapt new technology to meet customers' changing needs. ■

Thompson Tractor Company, Inc. specializes in the sale and service of Caterpillar products, including earthmoving, construction and materials handling equipment, and diesel and natural gas engines and gas turbines.

U.S. Pipe and Foundry Company

Water is the lifeblood of a community—the most basic need of residents, agriculture, and industry. An efficient and reliable supply of water is vital to growth and prosperity. For 100 years now, Birmingham, Alabama-based United States Pipe and Foundry Company has been supplying small towns and big cities throughout America with the pipes and fittings needed to keep the water flowing.

"You might say there's a little bit of Alabama in just about every state in the nation," says U.S. Pipe President Ralph E. "Red" Fifield. "It's generally buried underground where people can't see it, but it makes a very big difference in their lives."

Founded in 1899, U.S. Pipe is the nation's leading supplier of ductile iron pressure pipe and related valve, hydrant, and fitting products. The company operates six foundries located in Burlington, New Jersey; north Birmingham, Bessemer, and Anniston, Alabama; Chattanooga, Tennessee; and Union City, California.

U.S. Pipe enjoys an enduring reputation for excellence and innovation in both products and processes for the pipe-making industry.

Until the 1920s, cast iron pipes were individually molded and vertically cast in large circular pits—an inefficient operation requiring extensive finishing work. U.S. Pipe reengineered the process, purchasing the rights to a "centrifugal" pipe casting technique known as the deLavaud method—introducing molten iron into a rapidly rotating steel casting mold—and implementing it on a mass production scale. The new centrifugal system allowed U.S. Pipe to radically increase the quality and quantity of its output, ultimately revolutionizing pipe industry production standards.

In the 1950s U.S. Pipe once again transformed the pipe-making world with the invention of rubber-gasketed push-on joints—replacing the traditional lead-caulked variety—which were licensed for use in "restrained joint" water systems around the world. U.S. Pipe today manufactures an extensive line of restrained joints, pipes, and fittings, as well as the industry's foremost ductile iron pipe valves.

New ideas continue to flow at U.S. Pipe. Company engineers recently developed epoxy and polyurethane coatings and linings to extend the life of all their products. In 1999, U.S. Pipe introduced a line of highly durable, corrosion-resistant "fusion bonded" pipe, further demonstrating the company's commitment to industry leadership and product innovation.

Modernization efforts now underway in U.S. Pipe's valves, fittings, and fusion bonded product areas will further expand the company's capacity and capabilities. An innovative computer enterprise system linking the company's foundries and storage sites is already increasing production efficiency while providing

Water Environment Federation Cone. October 1998, Orlando, Florida, U.S. Pipe and Foundry's exhibit.

customers with a real-time link to their product orders.

U.S. Pipe employees are undergoing intensive training on all aspects of the business. The belief is that more knowledgeable employees will be more responsive and involved on the job, helping the company optimize every phase of its manufacturing and distribution process. "We have been blessed with exceptionally talented people over the years," Fifield says. "The more we invest in our staff, the better they can do their jobs and serve our customers. That's our number one priority: offering our customers better service than they can find anywhere else."

U.S. Pipe also believes in giving back to the communities in which it operates. The company is active in the Birmingham Chamber of Commerce and Metropolitan Development Board, as well as the Business Council of Alabama. U.S. Pipe sees education as the biggest challenge for Alabama and has become part of the Birmingham City Schools' "Partners in Education" program.

"Of the 76,000 businesses headquartered in the state of Alabama, U.S. Pipe is one of only 26 to celebrate a 100th anniversary," says Fifield. "We have a tradition of success that makes us very confident about our company's future. Water will always be vital to people's lives, and U.S. Pipe is prepared to keep that water flowing for another century and beyond." ■

U.S. Pipe and Foundry Co. General Office. 3300 First Avenue North, Birmingham, Alabama.

Quality Research

Quality Research in Huntsville, Alabama, is a shining example of the American dream at work. Powered by a dedication to customer service, hard work, and a supportive employee environment, Quality is a textbook example of business success.

Founded in 1988 by Dr. Dusit (Dusty) Charern, Quality Research provides information technology, modeling and simulation software, engineering and analysis, and training services and products. Working with defense, law enforcement, and many commercial clients, Quality's expertise includes operating and maintaining complex computing and network centers, classroom training in information technology and specialized subject areas, and developing high-fidelity computer models of weapon systems and analysis of those systems in immersive virtual environments.

Quality Research has seen its business grow by leaps and bounds since winning its first defense contract in 1990. It was recognized as the 52nd fastest growing private business in America by *Inc. 500* magazine in 1996. It doubled its business between 1997 and 1998 to a level of 22 million in sales. In addition to its headquarters in Huntsville, the firm also now has offices in Fort Leonard Wood, Kansas; Fort Eustis, Missouri; Fort Monroe, Virginia; Anniston, Alabama; Atlanta and Fort Benning in Georgia; Washington, D.C.; St. Petersburg and Orlando in Florida; New Cumberland, Pennsylvania; and Colorado Springs, Colorado.

Dusty Charern credits his company's fantastic growth to a focus on customer success and a talented pool of highly experienced employees.

"A large part of our growth comes from referrals," Charern says. "Our satisfied customers spread the word about Quality Research and they lead others to us. As the business grows, we continue recruiting the best talent in every discipline. We have the best people here," says Charern. "I challenge anyone or any company to try and match us."

Quality Research provides an employee-oriented work environment to attract the best people in the fields of engineering, computer science, strategic defense, software development, mathematics, physics, and information systems. Quality offers an outstanding employee benefit package and a share in company ownership to its people. Those who put in extra hours and extra effort create wealth for themselves and the company at the same time.

"I tell my people, I want this to be the last place you ever work," Charern says. "We all do well working together. There is no jealousy in our corporate community. We are the wind beneath each other's wings."

The State of Alabama may be a major beneficiary of the work going on at Quality Research in the next several years. Dusty Charern would like to extend his company's contacts with state government and agencies to help develop Alabama's infrastructure in information technology. As competition grows between states to attract new business and economic development, Quality could provide Alabama with an important edge.

If past accomplishments are any measure, Quality Research will be a company to watch in the new millennium. Charern says he hopes to push the company to $100 million in revenues by 2005, continue to build his infrastructure, recruit more proven winners to his team, and win more competitive contracts. Quality Research is also looking for opportunities to work with the community in developing niche products that can be brought to the market profitably.

"Our goal has always been to be the best corporation in the world," says Charern. "We will keep improving. We will continue to give our customers the best. We will continue to challenge and reward our people. I think we are definitely on the right track." ■

Dusty Charern, CEO of Quality Research, fosters an employee-oriented work environment.

Quality Research's work spans sophisticated business application, leading-edge visualization and animation, multimedia courseware development, advanced modeling and simulations, special purpose automation tools, and real-time software for various computing environments.

Mitsubishi Polysilicon

....

Aerial view of Mitsubishi Polysilicon Plant.

At the heart of every computer in the world is a chip made from silicon. Silicon is the most abundant element in the earth's crust next to oxygen, but only in its most pure form does it have the properties necessary to serve in electronics. That's where Mitsubishi Polysilicon of Mobile, Alabama, enters the picture.

Mitsubishi Polysilicon produces polysilicon that is 99.999999999 percent pure. Those are scientifically accurate numbers, not hyperbole. The company's product is the purest, most stringently fabricated silicon available in the world.

Mitsubishi Polysilicon is a wholly owned subsidiary of Mitsubishi Materials Corporation of Tokyo. Mitsubishi Materials has taken a leading position in the high-tech arena as a supplier of advanced electronic products, silicon wafers, and related products. The company is a prominent process manufacturer specializing in the smelting, refining, and fabrication of metals, as well as the production of cement and aluminum cans.

In 1995, continuing demand for polysilicon and a customer presence in the United States, created a need for a polysilicon production facility in the U.S. The Mobile site was selected for several reasons, such as the Alabama Industrial Development Program. This program helped ensure the company has a qualified, excellent workforce available. Mitsubishi Polysilicon employs 110 skilled personnel to perform the precise measurements and chemical processes necessary to purify the polysilicon. Alabama's affordable electricity rates were also important because of a large power consumption in the reduction process.

The presence of Degussa Corporation in Mobile is also a benefit to Mitsubishi. The two companies already have side-by-side facilities in Yokkaichi, Japan, that allowed them to share products. Degussa manufactures a substance used in the production of polysilicon, and a by-product of Mitsubishi's plant

Reduction Process.

is used by Degussa to make fumed silica. Mitsubishi built its Mobile operation on property right next door to Degussa.

The raw material for Mitsubishi Polysilicon is purchased from a supplier in Norway. This 98 to 99 percent pure metallurgical silicon is first processed in a chlorination and distillation process to remove the remaining impurities. The silicon from this process then goes to a reduction process, where it is deposited on the surface of electrically heated silicon rods. After four or five days, the rods are grown to the desired diameter. The rods are then sent to a finishing process, where they are first sized and then put through an acid solution to remove any remaining impurities. The polysilicon is then rinsed in ultrapure water and vacuum dried, inspected, and then carefully packaged for shipping to customers. Customer applications for its polysilicon are silicon wafers, photovoltaic cells, silicon targets for glass coatings, and silicon parts for semiconductor fabrication equipment.

Mitsubishi Polysilicon is committed to being a responsible corporate citizen. It has done this by participating in and contributing to community functions and organizations through the donations of its time, talents, and resources. The company is committed to environmental responsibility as well. Air emissions from the facility meet or exceed all local, state, and federal standards, and no process water is discharged into area waterways.

"We have found a wonderful home in Mobile," says Mike Hashimoto, who was the project manager and was later named president and CEO. "The citizens and the business community here have made us feel very welcome. We have found a fantastic workforce here—absolutely dedicated to getting the job done." Hashimoto says that Mitsubishi Materials corporate leaders in Japan have noted the quality of the employees in Mobile and plan for future growth at this site. ◼

Saginaw Pipe Co., Inc.

Since opening in 1983, Saginaw Pipe Co., Inc. quickly stepped forward as a leader in Shelby County industry. Now, after 18 years of sustained growth, they have taken their place among the leading steel distributors in North America. Saginaw Pipe is a full service distributor of steel pipe, square and rectangular tube, and wide-flange beams, and offers a full array of specialty fabrication services. Situated off Highway 31 in Saginaw, Alabama, just twenty miles south of Birmingham, they have built their reputation on quality products and fast, dependable service to their wide variety of customers throughout the United States, Canada, and Central America.

To meet the demands of their growing customer base, Saginaw Pipe has continued to add and upgrade services and has opened three branches, strategically located across the country, in Houston, Texas, Bloomington, Illinois, and Harrisburg, Pennsylvania, in addition to their Shelby County headquarters. Over the years, the Alabama facility has undergone numerous expansion projects, including one in 2000 which will add several new offices and another 100,000 square feet of warehouse space.

Started by the late E. E. "Pete" Raughley, Saginaw's local operations have grown from humble beginnings in a two-bedroom farm house and just under three acres of land to a 100-plus acre complex of offices, yard, warehouses, and fabrication facilities, employing over 140 employees. Their state-of-the-art equipment, including thirteen saws for both miter and straight cutting, and machines for threading, grooving, notching, sandblasting both O.D. and I.D., and wheelabrating (a process similar to sandblasting that cleans pipe by blasting it with steel shot), and a complete torch cutting system, gives them the ability to accommodate the most unique requests from their clients. An experienced team of certified welders and fitters are on sight, enabling them to assist in any projects their customers require.

Stocking a full range of sizes and specifications from most domestic and several foreign mills gives Saginaw Pipe the ability to meet

Material supplied by Saginaw Pipe Co., Inc. is used by many diverse industries, including equipment manufacturers and water tower constructors.

the needs of all its customers, from local pile drivers to international communication companies, from back yard welding shops to highway construction firms, from bumper posts installers to sign pole manufacturers, and from small town fabricators to big city utilities.

Regardless of the size of a customer's needs, Saginaw has built its reputation with quality products and prompt, reliable service. Some of the diverse projects for which Saginaw Pipe has supplied material include the Ronald Reagan Washington National Airport, the Cleveland Indians Stadium, the Baltimore Oriole's Camden Yards, Bush Stadium, Tampa Bay's Houlihan Stadium, the Smithsonian Institute at Cape Canaveral, Florida, and, of course, Disneyland. Locally, both pipe and tube were supplied to contractors working on projects at the Birmingham International Airport, the Riverchase Galleria, Legion Field, and the University of Alabama.

Year after year, Saginaw Pipe has posted record sales. Fiscal year 2000 continues in that trend. Current CEO Howard Wise attributes the consistent growth of Saginaw Pipe to its competitive pricing, quality products and service, and its employees' dedication, and their ability to anticipate and adequately prepare for changes in the market. As it has grown, Saginaw has not forgotten its ties to the community. Among the many projects in which it has taken part, Saginaw employees are particularly proud of their involvement with the Pig Iron Bar-B-Que Challenge, which annually raises money for the Children's Harbor at Children's Hospital in Birmingham. With its eye on the future and its emphasis on service, Saginaw Pipe Co., Inc. has positioned itself to continue as a leader in the steel industry throughout the twenty-first century.

Its large inventory and fleet of trucks enables Saginaw Pipe to respond quickly to the needs of all its customers.

American Cast Iron Pipe Company

Nearly a century ago, the American Cast Iron Pipe Company (ACIPCO) was just a bright idea by a young woman named Charlotte Blair.

Ms. Blair was familiar with the iron industry, as secretary in charge of sales for Dimmick, and she knew Alabama's natural resources of iron ore and limestone made a good foundation from which to start a new iron plant. She solicited a few financial backers, and by 1905, ACIPCO was an up and running pipe company. Ms. Blair was the first woman to sit on a corporate board in Alabama.

John Eagan, a Georgia businessman with strong Christian morals, was named President of the company. He later became the sole owner, and it is he who is credited with instilling in the company the same philosophies that have made ACIPCO one of the top companies in America, according to a recent article in *Fortune* magazine, "The 100 Best Companies To Work For In America."

Today, ACIPCO remains a privately held company that operates as a beneficial trust with employees as beneficiaries. But the company has grown considerably. According to the Birmingham Chamber of Commerce, ACIPCO is the largest manufacturing employer in the Birmingham area covering Jefferson, Shelby, Walker, and St. Clair counties. And the company has grown to be the largest individual ductile iron pressure pipe casting plant in the world.

ACIPCO employs about 3,000 people, who are dedicated to manufacturing a diversified product line for the waterworks, capital goods, and energy industries. These products include ductile iron pipe and fittings; fire hydrants, valves, and fire truck pumps; centrifugal cast steel tubes, static castings, and fabricated assemblies; electric-resistance welded steel pipe; and spiral welded steel pipe.

The company's corporate headquarters and principal plant covers 1,800 acres in downtown Birmingham. The company's products are produced and marketed worldwide through ACIPCO's four divisions: American Ductile Iron Pipe, American Flow Control, American Centrifugal, and American Steel Pipe. ACIPCO's five subsidiaries include American Specification Rubber Products in Alabaster; WATEROUS Company in South St. Paul, Minnesota; American Valve & Hydrant Manufacturing Company in Beaumont, Texas; Kristin Shipping Company in Birmingham, and American Spiral-Weld Pipe Company, LLC in Columbia, South Carolina.

ACIPCO's corporate philosophy is to respond to customer demand with premium quality products shipped in a timely manner at a fair and competitive price. Its dedication to meeting this goal has earned it the prestigious ISO 9000 certification.

ACIPCO's commitment to quality begins with its employees. The company's founding father, Mr. Eagan, set up the Eagan Trust, under which ACIPCO operates today. This program emphasizes a team-like relationship between management and employees. Representatives from throughout the company meet regularly with management to ensure that employees continue to have a voice in matters that affect the company and its employees.

Employees enjoy many exceptional benefits and services. Some of these include apprenticeship training in crafts and trades utilized at the company; a suggestion program as a means of improving current methods; organized intramural sports; in-plant training and tuition reimbursement for college study; professional counseling services; and a unique wellness program. ACIPCO has an on-site medical facility staffed with full-time primary care physicians, dentists, and pharmacists.

ACIPCO's century-long dedication to its customers, as well as its employees, is the driving force behind the company's success. ■

ACIPCO's facilities in Birmingham.

After desulfurizing, the iron is conveyed to either a 1300-ton or 1000-ton holding ladle.

Robinson Foundry, Inc.

Robinson Foundry, Inc. of Alexander City supplies castings to the automotive, marine, tractor, and construction industries throughout the United States. Its main line of business is aluminum automotive parts. The company has managed to grow at a steady rate, adding customers over the years by consistently reinventing itself to better serve those customers' needs.

"Men have been casting metal through one means or another for several thousand years," says company CEO Joseph H. Robinson Jr. "The industry is always changing, though. We are constantly seeking to improve the casting process and the environment in which it is accomplished."

The Robinson family has played a part in the foundry industry in Alabama for over 50 years. Joseph H. Robinson Sr. founded today's Robinson Foundry in 1946. The company's original business was producing ornamental objects of iron from a collection of patterns that Robinson owned, and castings were made from primitive, hand-operated machines. A while later, the company added soil pipe and fittings to its product line. Mechanization of the foundry allowed the production of valves, drains, and electric motor parts.

Robinson Foundry is unique in its ability to identify emerging markets and to adapt its production to meet these requirements.

Robinson Foundry, Inc. has been in existence for 53 years making grey iron, ductile iron, and aluminum castings for the automotive, agricultural, marine, and commercial equipment industries. The foundry is certified for the QS-9000 and ISO-9002 quality rating. Photo by McClellan Studio.

The company moved into the market for "net shape" high-technology parts when it introduced the "Lost Foam" process for iron casting. More recently, Robinson began using the "Lost Foam" process for aluminum parts to serve the automotive and marine markets. Robinson is now introducing new technology for the production of aluminum automotive safety parts in large quantities.

Robinson Foundry, Inc. has a positive impact on Alabama's balance of trade, as it sells 90 percent of its products out of state. At the same time, the company purchases more than 80 percent of its materials within Alabama. In Alexander City, the foundry provides numerous jobs as well as a source of revenue to electrical, parts, and packing suppliers and builders.

Future plans for Robinson Foundry include a high-technology facility for the twenty-first century that will quadruple the company's existing output and radically increase efficiency. Construction of the new plant is scheduled to begin in the year 2000.

"We look forward to serving more and more customers inside and outside the state with the increased capabilities of our new facility," Joseph Robinson Jr. says, "and we'll continue to develop new and better technologies to serve those customers in the years to come. This is an exciting industry to work in, and I think it's an exciting time for business all over the state." ∎

Robinson-Latva Company, LLP was created in 1998 to machine automotive quality aluminum castings with state-of-the-art technology equipment. This plant is certified for the QS-9000 and ISO-9002 quality rating. Photo by McClellan Studio.

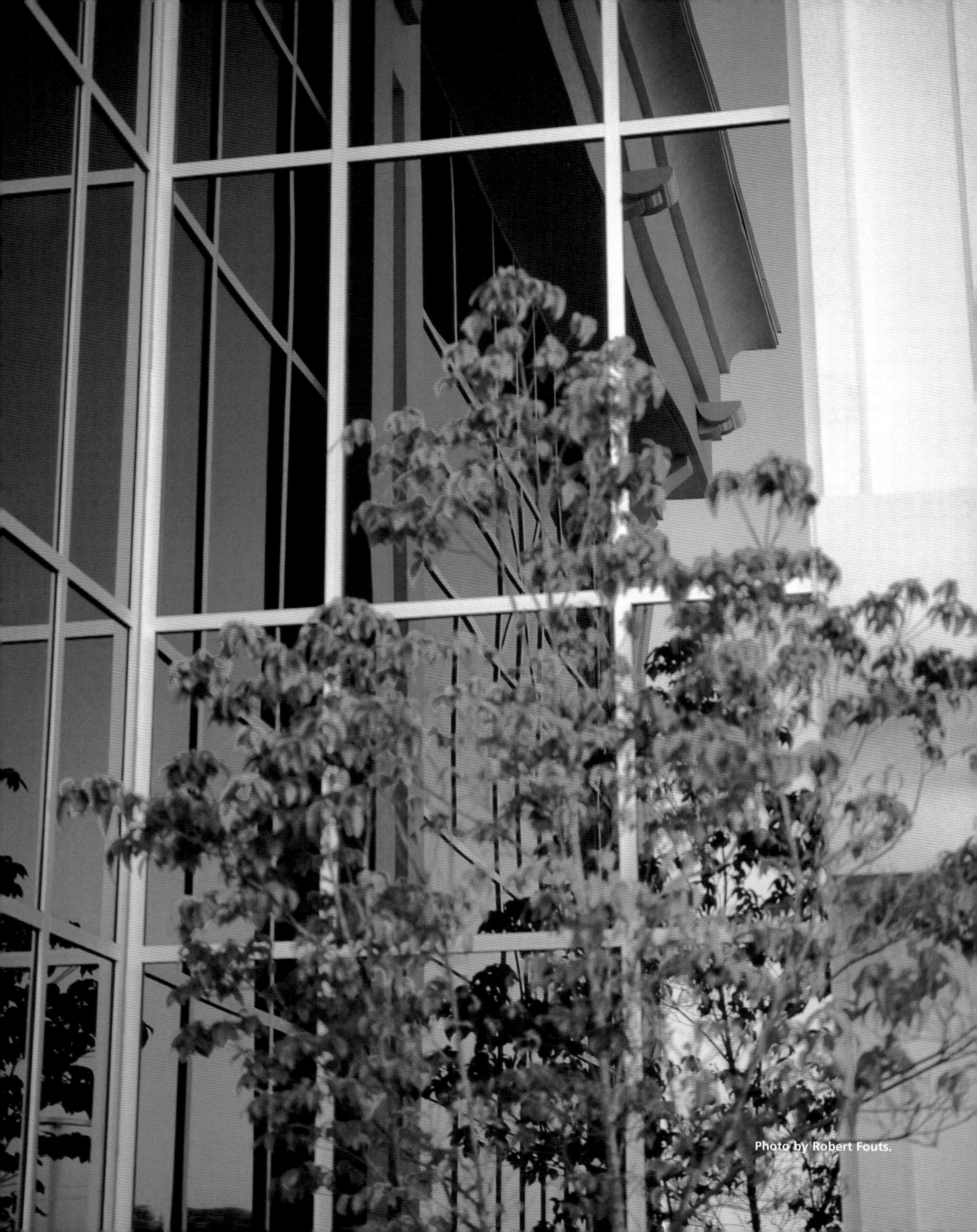

Photo by Robert Fouts.

Rheem began in Oakland, California as a manufacturer of galvanized drums. Then, with the purchase of the John Wood Water Heater Company in 1931, the business began an expansion mode that has continued to this day. Growing from their West Coast base, Rheem built and acquired six more water heater plants by 1940. In 1959 the company acquired Ruud Manufacturing Company, which resulted in a broader line of commercial products, and a second well-established brand from which to leverage growth.

By 1972, Rheem had consolidated its manufacturing to one Chicago facility and the newly constructed plant in Alabama. In 1989 the Chicago plant was closed as the Montgomery plant expanded. Today the Montgomery facility is producing more than the total amount the combined plants formerly produced.

Innovation has been vital to Rheem's success. Rheem produces water heaters that are dramatically different than those it made just 10 years ago. One of the major differences is energy efficiency. As consumers have learned that the water heater is the second largest consumer of energy after space heating and cooling, they have shifted purchase preference to Rheem's higher-efficiency products, which can save hundreds of dollars over the life of the product. Rheem has responded to the consumers' desire to enjoy more hot water with larger water heaters and faster recovery times. Rheem also produces unique state-of-the-art products such as the Marathon non-metallic water heater featuring a limited lifetime warranty.

One of the fastest growing departments in the company is research and development. Rheem anticipates that product and design changes will occur even faster in the future. The company currently expects more changes in the next five years than occurred in the previous 25 years.

Rheem Water Heater Division is one of three major divisions of Rheem Manufacturing Company, headquartered in New York, New York. Rheem Air Conditioning Division, based in Ft. Smith, Arkansas is a leading manufacturer of furnaces and air conditioners. Raypak, which produces commercial boilers and swimming pool heaters, is located in Westlake Village, California. ▪

Water heater exterior jackets are painted in a continuous flow process. Paint is applied as an electrostatically charged powder, providing thorough coverage and extremely consistent application. After being coated, the jackets flow directly through ovens resulting in a durable and attractive appliance-like finish. The controlled environment allows for virtually zero material waste in the painting process.

Product testing and quality assurance allows Rheem customers to enjoy the highest product quality in the water heater industry. Rheem conducts pressure continuity tests on 100 percent of products during production. The glass-lined interior of every water heater is visually inspected, further enhancing product quality and reliability.

Vulcan Materials Company

I t may be impossible to list all the different ways Vulcan Materials Company touches your life every single day. The roads you drive on, the foundation of your home, the food you eat, the medicines you take, and the water you drink are just a few examples of how the products made by Vulcan play an important role in everyone's daily life.

In addition to being the nation's leading producer of construction aggregates, Vulcan Materials Company is also one of America's leading chemical manufacturers. But this major national corporation started in 1909 as a small operation called Birmingham Slag. In 1916, Charles Lincoln Ireland, a banker from Ohio, purchased Birmingham Slag on the recommendation of his son, Glenn. The elder Ireland sent his three sons Glenn, Gene, and Barney, to run the operation. Glenn Ireland's son, Charles William Ireland, became president of Birmingham Slag in 1951 and immediately began looking for new growth opportunities. Growth required capital, which led to an important change for the company: its merger with a profitable New Jersey operation, Vulcan Detinning Company. This merger transformed Birmingham Slag into a public company with a listing on the New York Stock Exchange. The new company was called Vulcan Materials Company, and Charles Ireland's vision of creating a major national corporation was finally realized.

In the next four years, 1956 to 1960, Vulcan merged with a dozen more firms and gained thousands of stockholders. It was also during this time period that Vulcan entered the chemicals business through a merger with Union Chemicals and Materials Company of Chicago. The corporate framework and basic product mix of today's Vulcan Materials Company were set in place. Between 1970 and 1996, company chief executive officers W. Houston Blount and Herbert A. Sklenar continued leading Vulcan to obtain ever increasing shares of the construction materials and chemicals industries. Vulcan's current chairman and chief executive officer, Donald M. James, sees a continuation of the legacy established by his predecessors. "Vulcan has been a well-managed

Vulcan's Kingsport, Tennessee, plant is a state-of-the-art aggregates production facility.

company throughout its history. The challenge for those of us in a new generation of leadership in the company is to build on the successes of the past, to find opportunities to continue to build value for our shareholders, and to provide the leadership to achieve that goal."

Vulcan's construction materials segment today serves all parts of the construction industry. End uses for the company's products include highways and other public works, housing, and commercial and industrial facilities. In addition to crushed stone, which accounts for 75 percent of the construction materials segment's sales, Vulcan produces a diversified line of other aggregates and building materials and provides many other related products and services.

Although most of the company's facilities are in the United States, Vulcan is also a 50-percent partner in an international joint venture called The Crescent Market Companies, which supplies high quality limestone aggregates to counties along the U.S. Gulf Coast.

Vulcan's Chemicals Segment is a significant producer of basic

Raven's nest at Vulcan's Royal Stone Quarry near Richmond, Virginia. Vulcan Materials Company is a leader in the establishment of enhanced wildlife habitats at its operations.

industrial and specialty chemicals. Through its Chloralkali Business Unit, known as Vulcan Chemicals, it produces chlorine, caustic soda, hydrochloric acid, potassium chemicals, and chlorinated organic chemicals. Chlorine has thousands of applications, but it is best known for its use in purifying drinking water and in the manufacture of pharmaceuticals. Most of Vulcan's chlorine is used internally to produce chlorinated organic chemicals that are used as solvents and fluorocarbon (refrigerant) feedstocks.

Through its Performance Systems Business Unit, now known as Vulcan Performance Chemicals, it provides process chemicals for the pulp and paper and textile idustries, chemicals and services to the municipal, industrial, and environmental water management markets, and the custom manufacture of a variety of specialty chemicals. The products and services of Vulcan's Performance Chemicals business are marketed worldwide.

Vulcan Materials Company is steadfast in its commitment to the health and safety of its employees and to stewardship of the environment. Vulcan is actively involved in the Birmingham community and in the other communities in which it has operations. From its leadership in quarry beautification and the development of wildlife habitats to the creation of citizen advisory panels and the support of education, cultural groups, and charities, Vulcan and its employees are working to meet the challenges of corporate responsibility.

Vulcan Materials Company, which began by selling the byproducts of Birmingham's steel industry, has grown into a major publicly owned corporation. Its operations span the nation and its products sustain many of the country's most important growth industries. Vulcan stands as a proud symbol of a city that has grown from small beginnings to become a shining star of the South. ▪

Hager Companies

Hager Companies is one of the oldest family-owned and operated businesses in the United States. Hager has manufacturing facilities in Oxford and Montgomery, Alabama, producing Architectural and Consumer hardware. Hager has another plant in Mississippi and its headquarters is in St. Louis. The company was founded 150 years ago.

Charles Hager came to America in 1849 on a Norwegian freighter from Hamburg, Germany. New Orleans was the young blacksmith's first stopping point, and he was immediately drawn upriver to St. Louis, his primary destination. A massive fire had destroyed downtown St. Louis, and Hager found immediate work in the city's rebuilding efforts.

During the 1800s, St. Louis was the starting point for thousands of pioneers seeking new land and new lives in the West. Charles Hager helped send them on their way and outfit their farms and ranches, making metal wagon wheels, knives and hand-forged hinges and hardware for barn doors, gates, and fences in rural America.

The Hager Company grew as America grew, answering the needs of individuals, businesses, and government alike. When Americans went to Central America to build the Panama Canal, Hager was contracted to make the custom hinges for the locks. Hager also contributed heavily to the war efforts during World War I and World War II. The company produced a variety of materials for the military, and family members served during World War II.

August William (Bill) Hager, the great-grandson of the company's founder, decided to move the Consumer Goods Division of Hager Companies to Oxford, Alabama, in 1978. An existing building in the city of Oxford fit perfectly with the company's needs after a little remodeling. The plant manufactures hinges and related hardware, including door pulls, drawer pulls, safety hasps, and shelf brackets for the retail market. It currently employs around 200 workers.

Bill Hager moved the Architectural Hardware Division of his company to Montgomery in 1980, choosing the newly built industrial park in Hope Hull as a location. The major products of this facility are heavier grade hinges and related products destined for commercial

**August W. Hager III
Fifth Generation President.**

buildings. The Montgomery plant employs nearly 500.

Hager saw a number of advantages to locating these operations in Alabama. The manufacturing facilities are in close proximity to the raw materials needed. Alabama offers an excellent labor market with available skills to meet the company's needs. The state provided training for all of Hager's new employees and offered attractive tax credits and incentives for the relocation.

"Alabama puts us closer to our customers," says fifth-generation Hager President August William Hager III (Rusty). "Construction growth in the Southeast markets is outpacing the rest of the nation. Having our operations here in Alabama puts us at the center of all the activity and really reduces the cost of taking products to our customers."

Montgomery Manufacturing Facility.

CHAPTER 12

Business & Finance

Photo by Robert Fouts.

Alabama Farmers Federation and Alfa Insurance Companies

From the fertile fields of Alabama's rural communities to her bustling cities, the familiar red logos of the Alabama Farmers Federation and Alfa Insurance Companies shine brightly as symbols of strength and security. Whether embossed on a farmer's cap or displayed on the bumper of a soccer mom's car, the Alfa emblem represents a corporate family that's been protecting its members and policyholders for more than 75 years.

Anchored in the grassroots foundation of the Alabama Farmers Federation, the organization known as Alfa first emerged from the Alabama soil in 1921. Its mission: to promote the economic, social, and educational interests of rural Alabamians.

By holding fast to the simple idea of strength through unity, the Alabama Farmers Federation has grown from 30,000 members just 50 years ago to become the state's largest farm organization. But despite its phenomenal growth, Alfa continues to have a reputation for providing its 400,000 farm and nonfarm members with unsurpassed service at an exceptional value.

In a recent survey conducted by the Marketing Research Institute of Pensacola, Florida, Alabama voters gave the Alabama Farmers Federation a higher approval rating than any other political or membership organization in the state. Likewise, farmers were considered the most respected occupational group, earning an amazing 93 percent favorable rating. These high marks recognize the farmers who comprise Alfa's leadership, as well as the organization's unwavering commitment to the people of Alabama.

As the voice of Alabama agriculture, the Farmers Federation works with government officials at the state and national levels to increase profitability in farming and enhance the standard of living for rural residents. In addition, the Federation's Commodity Division coordinates education, promotion, and research activities with producers of every major agricultural crop grown in the state. The organization also encourages future farm leaders through its Young Farmers Division while keeping members informed through the Federation's communications department and field staff network.

Other benefits enjoyed by Alfa members include Blue Cross/Blue Shield group health insurance, savings on tires and farm supplies at AutoSave stores and more than 450 independent retailers, and access to Alfa's in-house commodity marketing service. The most popular membership benefit, however, is Alfa Insurance.

Founded in 1946 to provide farmers and rural residents with affordable fire protection coverage, Alfa Insurance has matured into a leader in the property/casualty and life insurance industries.

With more than a million policies in force, Alfa now offers a broad line of business, homeowners, automobile, and life insurance products through more than 360 service centers in Alabama, Georgia, and Mississippi. In Alabama, Alfa Insurance ranks in the top three in market share for both property and casualty insurance and life insurance.

In addition to Alfa's reputation for providing unparalleled claims service, the company's financial strength and growth has earned the property and casualty group an A++ rating from the A.M. Best Company, the nation's leading independent rating service for the insurance industry. Best also awarded the Alfa Life Insurance Corporation a superior A+ rating. Alfa's success, however, has not been the result of any one factor. In addition to its loyal customer base, which is rooted in the membership of the Alabama Farmers Federation, Alfa boasts one of the most dedicated customer service teams in the business and a solid financial footing that

Jerry Newby serves as president of the Alabama Farmers Federation and Alfa Insurance Companies.

By holding fast to the simple idea of strength through unity, the Alabama Farmers Federation has grown from 30,000 members just 50 years ago to become the state's largest farm organization with 400,000 farm and nonfarm members. Photo by Wade Collins.

awarded millions of dollars in scholarships for college students and helped fund eminent scholar positions at both Auburn University and Troy State University.

Alfa's greatest contribution to Alabama residents, though, lies not in its philanthropy or honest business practices, but in the harvest of benefits produced from seeds planted by the founders of the Alabama Farmers Federation. By helping preserve the family farm, the Alabama Farmers Federation ensures Americans will continue to enjoy the world's safest, most abundant, and most affordable supply of food and fiber. At the same time, the Farmers Federation helps keep taxes and utility costs low by encouraging good government at the state and national levels.

Perhaps that's why Alabamians feel good when they see the bright red Alfa emblem. They know behind the nameplate is an organization founded in wholesome principles and dedicated to the financial security of its members and policyholders. ■

enables it to weather natural disasters and fluctuations in the financial markets.

Supported by almost 900 employees at the company's home office in Montgomery, Alfa's 1,500 agents, managers, adjusters, and customer service representatives provide policyholders with personal, caring service. Alfa employees also are active in their communities, contributing their time and skills to improve the cities in which they live and do business.

Similarly, the leadership of Alfa and the Alabama Farmers Federation remains committed to improving the economic, social, and educational interests of all Alabamians. For that reason, Alfa and its employees have contributed more than $2 million to the Montgomery Area United Way, while helping the charity raise an additional $9 million in the past six years. In addition, Alfa has made donations totaling about $1 million to the American Red Cross, the Montgomery Zoo, Alabama Public Television, the Helen Keller Eye Research Foundation, and medical research projects at the University of Alabama in Birmingham.

Alfa also sponsors the Alfa Teacher of the Month Program, which awards $1,000 each month to an outstanding public or private school educator and another $1,000 to his or her school. In other initiatives to encourage excellence in education, Alfa gives the Alabama Teacher of the Year the use of a new car for one year, and the company has donated computers to schools and funded "Writing To Read" labs valued at almost $500,000. Alfa's partnership with education, however, extends beyond high school graduation. Together with the Alabama Farmers Federation, Alfa has

Supported by almost 900 employees at the company's home office in Montgomery, Alfa's 1,500 agents, managers, adjusters, and customer service representatives provide policyholders with personal, caring service.

The Business Council of Alabama

Fair courts. A skilled work force. Affordable health care. Sensible tax laws. Reduced regulatory burden. Balanced environmental policy. The impact of issues like these cut across the landscape of Alabama business and into the very heart of every company's ability to compete and grow in this state.

That's why nearly 5,000 Alabama business and industries of all shapes and sizes turn to the Business Council of Alabama for help on the issues that affect their bottom line. On the strength of a formidable membership and with the help of dedicated volunteer leaders from across Alabama, the BCA has earned a reputation for getting the job done when it comes to protecting Alabama's business community.

As Alabama's foremost association of business and industry, the BCA is always first to stand up for free enterprise. Independently, and as part of united pro-business coalitions, the BCA has led the way in the fight for key business issues such as tort reform and sales tax simplification. The Business Council played a key role in helping find a solution for the state's Franchise Tax crisis and continues to be at the front of the class in support of education reform, healthcare reform, tax and business license reform, and regulatory reform.

BCA members are corporate citizens making a difference in their communities. Photo by Paul Sumners.

In addition to its legislative activities, the BCA is involved in every progressive pro-business initiative under way in Alabama. BCA leaders serve on the distinguished Alabama Commerce Commission, which is implementing an aggressive long-term plan for growth and economic development. The Business Council provided the impetus for the Alabama Coalition for Tomorrow (ACT), which has established a legislative agenda designed to remove the roadblocks to economic development in communities across the state.

The BCA is also active with the Higher Education Partnership of Alabama to help determine how Alabama's colleges and universities can better meet the needs of business and industry. The Business Council is a member of the Partnership for Alabama School's Success, which is dedicated to increasing and sustaining higher standards and accountability in Alabama's public schools. And, the BCA is Alabama's only business organization to serve on the National Association of Manufacturer's National Industrial Council, where the BCA helps form federal policy and tracks nationwide trends that stand to impact Alabama.

Since its founding in 1985, the BCA has been Alabama's strongest advocate for free enterprise. Because the daily rigors of running a business keep most BCA members in the office or on the plant floor, BCA's respected governmental affairs staff is always on the political scene working for them—meeting with legislators, tracking bills, testifying at hearings, and representing the issues important to business and industry at every turn.

If it concerns business, it concerns BCA members. That's why the Business Council staff also works hard to keep those who have invested in keeping Alabama safe for business accurately informed and up-to-date on the issues they care about. The Business Council

Retired Gen. Colin L. Powell has been among the nationally acclaimed speakers to bring messages of leadership and excellence to Business Council of Alabama audiences.

is Alabama's first source for business news, keeping its members informed via monthly newsletters, weekly legislative bulletins, grassroots action alerts, informative conferences and workshops, and a state-of-the-art interactive web site.

In addition to aggressive representation and thorough information, BCA members also enjoy a variety of money-saving special benefits ranging from highly competitive workers' compensation insurance rates to discounted shipping rates, discounts for on-line tax filing, and member-only advertising discounts. These valuable membership benefits are another key part of BCA's mission to help make doing business in Alabama easier and more profitable.

BCA members make up one of Alabama's most far-reaching grassroots networks. The association's roster of informed and active business leaders is Alabama's most effective mechanism for building public policy that will enhance business bottom lines, create real economic growth, and improve the quality of life for all who live and work in Alabama. By defining the issues and encouraging thousands of business people to take action, the BCA has created a climate where lawmakers take note and recognize the strength of BCA's united and informed membership.

The fact is, good government is everybody's business and it takes a unified, well-focused effort to ensure it. ProgressPAC, the BCA's political action committee, is an example of that kind of effective coordination. ProgressPAC supplements the Business Council's legislative efforts by supporting candidates who are willing to stand up for issues that are important to Alabama businesses and the hundreds of thousands of people they employ.

ProgressPAC endorsements and contributions are decided locally by the BCA members who live and work with the candidates. They know, better than anyone, the candidates up close and personally and are best able to help identify the candidates who understand the issues of concern to Alabama's hardworking business people.

BCA staff members are always on call and ready to assist association members. Photo by Nancy Dennis.

ProgressPAC participation is the single best way for BCA members to ensure their voice is heard at election time. By leveraging the impact of a single contribution with the contributions of thousands of other concerned business people, BCA members have discovered time and again that they can, and do, make a real difference at election time.

Representation, education, and participation. A decade-and-a-half of solid unity and coordinated effort has put Alabama's business community front and center when it comes to policy-making in Alabama. The Business Council of Alabama is business at work for a better Alabama. ▪

Former BCA Chairman Ab Conner, center, and BCA Chairman Keith King (right) discuss federal business issues under consideration by Congress with U.S. Rep. Terry Everett during the BCA's Federal Fly-In. Photo by Nicholas Michaelson.

AmSouth Bank

Since its beginnings in 1873, AmSouth Bank has grown to become one of the top banks in the nation, fueling the growth of Birmingham as well as cities across the Southeast. AmSouth's success is built on its employees, who together have earned a reputation as "The Relationship People." Despite its international scope, AmSouth's banking philosophy is built on the most basic of business principles: understanding and meeting the needs of every customer.

The new parents who need to prepare for their child's college tuition. The professional who needs to establish financial security for retirement. The entrepreneur who needs financial advice and planning as she prepares to realize a dream. Or the multinational corporation whose leaders need proven performance for a myriad of financial needs. Each of them can expect professional one-on-one service from the employees of AmSouth Bank.

In the highly competitive world of banking, AmSouth has carved a niche for itself by developing programs and services to meet diverse needs. In the mid-1970s, AmSouth pioneered telephone bill paying services for retail customers in its markets. Today, customers can conduct their banking 24 hours a day, seven days a week, through AmSouth's Internet Banking and PC Banking services and TeleBanking Center. In 1999, the TeleBanking Center specialists handled more than 4.4 million calls. These "live" calls were in addition to the 27.2 million calls handled by the automated voice response system during the year.

From 1995 through 1998, AmSouth invested approximately $80 million in new technology to improve customer convenience, enhance the development of new products and services, and produce higher levels of service quality.

From free checking to flexible loans, AmSouth offers customers relationships that meet their many needs. With the power of an AmSouth relationship, customers can take advantage of checking accounts designed to meet their individual needs, a variety of credit products, and convenience services such as the AmSouth CheckCard and Overdraft Protection.

AmSouth is also a leader in providing innovative commercial banking products and services. The sophisticated Treasury Management services at AmSouth include state-of-the-art wholesale and retail lockbox equipment that provides customers the fastest possible access to accounts receivable. AmSouth is a recognized leader in international banking and maintains relationships with financial institutions in more than 100 countries on six continents. AmSouth has long held the President of the United States' "E Award for Excellence" for helping its customers develop and promote export business. Thanks to AmSouth, these businesses are

AmSouth's president and chief executive officer is C. Dowd Ritter. Photo by Gittings/Skipworth, Inc.

bringing important new revenue into Alabama in this era of growing global markets. In Alabama, AmSouth Bank's commitment to small business owners is illustrated by its designation as "Preferred SBA Lender" by the U.S. Small Business Administration.

AmSouth's Capital Management Division offers a wide variety of products to suit each customer's financial goals, including the AmSouth family of mutual funds. For more than 75 years, the trust and investment officers of AmSouth Bank have built solid relationships through personalized asset management, trust services, private banking, and estate planning.

Each month, AmSouth demonstrates its commitment to customer service by honoring AmSouth employees who go "beyond the call of duty" with the Chairman's Performance Awards. Honorees represent every area of AmSouth's business, from business bankers, investment bankers, and branch managers to the tellers. Reliance on employees as "The Relationship People" extends to

With more than 600 branches in eight states, AmSouth offers customers the relationships they need.

Perhaps nowhere is AmSouth Bank's commitment to relationships more evident than in its philosophy for how to do business. The philosophy is based on AmSouth's Basic Values that employees strive for daily: Do more than is expected; If something's wrong, make it right; Make time for people; Improve someone's life; Make a difference; and Do the right thing.

Six Basic Values, but powerful ones that drive AmSouth Bank and its employees to continue to find ways to meet the needs of customers and the community AmSouth serves. A booklet, distributed to employees, customers, and potential customers, provides a thumbnail view of these financial core values. Rather than share grandiose views of the complexities of banking, it outlines basic values of life. Among them? "Smile More." "Be Sincere." "Look for the Best in People." And the last entry: "Meet Needs."

In the end, it's what makes AmSouth Bank, and its customers, a success.

AmSouth's bottom line: all AmSouth employees participate in some type of performance-based incentive program; as they succeed, AmSouth succeeds.

To keep customer relationships fresh, AmSouth regularly asks for feedback. Comment cards distributed to hundreds of thousands of customers give a picture of how they rate AmSouth's products and services. Many of AmSouth's programs, services, and policies are a direct result of this customer input.

AmSouth also continuously measures more than 100 different quality indicators of high service performance. Again, many of these are the simple things that make up an individual customer's banking experience: how many times the telephone rings before it is answered, whether a customer service representative smiles and calls a customer by name, and error-free data entry.

AmSouth bankers build strong relationships with the communities they serve, volunteering their time and expertise to benefit the arts, education, economic development, health care, and more. AmSouth also provides significant financial contributions to support these community institutions and efforts.

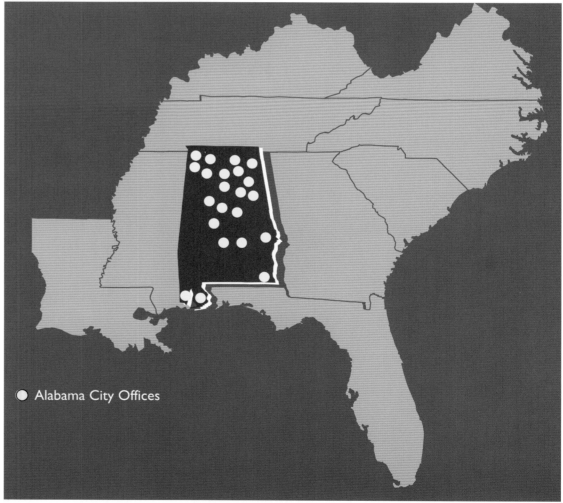

Alabama City Offices

Beyond its headquarters in Birmingham and offices across Alabama, AmSouth Bank serves financial needs across the Southeast.

Jemison Investment Co., Inc.

Jemison Investment Co., Inc. is a privately held holding company with a diversified portfolio of investments. The firm was founded in 1949 by John S. Jemison Jr., a descendant of one of Birmingham's most prominent families. After spending 15 years in New York as an investment banker with The Bank of Manhattan (now Chase Manhattan) and Goldman, Sachs and Co., Jemison returned to Birmingham to start what was to become Jemison Investment Co., Inc.

From the very beginning Jemison relied upon his ability to artfully construct the financing of his acquisitions and investments, utilizing both equity and various forms of leverage long before such techniques became popular. His personal integrity, absolute commitment to honesty, and highest ethical standards led to an impeccable reputation that ultimately became the firm's most valuable asset and resulted in his induction into the Alabama Business Hall of Fame.

Jemison was still active as chairman of the company at the time of his death in 1988. Today, Jemison Investment Co. is led by H. Corbin Day, James D. Davis, and J. David Brown III.

Day joined the firm as vice chairman in 1986 and became chairman in 1988. Prior to joining Jemison, Day spent 25 years at Goldman, Sachs and Co. and is well known on Wall Street and in national financial circles.

Davis joined Jemison in 1979 and became president in 1983. Prior to joining the company, he was with the accounting firm of Touche Ross & Co. (now Deloitte & Touche). Davis relies on his skills and experience in finance and general management in running the day-to-day operations of the holding company.

Brown, executive vice president, joined the firm in 1989 shortly after Mr. Jemison's death. Prior to joining Jemison, Brown was associated with the New York-based investment banking firm Cyrus J. Lawrence, Inc. and the international shipping company United States Lines, Inc.

With such a small staff, Jemison's involvement with its investments is limited to strategic planning, goal establishment, and

Jemison Investment Co., Inc. is a privately held holding company with a diversified portfolio of investments. The company is led by **H. Corbin Day (center), James D. Davis (top left), and J. David Brown III (top right).** Photo by Bondarenko Photography.

serving as a sounding board to each company's management team.

Jemison makes equity investments in two separate and distinct arenas. It seeks to acquire controlling interests in stable, well-managed, privately held businesses with revenues of $20 to $100 million dollars. It also looks for opportunities to purchase minority interests in smaller early stage ventures offering significant growth potential.

Unlike many of the firms with which it competes, Jemison's ownership allows it to take a long-term view to value creation. It operates without the need for predetermined exit strategies, which allows for a more patient approach to realizing its objectives. As a result, Jemison has interests in several companies that it has held for more than 20 years.

It is this unique element to its business which Jemison believes allows it to create a true partnership with the management teams of the companies in which it invests, a partnership which draws on the financial and strategic strength of Jemison and the operational strengths of its management to increase the value of the assets they own together. ■

COMSYS

COMSYS is a national information technology company offering project support and specialized project services tailored to meet the needs of business. With more than 4,000 consultants and associates nationwide, COMSYS has proven experience in a wide range of industries, including banking, defense, insurance, manufacturing, retail, state and local government, telecommunications, transportation, and utilities. COMSYS has served more than 1,000 customers, including 129 of the Fortune 500.

"When a company discovers it doesn't have sufficient internal resources to handle an IT project—or doesn't have staff with the necessary skills—we can precisely match their needs with the highest skilled consultants available," says Mark Williams, Vice President of Sales and Operations. "Our goal is to be *The One* resource when an IT manager calls for highly skilled IT professionals."

COMSYS has offices in Birmingham, Alabama and 17 other states from California to Florida. This powerful network can provide everything from IT staffing initiatives to management of turnkey projects.

The COMSYS service portfolio begins with project support. COMSYS can augment a customer's existing staff with individuals or teams to meet any size assignment. At this level, the customer maintains control and responsibility for project management.

COMSYS can also provide clients with specialized support services, assuming management and responsibility for projects. The experienced project managers from COMSYS are available anytime and anywhere, and will make certain that the customer has the right people to staff their project. Managers can work independently or right alongside the customer's employee team.

COMSYS allows its clients to partially or completely outsource development and maintenance of applications. These services can be done either onsite or offsite. COMSYS will also provide vendor management for clients, centralizing all processes and administration as well as staffing solutions.

The consultants and associates at COMSYS stay on top of current trends so they are prepared to meet customer demands. In addition, the company's placement process guarantees to match each client's IT needs with the right people for the job.

"We maintain a proprietary database of 250,000 resumes," says Williams. "After we take a thorough look at a customer's specific needs, we define the technical skills, platform needs, and industry experience necessary for the project and locate the right personnel. If we don't have the right match in our database, we tap into our national and global recruiting networks."

COMSYS—Birmingham Office.

After COMSYS has located, screened, interviewed, and tested candidates for a position, clients can review potential consultants before placement. COMSYS monitors consultant performance for the duration of the project.

COMSYS oversees support and management of each customer's IT resources so the customer can focus on the core of their business. COMSYS takes care of administrative responsibilities with affiliate contract vendors and provides centralized invoicing, reporting, auditing, order placement, and other systems that can reduce costs and improve quality.

High-quality customer service is a key to remaining competitive in today's marketplace, and COMSYS offers its clients a full suite of technologies, training, and documentation to ensure customer satisfaction. COMSYS can help businesses improve their relationships and interaction with customers through internet e-business solutions and a variety of other methods. COMSYS will also help streamline internal processes such as electronic purchasing that allow businesses to reduce and control costs.

COMSYS is an important partner to businesses in Alabama and throughout the nation. As information technology becomes more and more significant to every company's bottom line, COMSYS can be the secret to success. ■

Compass Bank

••

D. Paul Jones, Jr., Chairman and CEO, is leading Compass Bank's charge into the next millennium with an ongoing focus on service and innovation.

Where there's Compass, there's a way. That's the reputation Compass has forged for itself from the day it opened its doors in Birmingham in 1964. The company has achieved tremendous growth and outstanding financial performance over the years by offering innovative, competitively priced products and superior service.

Compass has revolutionized banking in Alabama during the last few decades. Compass spearheaded the effort to allow statewide banking in Alabama. After expanding its service to cover all regions of the state, Compass became the first in Alabama to purchase an out-of-state bank. Today, Compass operates more than 320 retail banking centers in Alabama, Florida, Texas, New Mexico, Arizona and Colorado.

Compass Bank understands the needs of business and offers a number of innovative products and specialized services to help its customers succeed. These services include commercial checking and savings, commercial money market accounts, treasury management services, business banking software, investment and brokerage services, equipment financing and leasing, retirement programs and pension plans, trust services, and interest rate protection products. As an SBA "Preferred Lender," Compass can also provide expertise and fast processing on SBA loan requests. This was one of the reasons that Compass ranked as one of the top 10 SBA lenders among banks in 1999. Overall, the seasoned professionals at Compass provide businesses with personal attention, developing innovative solutions to help companies move forward—on the local, national, or international level.

Across its markets, Compass has led the way in meeting customer needs. Compass was the first bank in Alabama to offer Saturday banking. Today customers can open accounts, apply for loans, or even a mortgage right over the phone through Compass' Telephone Banking Center. CompassPC®, Alabama's first online banking service, lets customers access and download daily account information, record transactions, and even transfer funds among

accounts. Add to this their Bill Payment and Presentment Programs, and the Compass customer truly has a wide range of options for controlling their finances.

Compass Bank's Web site offers both information and interactive materials. At www.compassweb.com customers can calculate their potential mortgage payments, apply and receive approval for credit cards, or request information and rates on a wide variety of Compass products—all through this online resource.

As more and more people began investing in the stock market and in mutual funds, Compass developed another online resource for its customers: CompassWeb Brokerage. CompassWeb Brokerage (www.compasswebbrokerage.com) was one of the nation's first online trading services. In addition, Compass Brokerage, Compass Bank's brokerage affiliate, offers comprehensive investment services through its personal investment officers and also makes available its family of proprietary mutual funds, the Expedition Funds.

Compass' unique services to individuals and businesses in Alabama and throughout its service areas have helped propel the company to tremendous growth. This expansion has rewarded Compass Bancshares shareholders with outstanding returns on their investment. Shares of Compass stock are traded on the Nasdaq market system, and at year end 1999, Compass recorded its 12th consecutive year of both record earnings and earnings per share.

Every day, the people at Compass are finding new ways to help customers with creative ideas and innovative solutions. Compass continues to stand at the cutting edge of technology and service. At the same time, through Compass Charities, Compass is helping find solutions to problems in Alabama through donations to nonprofit, charitable organizations. At the dawn of a new millennium, the message continues to be loud and clear: Where there's Compass, there's a way. ■

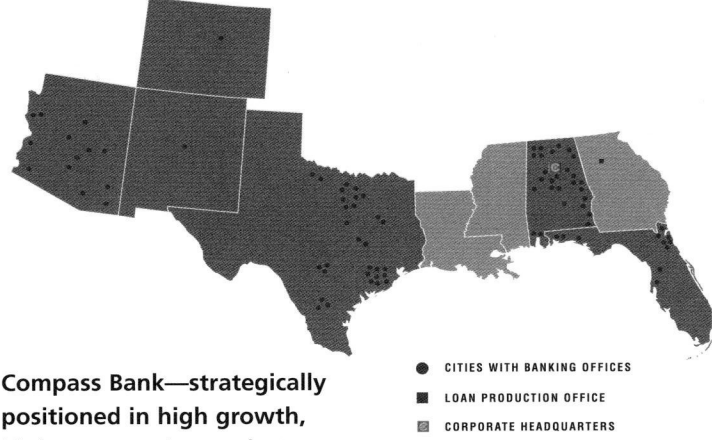

Compass Bank—strategically positioned in high growth, high opportunity markets throughout the Sunbelt.

● CITIES WITH BANKING OFFICES
■ LOAN PRODUCTION OFFICE
▣ CORPORATE HEADQUARTERS

Protective Industrial Insurance Company of Alabama, Inc.

P rotective Industrial Insurance Company has its foundations set deep in the history of the Magic City. At the turn of the century in Birmingham, the son of a former slave, Charles Morgan Harris, left school after the sixth grade to train as an embalmer. With the help of his sister, Hattie Davenport, he opened the Davenport and Harris Funeral Home in 1899. A quarter of a century later, Harris and his son Walter opened Protective Burial Society, the precursor of Protective Industrial Insurance Co. Today, Davenport and Harris is the oldest black-owned business in the state. Both companies have been open every day, 24 hours a day, since they were founded.

"We've never missed a payroll, never failed to pay a claim, never had a bad check in all those years," says Protective's Board Chairman J. Mason Davis, Jr., the grandson of C.M. Harris. Protective has a strong reputation for being fair and equitable to all of its stockholders. Davis admits that the family-owned company's profit margin might not be as great as it could be, but everyone at Protective can sleep well at night knowing they've treated all their customers fairly.

Protective Industrial Insurance Co. has succeeded over three quarters of a century through strong and conservative management, delivering a quality service at a reasonable price. The company began by offering only burial insurance, primarily to the low-income black community in Birmingham. In 1952, Protective expanded to become a "home service" company selling industrial life insurance policies with higher benefits. Premiums were paid in cash and collected by door-to-door agents on a weekly or monthly basis. This was the only choice available for many policyholders who lived from paycheck to paycheck on meager incomes.

Many insurance companies have abandoned the lower-income market in recent years, but not Protective Industrial Insurance Co.

J. Mason Davis, Jr., Chairman of the Board.

Davis says the company has also developed a broader clientele in recent years, however. Today, the company offers traditional whole life and term policies beginning at about $1,000. Protective also offers a small amount of supplemental health insurance. Protective's agents still provide service directly to the customer's home rather than relying on the mail.

"Our plan is to continue to increase the range of our insurance offerings and expand more into upper markets," Davis says. "But we will make the transition at a conservative pace."

Davis says Protective is also exploring opportunities to expand its business outside of Alabama. Currently, the company has seven offices in the state: Birmingham, Mobile, Montgomery, Tuscaloosa, Anniston, Selma, and Decatur.

Protective Industrial Insurance believes strongly in taking an active role in the community. Many of the company's board members also serve on the boards of organizations like the United Way, the Salvation Army, the Urban League, the YMCA, the American Heart Association, and the American Cancer Society. Protective's agents and other employees are also active in area churches.

Davis says he'd like to see Protective Industrial Insurance Co. remain a permanent fixture in the future of Birmingham and the state. While large companies have absorbed many smaller firms in recent years, the family members that govern Protective want to continue doing business the way they have in the past. "We feel we serve the community better this way," Davis says.

"Protective Industrial Insurance Co. is part of the heritage of this great state and this great city. We plan to be a part of its continuing growth and development as well." ■

Protective Industrial Insurance Co. has succeeded over three quarters of a century through strong and conservative management, delivering a quality service at a reasonable price.

Baldwin Mutual

• •

If you were a farmer in South Alabama during the early part of this century, you already had one strike against you. Insurance companies would not write coverage on farm buildings and structures due to their exposure to the Gulf Coast and its inclement weather. Most farmers and their families were barely able to stay afloat in those desolate times. With the future of the farming industry seemingly bleak in 1921, a group of 20 Baldwin County farmers merged together and formed their own insurance company. The result was Baldwin Mutual of Foley, Alabama.

From its early beginnings of 20 incorporators, with just one employee and one agent, to its present-day payroll of 35 employees and 300 agents statewide, Baldwin Mutual has become Alabama's only true mutual property casualty company, insuring both property and casualty. The company handles all of its own losses in-house with its own personal adjusters. This insures that the policyholder will be notified immediately, and an adjuster can be sent to visit the policyholder that very same day.

Governed by a nine-member board of directors and currently headed by Tim Russell, the mayor of Foley, Baldwin Mutual now insures thousands of families throughout Alabama. The mission of the organization today stays true to the mission when the company was first founded: To provide the finest insurance products available to its mutual policyholders at the most reasonable price possible. While the company is involved with reinsurance pools outside of Alabama, making it broader in scope, Baldwin Mutual remains a company that focuses squarely on Alabama families.

The secret behind Baldwin Mutual's success lies in its ability to relate to its customers. Being a mutual company, Baldwin Mutual is owned entirely by its policyholders. While this may be a common practice nationwide, no other property casualty insurance company in the state can make that claim. Even with the onslaught of technology and though its operations may span the entire state, the company still manages to maintain a "hometown" atmosphere with its policyholders. Each of the families covered by Baldwin Mutual experiences a person-to-person relationship with their individual agent, continuing the tradition which the company was founded on 79 years ago—personal service.

Baldwin Mutual also believes strongly in giving back to its community and remains civic-minded, with memberships in the South Baldwin Chamber of Commerce, the Business Council of Alabama, the United States Chamber of Commerce, and is one of the longest paying members of NAMIC.

Although Baldwin Mutual has been in business for eight decades, it has experienced its most celebrated growth over the last 20 years. Up until the early 1970s, Baldwin Mutual was content with staying a southern Alabama operation. Since that time, the company's growth has spread across the state with widespread success.

With a general movement into the total financial services picture, Baldwin Mutual is excited about the changes that a new millennium will bring to the world of insurance companies. The company can see itself as doing other financial services besides insurance soon, giving its customers even more for their money and ensuring even more concise coverage for every family in its organization.

From its meager inception, Baldwin Mutual has continued to flourish and grow in a market that is inundated with competition. And with its commitment to quality services on a personal level, its continued success in the world of insurance is practically guaranteed. ▪

From its early beginnings of 20 incorporators, with just one employee and one agent, to its present-day payroll of 35 employees and 300 agents statewide, Baldwin Mutual has become Alabama's only true mutual property casualty company, insuring both property and casualty.

Photo by Robert Fouts

CHAPTER 13

The Professions

Photo by Pat McDonogh.

Bradley Arant Rose & White LLP

A s the largest law firm in Alabama with over 170 lawyers practicing in virtually every area of law, Bradley Arant provides its clients with the broad range of expertise needed by businesses today. Since its founding in Birmingham in 1904, the firm has remained committed to its goals of providing the highest quality legal services to its clients, and understanding and addressing their needs. Bradley Arant's dedication to the achievement of these goals continues today from its offices located in Birmingham, Huntsville, and Montgomery, Alabama, and Washington, D.C.

Bradley Arant is a client-driven firm, and they measure their success by their ability to help their clients achieve success. They believe that they can best serve their clients and help them achieve their goals and objectives by becoming a true partner in their business endeavors. The firm represents a diverse client base that ranges from individuals to emerging business enterprises to established regional, national, and international companies, including nearly 100 of the Fortune 500 companies. Their clients come from a broad spectrum of industries, including manufacturing, financial services, construction, energy, oil and gas, health care, venture capital, real estate, technology, biotech, and insurance.

Through their client-focused practice groups they offer a diversified civil practice including environmental law, labor and employment, health care, employment benefits, construction and procurement, litigation, general corporate, mergers and acquisitions, emerging businesses, banking, bankruptcy and creditor rights, tax, estate planning, energy, trade regulation, international trade, securities, municipal finance, real estate, governmental affairs, white collar crime, intellectual property, and antitrust.

They take pride in the talent of their people and the depth of their experience and are committed to providing the highest s tandards of legal service to their clients. In recognition of this commitment, many of their lawyers have been selected for membership in professional organizations that recognize outstanding attorneys in particular fields, including the American Law Institute, the American College of Trial Lawyers, the American College of Tax Counsel, the American College of Trust and Estate Counsel,

the International Association of Defense Counsel, the American College of Construction Lawyers, the American College of Bond Counsel, the American College of Bankruptcy, the American College of Mortgage Attorneys, the Alabama Law Institute, the Southern Federal Tax Institute, the American Tax Policy Institute, and the American Bankruptcy Institute. Bradley Arant has more lawyers listed in the most recent edition of *The Best Lawyers in America* than any other Alabama law firm. Since 1923, the *Martindale-Hubbell Law Directory* has selected the firm to serve as the reviser of its *Alabama Law Digest*.

Standing, left to right: Susan Doss, John W. SmithT, M. Williams Goodwyn, Jr., John B. Grenier, A. H. Gaede, Jr., William L. Hinds, Jr., and Kenneth M. Perry. Seated, left to right: Brittin T. Coleman and Michael D. McKibben.

Since its inception, Bradley Arant has promoted the development of Alabama. One of the firm's earliest partners, John P. Tillman, was the first president of the Birmingham Bar Association. Hugh Morrow became the president of one of the pioneer firms in the area—Sloss Sheffield Steel & Iron Company, now U.S. Pipe & Foundry. Bernard Monaghan played a key role in the creation of Vulcan Materials Company and later became its president and chief executive officer. Douglas Arant was one of the leaders who helped guide the community through the turbulent 1960s. Former partners are the current Chief Executive Officers of Vulcan

In 2002 Bradley Arant will move to a new office tower to be built on the former Federal Reserve Bank property in downtown Birmingham.

Materials (Don James) and Energen (Mike Warren). Members of the firm have also been involved in the preparation and implementation of essential legislation at the state level in the areas of education, tax reform, and municipal finance.

Today, Bradley Arant is active in representing the core industries that are shaping Alabama. Banking has become a major growth industry during the past decade, and Bradley Arant consistently ranks in the top 10 firms in the nation in the number of mergers and acquisitions handled in that industry. Among other banks, the firm represents SouthTrust Bank and has performed all the merger and acquisition work for that rapidly expanding company. The firm also plays a large role in the construction business in the state. Bradley Arant performs work for most of the major builders in the area, as well as for construction firms throughout the Southeast. It is are also closely involved in the medical community in the city, representing Children's Hospital, Medical Center East, University Hospital, and the UAB Health Services Foundation, among others. The firm also believes in the potential for new business in the state, and recently formed an Emerging Business Team that is committed to assisting entrepreneurs, investors, and emerging companies with the full range of legal issues they face.

Beyond the role they play in the growth and development of the state, the lawyers and staff at Bradley Arant contribute to the quality of life in the community through their active participation in the Birmingham Area Chamber of Commerce, the Huntsville-Madison County Chamber of Commerce, United Way, the Birmingham Museum of Art, the Alabama Symphony, the Huntsville Public

Library Foundation, Children's Hospital, Alabama Public Television, and other civic organizations. Bradley Arant partner Jim Rotch is author of the Birmingham Pledge, a worldwide effort to eliminate racial prejudice. The firm has been heavily involved in the Partners in Progress (Adopt-A-School) program from the very beginning, providing 40 to 50 tutors throughout the school year to help students at Powell Elementary School in Birmingham, and was recently awarded the Liberty and Justice Award for these efforts.

In the summer of 2002 Bradley Arant will move its Birmingham office to a new office tower that is a part of the Federal Reserve Bank Property Development. The firm is pleased to be a part of this new project, which is the largest new multi-tenant development in downtown Birmingham since 1988. Bradley Arant is proud to be a part of the history of this state and looks forward to helping meet the challenges facing Alabama in the future. ▪

The Huntsville office of Bradley Arant Rose & White is located in the prestigious AmSouth Center.

Balch & Bingham LLP

Huntsville Office from left to right: David B. Block, Daniel M. Wilson.

Founded in Birmingham in 1922 by Judge William Logan Martin, Balch & Bingham LLP celebrated its 75th anniversary on October 1, 1997. The firm presently maintains two offices in downtown Birmingham, along with locations in Huntsville and Montgomery and in Washington, D.C. With these locations in Alabama's centers of government, commerce, and technology and in the nation's capital, Balch & Bingham LLP's attorneys offer statewide and national representation for its diverse group of state and regional clients.

Balch & Bingham's practice in the utility and energy industries is nationally recognized. The firm represents clients involved in oil and gas exploration and production, and coal and other minerals development. Balch & Bingham LLP serves electrical, gas, and telecommunication utility service providers, as well as independent power producers.

Additionally, the firm represents a number of local, state, regional, national, and international clients in industries including banking and financial services, construction, education, government, health care, high technology, insurance, manufacturing, real estate, retail, and sports.

The clients which Balch & Bingham LLP represent in these industries include internationally renowned concerns. The firm represents a number of companies listed on the Fortune 500 and those traded on the NASDAQ and Dow Jones exchanges.

Balch & Bingham LLP's full-service capabilities include representation of its clients in all the following practice areas: administrative law, alternative dispute resolution, antitrust, corporate, employment and labor, environmental, intellectual property,

litigation, mergers & acquisitions, products liability, public finance, securities, and taxation.

The many honors that have been bestowed upon the attorneys of Balch & Bingham LLP attest to the excellence of service provided by the firm. Several of the firm's attorneys are listed in *The Best Lawyers in America*. Several partners have served as Bar Examiners for the Alabama State Bar. The firm's attorneys have been elected by their peers to membership in organizations which recognize their knowledge and experience in the field of law in which they practice, including Fellows of the American College of Trial Lawyers. A number of the firm's attorneys serve as adjunct instructors at area law schools, and many participate regularly as panel members and speakers at seminars conducted for other attorneys or for laypersons, especially in the business community. Many have served as presidents of the American Bar Association and the Alabama State Bar committees and sections in their areas of practice. Several of Balch & Bingham's attorneys have been called to testify as expert witnesses before legislative bodies in their area of practice. Other attorneys from the firm have been involved in drafting the legislation and regulations which currently govern and regulate the industries they serve.

Balch & Bingham LLP's attorneys serve as active partners in their clients' businesses, providing counsel and proactive representation. Attorneys are deeply involved with the industries they

Montgomery Office from left to right: Charles B. Paterson, Malcolm N. Carmichael, Leslie M. Allen, David R. Boyd, John S. Bowman, Sr., Sterling G. Culpepper, Jr., Michael D. Waters, Dorman Walker, Donald R. Jones, Jr., and Warren H. Goodwyn.

serve, from writing for trade publications to writing and lobbying for key legislation and even serving on boards of directors. Balch & Bingham LLP's proactive strategy extends to providing newsletters, white papers, and seminars that apprise clients of changes in the law that could affect their businesses.

Balch & Bingham LLP's support staff and administrative personnel are also key resources for clients. The firm maintains one of the largest and most diverse law libraries in the Southeast, with access to the latest research technology such as WESTLAW, LEXIS, CD-ROM products, and the Internet. Balch & Bingham LLP supports its legal staff with cutting-edge technology, including document management systems, electronic billing, electronic mail, and interactive litigation support systems. The firm maintains one of the most extensive and most frequently updated websites of any law firm in the state, providing links to state and federal court decisions and many other legal-related sites.

Balch & Bingham LLP's Washington, D.C. office, which opened in 1991, offers another unique resource to clients. The firm's

Birmingham Office from left to right: James F. Hughey, Jr., H. Hampton Boles, William S. Wright, Richards L. Pearson, Lois S. Woodward, Jesse S. Vogtle, Jr., Suzanne Ashe, Phillip A. Nichols, Leonard C. Tillman, Randolph H. Lanier, William E. Shanks, Jr., Robert L. Loftin, III, Walter M. Beale, Jr., and Timothy J. Tracy.

attorneys in the nation's capital represent clients in legislative and regulatory arenas. They also bring matters before the executive branch of government, the federal courts, and federal agencies.

Balch & Bingham LLP is committed to providing today's corporate consumer with outstanding legal work and excellent service. The firm conducts regular customer reviews to judge each client's satisfaction with the legal services provided and their relationship with the firm.

The attorneys of Balch & Bingham LLP believe in serving their community as well as their clients. The firm has a long-standing commitment to the Adopt-A-School program, to PATH, and to the Explorers program of the Boy Scouts in Birmingham. The firm has also participated as a corporate sponsor in the Bruno's Memorial Classic Senior PGA event, which benefits numerous local charities.

Balch & Bingham LLP's presence touches all of Birmingham's major growth industries: banking, construction, and health care. The firm is also involved in the growth of the city through its representation of companies in real estate development, from residential areas to shopping centers and regional malls, office buildings, and other commercial structures. By providing solutions for Birmingham area businesses of all sizes and in all industries, Balch & Bingham LLP is playing an important role in the life and in the quality of life found in the Magic City. ▪

Left to right: Alan T. Rogers and Michael L. Edwards. Balch & Bingham LLP.

Sherlock, Smith & Adams, Inc.
ARCHITECTS • ENGINEERS • PLANNERS

The future in outpatient care—hospital without beds. Ambulatory Health Care Center, Maxwell AFB, Alabama.

From Montgomery's Garrett Coliseum, a landmark design achievement built in the early 1950s, to the largest ambulatory healthcare center ever undertaken by the United States Air Force, Sherlock, Smith & Adams, Inc. has proven itself worldwide as a firm of firsts.

Established in Montgomery in 1946, the young firm, under the guidance of innovative designers Morland Smith, Chris Sherlock, and Dick Adams, hit the ground running, rapidly earning a reputation for forward-thinking, progressive work.

But, from the start, SS&A has known there is more to the business than good design. The company's founders established a corporate culture founded on client service, responsiveness, and integrity that holds fast today. In fact, the firm's uncompromising commitment to service has helped ensure that today's SS&A design professionals maintain strong business relationships with some of the firm's earliest clients.

Based in Montgomery, Sherlock, Smith & Adams has earned an international reputation as one of the world's finest full-service architectural, engineering, and planning firms. The company has enjoyed more than a half-century of success, earning acclaim for award-winning designs of public buildings, educational institutions, hospitals and healthcare facilities, recreational facilities, churches, and more. Ground-breaking designs, such as a chain of rural Kentucky hospitals in the 1950s, to the more recent Madigan Army Regional Tertiary Care and Teaching Hospital in Ft. Lewis, Washington—the largest healthcare facility ever built for the U.S. military—have consistently ensured SS&A's stature as one of the nation's foremost institutional design firms.

But a strong diversity of Alabama projects has made SS&A an important contributor to the architectural landscape of its home state. Included in the firm's local portfolio are such notable structures as the Monroe County Courthouse, Eaves Memorial Coliseum in Auburn, Veterans Affairs Hospitals in Birmingham, Montgomery, Tuscaloosa, and Tuskegee, the Cheaha State Park Lodge, Bryant Hall at the University of Alabama, the Maxwell Air Force Base "Super Clinic" in Montgomery, and historic renovations at Montgomery's Huntingdon College and Troy State University.

The company's expertise on the educational front earned the notice of state leaders and gained the firm responsibility for monitoring and administering the massive statewide removal of portable and substandard classrooms. These kinds of projects, coupled with the firm's success on major international projects as far away as Turkey and Italy, exemplify the company's varied design expertise and production flexibility.

SS&A clients are served by proven, hard-working professionals. The company employs more than 90 professionals at two locations in Montgomery and Birmingham. To ensure cost-efficiency and quality production, SS&A has recently invested more than $1 million in technology and equipment upgrades.

A proven leader in its industry, SS&A has also taken a front seat as one of the state's most generous corporate citizens. The company focuses on diversity, coordinates mentoring programs for students and aspiring designers, contributes time and financial resources to enhance the local influence of the arts, and participates actively on behalf of small business and education on the political front. The company has, in fact, received its community's most prestigious business award, having been named Montgomery's Small Business of the Year.

As SS&A enters a new century and embarks on its fifty-fourth year of service, the firm remains committed to its heritage as a firm of firsts. Whether it is progressive new design initiatives, staff quality, customer service, or community leadership, Sherlock, Smith & Adams, Inc. remains committed to working hard to set a standard of excellence in every facet of its business. ■

"Design and Project Management Services When You Need Them."

A number of students in the UA Techno-M.B.A. program work on EIL projects with the faculty. The Techno-M.B.A. program is ranked fourth nationally by *ComputerWorld*.

Alabama Productivity Center

Two years ago, a county commissioner from rural Pickens County, Alabama, made an urgent appeal for help to The University of Alabama. The county had a serious financial crisis, and citizens held the county government in low esteem. What were county leaders to do?

The University moved quickly, working through the Alabama Productivity Center (APC) to form a partnership with the citizens of Pickens County. The partnership worked to improve the efficiency and productivity of county operations, and most importantly, to increase citizen involvement in county operations.

Earlier this year, the County Commission approved a resolution thanking UA for its "significant contributions" and for the "vital partnership" that led to a more efficient and productive county operation. The resolution went on to thank the University for helping the county be "good stewards of the taxpayers' money."

When approached by Pickens County officials, the Alabama Productivity Center, part of the Culverhouse College of Commerce and Business Administration, put together a team of business college faculty, staff, and graduate students. The UA team recommended forming a blue-ribbon committee of county citizens to become involved in county operations.

The UA team, led by Dr. David Miller, APC director, included George Hamner, regional manager of the Manufacturing Extension Partnership, and Robert Allen, director of UA's Executive M.B.A. Program, along with several graduate students. The team spent more than 200 hours examining each aspect of county government, looking for better ways to carry out county functions, looking for ways to save money, and asking county employees to

The Center for Green Manufacturing explores methods of environmentally prudent manufacturing.

The Center for Freshwater Studies brings together scientists from many disciplines in crucial research funded by the National Science Foundation.

recommend better ways to accomplish their jobs.

"It was an exciting experience to see citizen involvement and commitment to better governing, and to see the responsiveness of elected officials wanting to find better, more efficient ways of doing the job," Miller said.

APC, a nonprofit organization, was established in January 1986 by UA and Alabama Power Co. The center uses University educational resources and research capabilities to improve productivity and stimulate economic development within the state.

Center for Business and Economic Research

The popular and eagerly awaited annual *Economic Abstract of Alabama* will be published early in January 2000. The abstract, published by UA's Center for Business and Economic Research (CBER) in the Culverhouse College of Commerce and Business Administration, is a fixture in most business libraries around the state. It features sections on Alabama agriculture, communications, construction, education, employment, finance, foreign trade, health and human services, income, manufacturing, mineral industry, population, price indexes, transportation, and other vital statistics. *Outlook*, also published by CBER, will be out early next year. Published annually since 1980, *Outlook* gives the state's business leaders vital information on the U.S. and state economies, provides data on the state's metropolitan areas, and projects tax revenues.

CBER is headed now by Dr. Carl E. Ferguson Jr., who earlier this year was named associate dean for research and technology at the Culverhouse College of Commerce and Business Administration. Ferguson brings a strong background of research and scholarship to CBER.

CBER was created in 1930 and has since engaged continuously in research programs to promote economic development in the state. The center serves as Alabama's central reservoir for business, economic, and demographic data. ▪

Auburn University

"Auburn's mission is defined by its land-grant traditions of service and access. This university is dedicated to Alabama's economic and social growth. As we enter the twenty-first century, we are focusing particular attention on seven 'Peaks of Excellence,' which represent program areas with tremendous potential. Fisheries and allied aquacultures, poultry science, biological sciences, detection and food safety, transportation, information technology, and forestry and wildlife sciences can play a critical role in the future economic development of our state and maintain national stature for Auburn as an academic institution."

—William Muse, President
Auburn University

Auburn University's charter dates back to 1856, although the doors first opened in 1859 for 80 students. Today, more than 22,000 students attend AU, which counts some of the most respected scientists and agriculturists as its alumni.

U.S. News & World Report magazine ranked Auburn University 38th overall among the nation's top 50 public universities in its annual rankings for 1999-2000. AU improved its ranking from 40th in the magazine's 1998-99 issue. Auburn was the only university in Alabama on the list.

Auburn University is committed to providing its students with a broad general education with a focus on enhancing personal and intellectual development. In addition to the goal of academic excellence, Auburn's emphasis on research manages to capture the world's attention. Auburn research has been playing a significant role in the advancement of medical and scientific innovation for several decades, and changing the way that most people worldwide live their lives.

Auburn's emphasis on research manages to capture the world's attention. Auburn research has been playing a significant role in the advancement of medical and scientific innovation for several decades, and changing the way that most people worldwide live their lives.

One of the most lucrative career fields for today's student is computer technology, and Auburn is at the forefront of this revolution.

Auburn became the first university in the Southeast to offer the Bachelor of Software Engineering degree and the Master of Software Engineering degree. These two programs will give AU graduates the ability to design, analyze, maintain, and implement software systems.

The university has received international attention through its diligent work on a microchip able to monitor the safety and freshness of food products. Other studies are being conducted to produce a kit for food inspectors to assure the safety and quality of meats.

"The poultry industry as a whole in Alabama has seen a phenomenal growth over the last two decades, making it one of Alabama's largest industries. Its success would not have been possible without the assistance of Auburn University's Poultry Science Department, and the poultry industry has served our industry through new products, new markets, and new jobs, and has served our state's citizens through the development of safer and more nutritious food, as well as a safer and cleaner environment."

—Johnny Adams, Executive Director
Alabama Poultry and Egg Association

Veterinary medical researchers are working to extract food-borne pathogens from cattle herds. AU's research team has discovered a method to extract the E.coli bacteria from meats while leaving the essential vitamins in ground beef intact.

Still other researchers at Auburn University are studying the relationship between obesity and chemical balance in the body as it relates to the hormone leptin.

Another important area of focus at Auburn University is the progress made by AU's wildlife and fishery departments. Its transgenic fish research could eventually lead to a disease-free species of catfish, which has furthered Auburn's international reputation in fish parasitology.

"Auburn University has made, and continues to make, significant contributions to the state of Alabama, but none has been more visible beyond Alabama boundaries than those contributions made through the Department of Fisheries and Allied Aquacultures. Aquaculture, particularly catfish farming, has been a bright spot in American agriculture, a kind of agriculture that did not even exist 50 years ago.

"Auburn University's fisheries program has supported aquaculture to its present status and is recognized worldwide for its teaching, research, and extension programs. The relationship between the

Auburn University is committed to providing its students with a broad general education with a focus on enhancing personal and intellectual development.

Department of Fisheries and Allied Aquacultures and the Alabama Catfish Producers, a division of the Alabama Farmers Federation, has allowed the catfish industry to identify future research needs, select priorities, and find solutions to the problems that has allowed for orderly industry development strategies for rural America and other parts of the world. Aquaculture can and should be integrally linked to a healthy environment. With Auburn University's continued support, I believe the industry can achieve these goals."

—Jimmy Carlisle, Director
Alabama Catfish Producers

Auburn's freshwater fisheries program, Fisheries and Allied Aquacultures, continues to be rated one of the top programs in the country by its peers. Its recent studies include experiments with genetically altered fish as an alternative to the increasingly diminishing saltwater fish. It is safe to say that without Auburn University and its vast research, Alabama's $75-million catfish industry might not be the lucrative force that it is today. This research has helped expand Alabama's catfish industry from 8,000 to more than 24,000 acres in production, producing 40 million catfish annually.

Auburn University's research has also played a large role in today's world of textiles and apparel. Within the last few years, an AU researcher has developed a new bullet-proof material that will provide more protection and comfort to the wearer. In addition, research at Auburn has been an important factor in increasing the safety, performance, and comfort of barrier garments used in medical professions, industry, and the military. These garments protect the wearer from hazards, and in some cases protect equipment from the wearer.

Auburn's forestry researchers have also played an integral part in the progress of Alabama. Currently, studies are being conducted to find methods of enhancing tree growth on an experimental 10-acre plot. AU chemical engineers are developing ways to improve wood pulping and pulp bleaching to avoid harm to the environment and increase energy efficiency. With pulp and paper representing Alabama's largest value-added manufacturing segment,

Auburn's College of Engineering is proud to be the home of the Pulp and Paper Research and Education Center.

"Auburn University's School of Forestry and Wildlife Sciences has been Alabama's only accredited degree program (in this field) since 1945. The School's outstanding faculty provides leadership in teaching, research, and extension to Alabama's forest management, forest science, landowners, loggers, and other professionals in forestry-related communities. AU graduates in forestry and forest engineering have been proven to possess the knowledge and skills necessary to meet the needs of the primary employers of foresters in the state and to progress as leaders in their chosen field."

—John McMillan, Secretary/Treasurer
Alabama Forestry Council

Auburn also has been finding answers to some of the biggest problems in the textile industry. While there are only four universities in this country studying textiles and the apparel industry as a whole, AU has the distinct honor of being part of the National Textile Center. The center conducts research that can be used to create solutions to some of the textile industry's biggest concerns, from consumer wants and needs to textile components.

Auburn recognizes that the solution to keeping textile jobs in Alabama and the Southeast is technology management through engineering innovation. The Department of Textile Engineering works closely with the College of Human Sciences through the National Textile Center and provides extensive research that benefits all three parties. The Department of Textile Engineering also has ties to Alabama industry through contracts and grants distributed to businesses throughout the state.

For many, Auburn's heritage has become an integral part of countless families. While the university has a rich history behind it, Auburn has demonstrated that it has its sights set clearly on the future. Auburn University has earned its reputation as one of Alabama's most treasured institutions.

"The Alabama Farmers Federation and Auburn University have shared a mission to serve Alabama farmers and the $4.2-billion agricultural industry in this state. Auburn has been, and continues to be, invaluable in providing the support Alabama agriculture needs. Helping farmers provide a plentiful, safe, and economical food supply is a mission that serves everyone. Auburn University has provided us with some of the leading CEOs, scientists, astronauts, government leaders, and farmers across America."

—Doug Rigney, Executive Vice President
Alabama Farmers Federation

The University of Alabama in Huntsville

The University of Alabama in Huntsville is the university for your future. Whatever one's interests, goals, or aspirations, UAH helps shape a student's future and the world around him or her. UAH students and faculty define and build the future at a special university that takes the strengths of its world-class research programs and brings that knowledge into the classroom.

UAH is a university building on its traditional strengths. It is a university merging the sciences and humanities. UAH embraces new branches of science and engineering that cross the traditional lines between the disciplines.

The vision and dream of UAH was born from the dreams and vision of pioneers whose rockets carried humans into space, the moon, and beyond. UAH has since developed into a nationally recognized institution of higher education, valued for its research and prized for educational opportunities.

UAH thrives on the synergy among academia, government, and business. The university complements the research and development needs of local government entities and private industry and answers the community's need for advanced educational opportunities in science and engineering.

While UAH continues to excel in its scientific and engineering capabilities, the university also offers outstanding programs in liberal arts, administrative science, and nursing.

UAH is a key participant in one of the nation's major international centers for advanced technological research and uses its position in this environment to provide unique opportunities and

Today, 7,000 students take advantage of UAH's 62 degree-granting programs that meet the highest standards of excellence, including 35 bachelor's degree programs, 17 master's degree programs, and 10 Ph.D. programs through its five colleges.

UAH is committed to maintaining an academic community of the highest quality, and to providing an environment that facilitates intellectual, cultural, personal, and professional growth.

creative programs for students, faculty, and the community.

UAH is committed to maintaining a diverse academic community of the highest quality, and to providing an environment that facilitates intellectual, cultural, personal, and professional growth. UAH fosters leadership, creative and critical thinking, clear communication, a respect for knowledge and the pursuit of truth, and an engagement in the challenge and pleasure of a lifetime of learning. UAH, through its graduates and its programs, contributes to economic advancement, health care, cultural enrichment, and the quality of life of the region, state, and nation.

UAH President Frank Franz remarked: "We must maintain and

extend our pre-eminence in research, particularly with emphasis in science, engineering, and technology, balanced with fostering and developing our high quality programs in liberal arts, nursing, and business. Our university is an institution with remarkable success already achieved, but with even greater potential for the future. Our faculty and staff are talented and productive; our students rank among the most dedicated and successful in Alabama; and our performance in research is extraordinary."

Today, 7,000 students take advantage of the 62 degree-granting programs that meet the highest standards of excellence, including 35 bachelor's degree programs, 17 master's degree programs, and 10 Ph.D. programs through its five colleges: Administrative Science, Liberal Arts, Engineering, Nursing, and Science.

Students also get extraordinary opportunities to apply their knowledge. The university received more than $44 million in revenues for active research projects during 1999. Sponsors of that research include federal and state agencies, academic institutions, industry, and private foundations. Research is conducted within the individual colleges or through UAH's 17 independent research centers, laboratories, and institutes. Major interdisciplinary research thrusts include applied optics, propulsion, space plasma and aeronomics, space physics and astrophysics, earth system science, information technology, management of science and technology, microgravity and materials, and automation and robotics. Many UAH students work on these projects. Many others work in

UAH is a key participant in one of the nation's major international centers for advanced technological research and uses its position in this environment to provide unique opportunities and creative programs for students, faculty, and the community.

professional positions in the community as co-op students or regular employees.

In student life, the university provides activities outside the classroom such as intramural and intercollegiate sports, fraternities and sororities, choir and music ensembles, and theater productions. The university has more than 100 clubs and organizations, including the World Issues Society, Circle K, the Society for Ancient Languages, the Association for Campus Entertainment, the Student Government Association, and professionally oriented clubs and societies in almost every discipline. Greek life ranges from social activities to service projects for local and national charities. There are six national fraternities and five sororities at UAH.

Athletics are a highly charged blend of competitiveness and the ideal of the student-athlete. The university is home to 12 NCAA men's and women's sports programs. Many of them are highly competitive in their endeavors, including two national championships by the men's ice hockey team.

It took a unique community like Huntsville to create a university like UAH. In many ways, the university is a reflection of the needs of this high-tech community. "UAH is the result of the special character of Huntsville," says Dr. Franz. "The interaction among the university, federal agencies, and the community is crucial to our success. And the university's success is also crucial to the success of Huntsville."

UAH is a shining star on Huntsville's horizon, expanding the universe of opportunities for both students and the high-technology community that surrounds it. ▪

UAH, through its graduates and its programs, contributes to the quality of life and cultural enrichment of the region, state, and nation.

The University of Alabama at Birmingham

T he campus that would become the University of Alabama at Birmingham consisted in 1969 of a few blocks in the south corner of a city whose industrial base had rusted away. Birmingham was changing, and found itself challenged with meeting the demands of a growing urban community that needed higher standards of education, quality health care, and diversification of an economy once based on heavy industry.

UAB's early leaders understood that kind of transformation would be accomplished only through tireless effort, ambitious dreams, and a sturdy will. That same year, an extension center with some 5,000 students became an independent campus within the University of Alabama System and named its first president. It was the vision of that president, Dr. Joseph Volker, for UAB to not only touch the lives of people on a local, national, and global level, but to regularly contribute to, and raise, the standards of excellence in teaching, research, and health care.

"We would do Birmingham a great disservice," Volker said, "if we dreamed too little dreams."

Today UAB is at the very heart of the city's medical, educational, and economic renaissance, encompassing 75 city blocks in a revitalized Birmingham economy ignited and nourished by a thriving health services industry.

UAB enrolls 16,000 students in schools of arts and humanities, business, dentistry, education, engineering, health related professions, medicine, natural sciences and mathematics, nursing, optometry, public health, and social and behavioral sciences. UAB also is home to a large graduate school and a world-renowned health care complex.

Ranked as one of the top research universities in the nation, UAB's $300 million extramural funding annually exceeds that of

The historic Honors House is home to UAB's nationally acclaimed Honors Program, which enrolls about 200 students each year in an innovative series of interdisciplinary courses.

all other Alabama universities combined. Its worldwide reputation for innovative research, patient care, and education is paralleled by its community leadership and contributions to the welfare of Alabamians.

Energizing the Economy

UAB is Birmingham's largest employer and the second largest employer in the state, with one in every 10 jobs in the Birmingham area resulting from UAB's presence. Its annual direct and indirect economic impact on the Birmingham area is nearly $2 billion; revenues to local governments from university-related influences are estimated at $99.06 million; and about $30.6 million of state funds supplied to area governments are attributed to the UAB-affiliated portion of the community, including public education funds.

UAB exerts a strong influence on job creation and retention.

In addition to UAB's 12 schools, 75 interdisciplinary centers offer its 16,000 students the chance to join faculty in the exploration of such diverse issues as aging, the environment, urban affairs, and telecommunications.

The UAB Research Foundation patents and licenses faculty discoveries for commercial use; it works closely with the Office for the Advancement of Developing Industries (OADI) incubator to create and nurture high-tech businesses at its 67,000-square-foot facility in the UAB Research Park in Oxmoor Valley. The 36 graduate companies, comprising computer technology, biotechnology, biomedical technology, and pharmaceutical industries, have created more than 1,200 jobs, and generated an annual sales volume averaging nearly $40 million over the past few years.

Local entrepreneurs seek guidance from the UAB Small Business Development Center, and the Center for Labor Education and Research studies workplace issues and provides expertise on labor-management negotiations, hazardous material handling, federal labor laws, and more.

UAB's 75-block campus is located just blocks from Alabama's financial, corporate, and economic hub, ensuring students easy access to an active campus life and plenty of internships, jobs, and volunteer work in every field.

Faculty and Students

UAB's faculty includes more than 1,800 full-time members, 91 percent of whom have terminal degrees. The students they teach represent a rich blend of ages, cultures, and backgrounds. More than 650 students from about 90 countries tender unique perspectives on life and learning.

The UAB Honors Program enrolls about 200 students each year in an innovative series of interdisciplinary courses taught by teams of faculty with a variety of expertise.

UAB's faculty includes more than 1,900 full-time members, 91 percent of whom have terminal degrees.

UAB faculty do more than teach. They write, research, invent, discover, and bring their firsthand knowledge to the classroom. For example, UAB faculty are perfecting a device to detect microscopic fossils on Mars, pioneering HIV and AIDS studies, tracking terrorist activity, and pursuing genetic treatments for cancer and other diseases.

There are more than 75 interdisciplinary centers at UAB, where faculty and students explore such diverse issues as aging, the environment, urban affairs, and telecommunications. UAB is the only university in the state to earn the Carnegie Foundation "Research I" classification, grouping it with Duke, Harvard, and Johns Hopkins. Yet its tuition is affordable and below the national average, making UAB an outstanding educational value.

Partnership with the Public

UAB's comprehensive educational mission extends into elementary and secondary classrooms across the state and other Alabama colleges and universities.

One example involves the Birmingham school system, which has joined forces with UAB and the National Science Foundation to improve student test scores by emphasizing practical math skills children use daily.

Through UAB's Center for Community Outreach and Development (CORD), high-school students from all over Alabama participate in hands-on, high-tech experiments in an authentic molecular biology lab at Birmingham's McWane Center.

The UAB Urban Education Initiative is a collaboration between the UAB School of Education and six metro-area school systems to prepare teachers and administrators to work with inner-city

The UAB Blazers field 17 intercollegiate teams as a Division I member of the NCAA and a founding member of Conference USA. Blazer football matchups routinely include highly competitive schools like Missouri and Virginia Tech.

children facing social and family problems that can thwart academic success.

The UAB Center for Educational Accountability is the nation's first program devoted to assessing the long-term impact of state and national policies and educational innovations on school achievement, student retention, and graduation rates.

Connecting with Corporations

UAB also partners with corporations to ensure a well-trained and knowledgeable workforce. For K-12, the UAB School of Education is redesigning its teacher-education program with a grant from the BellSouth Foundation. One component, teacher-development sites, will enable educators and administrators to share the responsibility with UAB faculty for teacher education and school renewal.

UAB and the corporate community forge paths to improved educational opportunities and quality of life. Business leaders serve on advisory boards of UAB schools and provide internships and cooperative learning opportunities. The Alabama Power Foundation, for example, has committed almost $500,000 to fund scholarships for engineering students.

Serving the Public Welfare

Partnerships extend into the civic arena, where the university enthusiastically serves.

The Center for Urban Affairs provides research and technical assistance to community organizations and federal, state, and local governments. The center's faculty and staff also conduct business-retention surveys and demographic and land-use analyses.

Through the UAB/Titusville 2000 Project, the university is helping community leaders find solutions to problems facing the historically African-American urban community of 6,000 people. New homes, job and family counseling, and an after-school educational program have emerged.

The health and safety of Birmingham's youth also concern the university. The UAB Drug Store brings together professionals in law enforcement, medicine, and counseling who present middle-school students with realistic demonstrations and straight talk about the legal, social, and physical consequences of substance abuse. Since the UAB Drug Store began in 1995, the program has

Women at UAB compete and routinely take home individual and team competition and scholastic honors in basketball, cross country, golf, rifle, soccer, softball, synchronized swimming, tennis, track and field, and volleyball.

UAB is the only university in the state to earn the Carnegie Foundation "Research I" classification, grouping it with Duke, Harvard, and Johns Hopkins. Yet tuition is affordable and below the national average, making UAB an outstanding educational value.

become a model for other drug-education programs across Alabama, in California, and Oklahoma.

Boosting the Arts and Entertainment

UAB's spectacular Alys Robinson Stephens Performing Arts Center opened in 1996, and attracts stars of music, theatre, and dance to its stages. The center's spacious concert hall hosts special performances of the Alabama Symphony Orchestra, the UAB choirs, and music ensembles. Since its opening, the center has become a home to the performing arts, and features not only the 1,300-seat concert hall, but also three new venues—the 130-seat Odess Theatre, the 350-seat Sirote Theatre, and the 175-seat Reynolds-Kirschbaum Recital Hall. The public is also invited to attend productions by the UAB departments of theatre and music, which regularly feature guest directors and performers from across the nation.

Cutting-edge industry meets the classroom in UAB's music technology program. In 1997, UAB launched its recording label, UAB Entertainment!, with the release of *UAB Gospel Choir—Live*, and two publishing companies, UAB Music Publishing and SWC Music Publishing. All are joined in UAB's Stevie Wonder Center for Computing in the Arts, a teaching and recording facility named for the entertainer who helped raise funds for its construction.

The visual arts also thrive at UAB in juried student exhibitions and the UAB Visual Arts Gallery, a permanent collection of more

than 300 works by established artists. The Department of Art and Art History also holds the Barker Triennial Outdoor Sculpture Competition; many of the fine sculptures now enhance the UAB campus.

Rounding out the UAB experience is UAB Blazer athletics, fielding 17 intercollegiate teams in 10 sports as a Division I member of the NCAA and a founding member of Conference USA. The Division I-A Blazer football team thrills fans with action against state rivals as well as national powerhouses such as Nebraska, Kansas, and Virginia Tech. And each home game in historic Legion Field brings a performance from the award-winning UAB Marching Blazer Band.

Since hitting the hardwood for the first time in the 1977-78 season, the UAB Blazers basketball team has captured numerous conference titles and participated in postseason play in all but four of its seasons. Each year, the Blazers basketball squad plays some of the toughest teams in the country, including Cincinnati, Louisville, and DePaul.

UAB is a vital part of the economic, intellectual, cultural, and social life of Birmingham. In just 30 years, the enterprise has exploded into one of the largest universities in the state and has become a bastion of education, research, and service. UAB's future, like that of the city it calls home, promises to be even brighter. ∎

UAB's spectacular Alys Robinson Stephens Performing Arts Center opened in 1996, and attracts stars of music, theatre, and dance to its stage.

The Troy State University System

At his October 1990 inauguration as chancellor of the Troy State University System, Dr. Jack Hawkins Jr. made this prediction:

"Troy State University in the year 2000 will not be classified simply as a regional university. It will be worldwide in outreach, international in perspective. The measuring stick of educational progress no longer is our Southern neighbors—we now compete in a global village."

Dr. Hawkins' vision has been proven correct. The Troy State University System has overcome obstacles and seized upon challenges to develop its service and its stature in the state and the world community. Initiatives begun during the 1990s will guarantee the System's success for many years to come.

Excellence is a tradition at Troy State University. Since it was founded more than 113 years ago, the University has been a leader in academics, administrative efficiency, student activities, athletics, and affordability. This leadership has been recognized by a variety of individuals and organizations throughout the Southeast and the nation, including *Money* magazine, which recently named TSU one of the top 25 "best buys" among the country's public universities and colleges.

Established in February 1887 as the Troy Normal School, Troy State University has developed from simple beginnings—128 students enrolled that first year—to become a worldwide educational system. The Troy State University System now serves approximately 18,000 students on campuses located in Alabama and across the globe. Troy State University is the flagship campus of the System, which also consists of a branch campus in Phenix City; University College, which offers degree programs at 50 military installations and metropolitan sites in 12 states and 5 nations; and 2 independently accredited universities, Troy State University Dothan and Troy State University Montgomery. While Troy's first students were proud to earn their teachers' certificates, current students have a few more choices: the System now offers associate's, bachelor's, master's, and education specialist degrees.

Building on its Normal School origins, Troy State University followed a steady course of growth as it developed to meet the changing needs of its students and the communities and region it served. The institution became Troy State Teachers College in 1929 and Troy State College in 1957, before being named Troy State University in 1967.

The Palladium, which rests atop Bibb Graves Hall, has become one of Troy State University's enduring landmarks.

Today, TSU prepares students in a variety of fields in the arts and sciences, fine arts, business, communication, applied science, nursing, and allied health sciences. And the University has maintained its legacy as a trainer of teachers—its education graduates lead classrooms across Alabama and the Southeast. TSU, which is situated on a 577-acre campus designed by the architects of New York's Central Park and the Biltmore Estate, offers almost 70 majors, more than 30 minors, and 10 preprofessional programs to its traditional-age student body. Small classes are the rule and faculty members know their students by name. Students enjoy the benefits of an attractive, well-equipped small college campus with many extras found only at larger universities.

Troy State University Dothan and Troy State University Montgomery have thrived by recognizing the unique educational needs of their communities. The two universities, which got their start as

Opened in fall 1998, the $6.5 million TSU Science Center was a key part of the System's massive building campaign in the late 1990s. The cutting-edge facility represents the University's commitment to build Alabama's premier undergraduate program in the sciences.

The Troy State University Montgomery campus is highlighted by the newly dedicated Curry Commons. The Commons centerpiece is a clocktower featuring an eternal flame representative of the Troy State University System.

outreach programs for military personnel at Fort Rucker and Maxwell Air Force Base, respectively, have developed programs specially suited to their nontraditional student populations. The use of night classes, business-and-industry partnerships, distance education technologies, and other measures has resulted in innovative programs for working adults.

The 1990s were difficult years for higher education in Alabama. Significant cuts in state funding, demographic changes in the state's population, and free-tuition scholarship programs in neighboring states led to decreases in enrollment in many of Alabama's colleges and universities.

The Troy State University System met these challenges and thrived despite them. Troy State University's new emphasis on the recruitment of international students brought hundreds of foreign students—and an array of languages and cultures—to southeast Alabama. The universities in Dothan and Montgomery strengthened their unique missions of service to their cities' adult learners. Academic and administrative efficiency were practiced throughout the System, as outdated programs were replaced with new, cutting-edge programs responsive to the needs of today's students; a 1998 study by the Alabama Commission on Higher Education determined that TSU led the state in program efficiency and viability.

As a result of these efforts, the System's enrollment increased dramatically between 1989 and 1999. Enrollment increased by 32 percent in Troy, 22 percent in Montgomery, and 10 percent in Dothan, while University College enjoyed a 15 percent increase during the decade.

The System's growth has been the result of leadership and vision. With unpredictable state funding, the System placed increased emphasis on private giving during the 1990s. Over the course of the decade, private giving nearly quadrupled, and endowments in the TSU Foundation more than tripled. To enhance the fund-raising effort, Troy State launched its first system-wide capital campaign—the Quest for Excellence—in February 1997. The three-year campaign was designed to fund five key areas: facilities, technology, student support, faculty support, and academic support; by the time it concluded, the campaign had raised $21.2 million, exceeding its goal by more than $3 million.

Funding successes allowed the Troy State University System to initiate a number of major building projects during the 1990s. More than $26 million was invested in TSU's physical plant between 1996 and 1999, including the TSU Science Center, the Claudia Crosby Theater, Richard M. Scrushy Field at Memorial Stadium, the Adams Student Center, and venerable Shackelford Hall. The construction projects have boosted TSU's academic facilities and enhanced quality of life for students. The new $6.3-million Rosa L. Parks Library and Museum, scheduled to open in 2000, will serve as a technology and resource center for the university in Montgomery. On the Dothan campus, a $6.5-million Library/Technology Building, scheduled to open in January 2001, will provide a cutting-edge research and resource facility for the university's faculty and students and for the community as a whole.

At Troy State University, the tradition of excellence continues. ■

The many faces of Troy State University are as diverse as the Earth itself. TSU has students from 45 states and 52 foreign countries.

Auburn Chamber of Commerce

Auburn is a thriving community with a unique spirit. Its blend of small-town charm and big-city benefits entices people from all walks of life. The commitment and positive attitude of Auburn's residents, city government, Chamber of Commerce, and local businesses make Auburn one of the most progressive cities in the South.

Located in east central Alabama off Interstate 85 between Montgomery and Atlanta, Auburn is best-known for being the home of Auburn University. *U.S. News & World Report* ranked Auburn University among the nation's 50 top public universities in 1998-99 in providing a superior education at a modest cost. Its extensive athletic department includes a museum and Hall of Honor for its ever-popular Southeastern Conference athletic teams.

Education has been a priority at Auburn since its founding in 1836. Its public school system is one of the best in the state. The city and community place emphasis on education through nationally recognized programs such as Foundation for Auburn's Continuing Enrichment in Schools, the Academic Venture Program, and the International Baccalaureate Program. Public school students consistently score above the state and national averages in all areas of the Stanford Achievement Test.

Quality, advanced education is available to even the youngest students. One of the few Blue Ribbon Schools in the Southeast, the Auburn Early Education Center provides children with meaningful, integrated experiences which nurture their natural learning processes.

As one of the fastest-growing towns in Alabama, Auburn abounds with businesses and job opportunities.

Downtown Toomer's corner is a symbol of time-honored tradition.

The City of Auburn and its Industrial Development Board have been successful in the recruitment, expansion, and retention of industries over the last decade. In the past five years, 2,200 jobs have been created in the community. Many of these industries are located in the Auburn Technology Park, consistently recognized as one of the finest in the Southeast.

A growing business itself, the Auburn Chamber of Commerce acts as the glue that binds area business people and the community through numerous interactive programs and special events. The Chamber has a consistent average of about 750 members and more than 1,300 contacts who make serving the community a priority.

Auburn's growth spurt isn't just commercial and industrial; it is also residential. Auburn Parks and Recreation works with the city to make it an attractive and enjoyable place to live. The Jan Dempsey Community Arts Center encompasses all of the various art disciplines. For active lifestyles, Auburn offers three recreation centers, the Boykin Community Center, the Auburn Soccer Association, a youth softball complex, and a state-of-the-art city softball complex, which has been recognized as one of the premier complexes in the nation by *USA Softball Magazine* and softball officials.

Parks like Kiesel and Chewacla State Park offer serene walking trails, picnic areas, and plenty of places to play and relax. Recently, the Auburn community raised $150,000 and volunteered for six days to build a neighborhood playground benefiting young and old alike.

Auburn's council-manager form of government welcomes continued growth and has long-term plans for the infrastructure of the community. The dynamic relationships among the residents of the community, the university, and the city create a chemistry that makes Auburn more than just a place to live. It is a way of life. ∎

Samford Hall is a symbol for the quality of Auburn University. Quality education continues to be a priority for the Auburn community.

Auburn Early Education Center is Auburn's Blue Ribbon School.

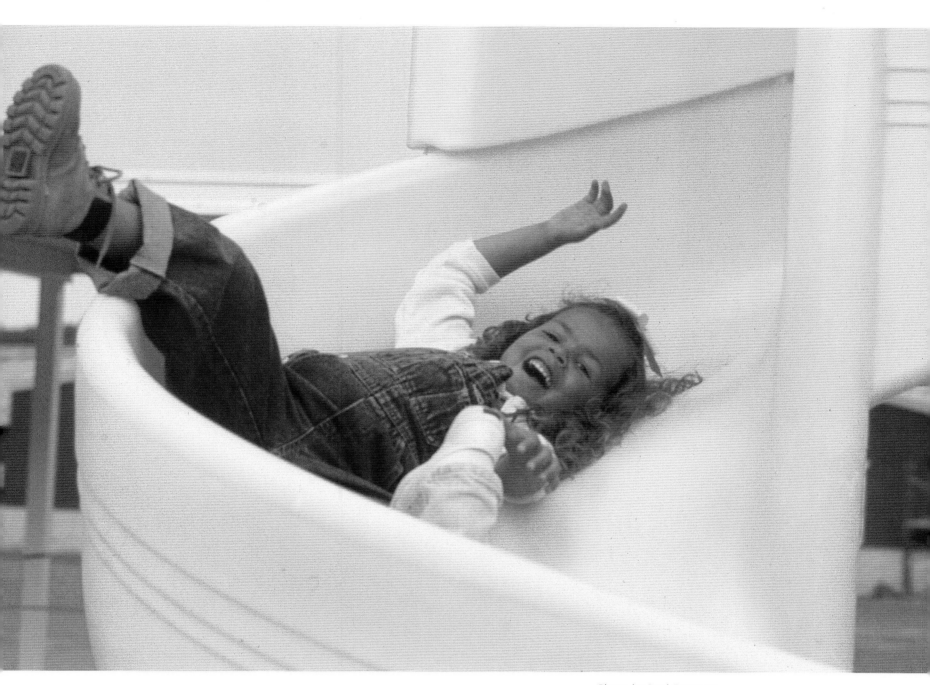

Photo by Paul Sumners.

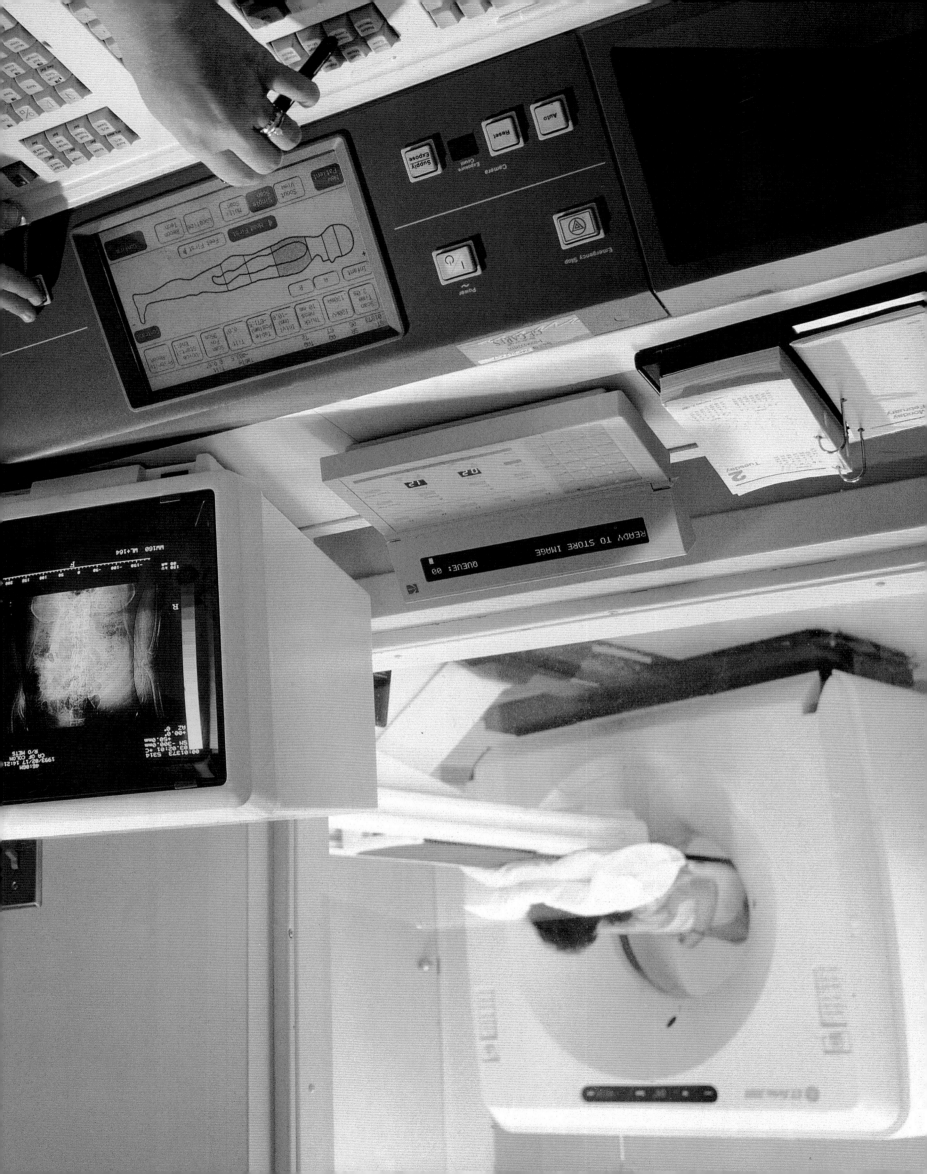

CHAPTER 16

Health Care

Photo by Robert Fouts.

Noland Health Services

In 1913, Dr. Lloyd Noland came to Jefferson County, Alabama, at the invitation of the Tennessee Coal, Iron and Land Company to address the public health needs of workers who suffered from smallpox, typhoid, and other epidemic diseases. Noland had recently served during the construction of the Panama Canal, helping to eradicate the malaria and yellow fever that plagued Americans working on the project. Soon after arriving in Birmingham, Noland realized there was a need in the community for more complete health care and presented to TCI&L his vision for a health system to address those needs. The result was a $750,000 health care facility, an investment greater than the entire state budget for public health at the time. Noland Health Services today follows the legacy of Dr. Noland. A private, not-for-profit health care organization that was founded in 1951, Noland Health Services is dedicated to identifying and meeting the health needs of the people and communities it serves by providing high quality health and educational services in a compassionate, efficient, and cost-effective manner. The organization is a pioneer in establishing special services and programs to meet the needs of the elderly and other unique patient populations.

Noland Health Services has sponsored comprehensive research to identify both the health status and the health care needs of West/Southwest Jefferson County and a portion of surrounding counties. This community health profile, including information on such topics as cardiovascular, respiratory, diabetes, cancer, mental health, and functional health, serves as a reference for the organization's planning for health care development and patient services.

Long-term acute care service is one growing need identified by

(left to right) Noland Health Services Planning & Development Officer Pam Nichols, President Gary Glasscock, and CFO Gary Goff review retirement community plans.

Noland Health Services. To serve patients that require extended care due to chronic diseases or complex medical conditions, The Long Term Care Hospital at Jackson (LTCH) in Montgomery, Alabama was established. The LTCH is a Medicare certified acute care referral hospital providing specialty services.

The LTCH serves individuals that require hospital care that typically will exceed 25 days. An evaluation team, which includes a physician, registered nurse, respiratory therapist, case manager, and pharmacist, assesses all referred patients prior to admission. The patient's progress is monitored and directed on a regular basis using an interdisciplinary holistic approach to treatment, including specialized nursing care and advanced therapies to promote optimal recovery. While the LTCH serves a large number of patients over the age of 65 who have Medicare coverage, it also treats individuals with other forms of health care insurance. Noland Health Services is developing two additional long-term acute care hospital facilities in Jefferson County, as well as evaluating other needs throughout the state.

Noland Health Services is also developing The Oaks on Parkwood, a comprehensive retirement community in Southwest Jefferson County. The $50-million, 100 acre community will provide many living options for a burgeoning retirement population, including individually owned garden homes and town homes, independent living apartments, assisted living, an Alzheimer/dementia

The Long Term Care Hospital at Jackson serves patients that require extended care due to chronic diseases or complex medical conditions.

care center, a nursing home, and other medical facilities. Planned living units will accommodate over 500 residents. Multiple levels of health services will be available to residents. The Oaks on Parkwood will provide seniors with a community setting that promotes independence, security, and dignity, and allows them to stay in the same community should their needs change. Recreational amenities, including walking trails, a swimming pool, a fitness facility, and other accommodations, will make the retirement community a very attractive location for seniors.

Some patients completing hospital treatment are not quite ready to return to independent living. The Noland Center at Carraway is an innovative subacute facility on the campus of Carraway Methodist Medical Center in Birmingham designed to accommodate these individuals. The Noland Center at Carraway offers a full range of skilled services, including restorative nursing, nutrition counseling, social services, recreational activities, and individualized therapies. The goal of The Noland Center is to help patients improve and/or restore their level of functioning to the fullest potential. Health professionals throughout the region refer patients to the Noland Center. A major goal is working with other health care providers in a collaborative relationship which strives to meet both the needs of patients, their families, and members of the patients health care team.

Maintaining good health for seniors is an important goal of Noland Health Services. The Hueytown Senior Citizens Center is the result of a partnership with the city of Hueytown. The 6,000-square-foot center is designed to serve as a hub of activities for Hueytown's senior citizens. Activity programs address health and wellness, social, recreational, and educational needs of seniors. In

The Noland Center at Carraway provides individualized therapy designed to improve or restore the patient's level of functioning.

addition to a general meeting/recreation area, kitchen, reading area, video room, and outdoor recreation area, the center houses The Noland Senior Wellness Center. As trends in health care increasingly move toward convenient community care with an emphasis on wellness and prevention, The Noland Senior Wellness Center follows that same trend in serving a growing senior population. Programs and services include health screenings, health teaching for management of chronic conditions, wellness and fitness programs, as well as a health library.

Noland Health Services serves the educational needs of health care professionals, including doctors as well as patients. A nationally recognized provider of continuing medical education for physicians, the organization is accredited by the Accreditation Council for Continuing Education (ACCE). The program serves approximately 2,000 physicians per year from around the nation and awards more than 10,000 hours of CME credits. From Pediatricians to Geriatricians, Noland Health Services helps to keep physicians up to date on the latest advances in medicine.

Dr. Lloyd Noland came to Alabama to serve the critical health needs of his time. His legacy continues to this day in the work of Noland Health Services. Through innovations in health care services, from hospital facilities to retirement communities, Noland Health Services continues to provide solutions for Alabama's changing health care needs. ■

Noland Health Services is a pioneer in establishing special programs and services to meet the needs of seniors.

Blue Cross and Blue Shield of Alabama

· ·

More than 1 million transactions take place during a typical day of operation at Blue Cross and Blue Shield of Alabama. This figure includes over 22,000 customer service phone calls, more than 192,000 processed claims, and more than 126,000 processed Medicare claims.

These impressive numbers are indicative of the strong presence Blue Cross and Blue Shield of Alabama enjoys with Alabamians; but for an organization known by its customers as "The Caring Company," the numbers tell only part of the story.

"Customer First"

"Every claim, every phone call, every e-mail, every piece of correspondence represents a person to us," says Dick Jones, the company's president and chief executive officer. "'Customer First' is one of our corporate values, and it's not just a slogan. From day one, we truly stress this philosophy to every one of our associates, from the mail room to the board room. It's our goal to provide each customer the highest possible value for the health care dollar, and to treat each person with a sense of urgency and compassion."

A Presence More than 60 Years Ago

Blue Cross and Blue Shield of Alabama has been in the business of maximizing its customers' health care dollars for over 64 years. During the era of the Great Depression, when the availability of health care suffered in Alabama, a group of physicians and hospital representatives founded The Hospital Service Corporation. When that company—now known as Blue Cross and Blue Shield of Alabama—was formed in 1936, there were only six employees on staff. Now more than 3,000 employees strong, the Birmingham-based company also has district offices in Huntsville, Mobile, and Montgomery, as well as satellite offices throughout the state, including Tuscaloosa, Andalusia, Florence, Anniston, Gadsden, Dothan, Opelika, Selma, and Foley.

A Strong Local Presence

Today, Blue Cross and Blue Shield of Alabama provides health and dental coverage to more than 2.8 million people. Its list of customers includes more than 20,000 companies, from most of the state's largest corporations to businesses with as few as two employees.

The U.S. Government is also one of Blue Cross's customers, by virtue of the company's role in the administration of the Federal Employees Program and the Medicare program. In addition to administering both Medicare benefits for the state of Alabama, Blue Cross also serves more than 2.3 million other Medicare beneficiaries throughout the country. The company handles Part B Medicare for the state of Georgia, and assists in the processing of Part B Medicare

**"It is our goal to provide each customer with the highest possible value for the health care dollar."
—Dick Jones, President and Chief Executive Officer.**

claims for Puerto Rico. Blue Cross is also involved in administering Part A Medicare benefits for the states of Iowa and South Dakota, and serves as the regional Home Health Intermediary for 15 states and the District of Columbia.

The company introduced its first preferred provider organization, the Preferred Care network, in 1984. Preferred Care remains the largest preferred provider network in Alabama, and is regarded as one of the largest and most successful in the nation. The program includes over 8,000 Preferred Medical Doctors and 100 percent of the state's hospitals.

A Strong National Presence

By far the largest health care benefits plan in Alabama, Blue Cross and Blue Shield of Alabama also commands a national presence in its industry. Over 30 percent of the company's business is comprised of national customers.

Blue Cross and Blue Shield of Alabama works in cooperation with other Blue Cross and Blue Shield Plans across the nation to provide consistent health care benefits to its customers regardless of where they receive medical services.

The company also offers nationwide prescription drug coverage through the Participating Pharmacy Program, a pharmacy network that includes 98 percent of Alabama's pharmacies, along with more than 38,000 pharmacies across the nation.

Increased Presence through Technology

Blue Cross utilizes the latest in computer technology to help perform and track the one million-plus transactions it handles each day. For example, 85 percent of the more than 42 million claims processed by Blue Cross in 1998 were either filed or scanned electronically. But technology is more than just a means to improve productivity for Blue Cross. It also helps the company reduce costs and improve the quality of care for its customers.

Specially developed software applications allow Blue Cross to manage health care costs and services for its customers. These computer programs are used to track health-related information according to factors such as demographics, geography, procedures, and costs. Sharing this information with providers helps Blue Cross and the provider community in Alabama work together to address and resolve health care issues.

The company has also developed a medical information network, called InfoSolutions. This database and secure on-line network allows Blue Cross, physicians, hospitals, pharmacies, labs, and other health care providers to communicate and share information with one another. This means physicians are able to input and access a patient's medical history and make more informed decisions; unnecessary and duplicate tests can be eliminated; and claims can be filed and processed faster. These are just some of the ways InfoSolutions stands to enhance the practice of medicine in Alabama.

A Community Presence

Blue Cross also demonstrates leadership in community efforts. A spirit of community service and volunteerism is strongly encouraged among its associates, as evidenced by the fact that Blue Cross consistently ranks among the top Alabama companies in fair-share giving to the United Way. Blue Cross also provides its associates scores of company-sponsored community service activities and other opportunities for community involvement.

Be Careful Be Safe is a health and safety awareness campaign begun by the company in 1997. While this formal campaign is relatively new, the company has long maintained a strong tradition of supporting efforts that promote the health, safety, and wellness of the citizens of Alabama, especially children.

The company's biggest commitment to the community can be found in the establishment and support of the Alabama Child Caring Foundation. Since 1988, this nonprofit foundation has provided health care coverage to Alabama children who would not otherwise receive the health care they need. Blue Cross provides all the administrative expenses for the Foundation and matches all contributions dollar-for-dollar. The company also administers the All-Kids program, Alabama's version of the federally funded Children's Health Insurance Program.

Unrivaled expertise, nationwide provider networks, cutting edge technology, a unique "customer first" philosophy—these are the reasons Blue Cross and Blue Shield of Alabama has earned and maintained its reputation and presence in the health care benefits industry. And today, the company is helping shape the way health care is delivered in Alabama—and beyond. ■

The UAB Health System

Recognized worldwide for its excellent patient care and groundbreaking research, the University of Alabama at Birmingham Health System has fueled the remarkable growth of UAB—and the expansion of Birmingham's economy— since its roots were first formed in the 1940s. The Health System now boasts one of the premier academic medical centers in the nation, along with a growing network of clinical facilities.

Extraordinary Expansion

At the height of World War II, momentum gathered throughout the South to upgrade medical education opportunities. By the summer of 1945, the University of Alabama School of Medicine had been established in Birmingham at the 17-story Jefferson Hospital. This school was the seed that would flower into the University of Alabama at Birmingham.

Thus began the enterprise that would become the largest training ground in the state for health care providers. Throughout the next 35 years, UAB continuously anticipated the needs of Alabama's citizens and provided the educational and training experiences necessary to meet the expected demand. The university added a dental school in 1948, a nursing school in 1967, an allied health school and an optometry school in 1969, and a public health school in 1981.

None of this expansion would have been possible without the exciting research activities and innovations in patient care that were occurring at a rapid pace. Physicians who were destined to become world leaders in their fields came to Birmingham to join the fledgling medical school. One of these giants, Dr. Tinsley R. Harrison, who joined the faculty in 1950, had an approach to medicine that differed from that of most of his contemporaries—he believed in focusing on the patient, rather than the disease. This philosophy eventually spread throughout the world as a result of his book, *Principles of Internal Medicine*, now the most widely acclaimed textbook in internal medicine.

The recruitment of nationally prominent physicians continued with the additions of Dr. Walter B. Frommeyer, a renowned hematologist; Dr. Basil Hirschowitz, the developer of the fiberoptic gastroscope; and Dr. S. Richardson Hill, who initiated laboratory research concentrating on metabolism of adrenal steroids.

The UAB Health System is Alabama's largest health care provider.

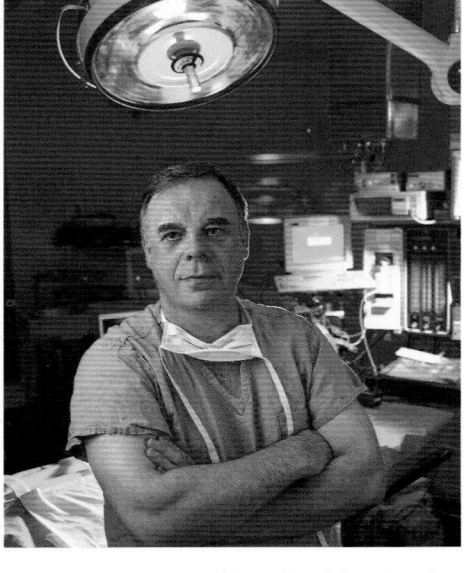

UAB surgeon Dr. Kirby Bland is a leader in the treatment of breast cancer.

A breakthrough in faculty recruitment came in 1966, when nationally recognized cardiovascular surgeon Dr. John W. Kirklin joined the medical school's faculty. Raised in Rochester, Minnesota, where his father was a radiologist at the Mayo Clinic, Kirklin was considered virtually unrecruitable by many major medical centers. His arrival put UAB on par with all other major academic medical centers in terms of recruitment of nationally and internationally recognized faculty.

In 1996, the UAB Health System was formally created to coordinate all of UAB's health resources. The Health System comprises UAB Hospital, The Kirklin Clinic, the University of Alabama School of Medicine, the Callahan Eye Foundation Hospital, and Viva Health, Inc. UAB also has family medicine clinics in surrounding communities to meet the daily health care needs of its patients.

In order to continue providing the world-class, state-of-the-art care that UAB is known for, the UAB Health System has embarked on

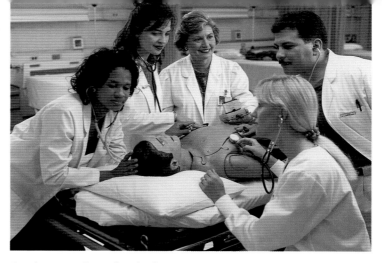

Students at the School of Medicine at UAB learn advanced life support.

several ambitious building projects. A major building project, scheduled to be completed in 2003, will add nine floors and 825,000 square feet to UAB Hospital. The project includes plans for a new emergency room, new and enlarged operating theatres, laboratory space, and critical care units.

In 2001, the Hugh Kaul Genetics Human Building will be completed. That building, constructed at a cost of $37 million, will house the Howell and Elizabeth Ann Heflin Center for Human Genetics. It will be among few centers in the nation to offer a complete array of genetics services under one roof.

A Reputation for Excellence

The hub of the Health System is the UAB Hospital and The Kirklin Clinic, located in the heart of Birmingham. The 900-bed hospital houses the state's only full-service organ transplant program and a full range of specialty services, including eight that were ranked in *U.S. News & World Report*'s 2000 "Best Hospitals" issue. UAB Hospital also was the recipient of the 1999 Alabama Quality Award in the Healthcare category, which is patterned after the Malcolm Baldridge Quality Award. It also was a winner, in 1999, of two Consumer Choice Awards from the National Research Corporation. During the same year, UAB Hospital was recognized as one of the top 100 Cardiovascular Hospitals by HCIA and the Health Network.

The UAB Health System is recognized worldwide for its excellence in clinical care, education, and research. A few of its distinctions include:

• One of only 14 National Institutes of Health designated Neonatal Network Centers, which specialize in the care of high-risk newborns.
• One of only 23 burn centers in the nation verified by the American College of Surgeons.

The Lister Hill Library serves students of UAB's six professional schools.

• One of the first cancer centers in the United States with standards high enough to earn a "comprehensive" designation from the National Cancer Institute—a designation awarded to only 37 centers in the nation.
• UAB Hospital houses the busiest kidney transplant program in the world. In 1999, the hospital performed its 5,000th kidney transplant as well as its 600th liver transplant.
• UAB's Department of Surgery was awarded $6 million from the federal government to create a coordinated trauma system for the state of Alabama.

The Kirklin Clinic is the focal point of outpatient care in the Health System. The clinic houses 35 specialty medicine clinics with more than 700 physicians, treating more than 450,000 patients each year. UAB faculty, residents, and advanced medical students also see patients in clinical settings in Huntsville, Montgomery, Selma, and Tuscaloosa.

The Frontiers of Research

Leadership in the health care field requires a commitment to research, and UAB ranks among the nation's top 20 institutions in funding from the National Institutes of Health (NIH), receiving some $300 million for sponsored research each year.

In addition to the basic research necessary to fully understand how the human body functions (and what causes it to function abnormally), UAB research extends to behavioral and sociological issues. For instance, UAB was recently a lead institution investigating the hesitation of African-Americans to participate in clinical trials. The resulting information helped researchers recruit African-Americans into research projects investigating high blood pressure, diabetes, possible vaccines for AIDS, community-based breast cancer education programs, and countless others.

UAB's Center for AIDS Research made international headlines in 1999 when researchers discovered the origin of HIV-1, the virus that causes AIDS. That finding is just one of many made at UAB as researchers pursue a cure and a preventive vaccine for AIDS.

In the field of cardiovascular disease, UAB reached a milestone in 1997 when it performed its 500th heart transplant. Ranked among the top centers in the nation for survival rates, UAB is the national coordinating center for heart transplant data from the leading programs around the nation.

UAB is helping to wage the war on cancer. With the only Comprehensive Cancer Center in a four-state region, UAB treats more than 3,000 new patients each year. Currently, researchers are using genetic strategies to treat cancers of the brain, colon, head and neck, and gynecologic cancers.

UAB neurology researchers are some of the nation's leaders investigating how to limit the damage caused by stroke. UAB was one of the original investigation sites exploring when best to give the clot-busting drug TPA to dissolve blood clots causing the blockage in the brain. Researchers at UAB also published the first study on the use of angioplasty as an effective treatment for some strokes.

Leadership in research requires not only cutting-edge investigation, but also the dissemination of the resulting information to the next generation of caregivers. UAB takes the knowledge gained in the laboratory and shares it with its students—both in the classroom and in clinical settings. This bench-to-bedside transfer of research into practice provides patients the best care that contemporary medicine can offer.

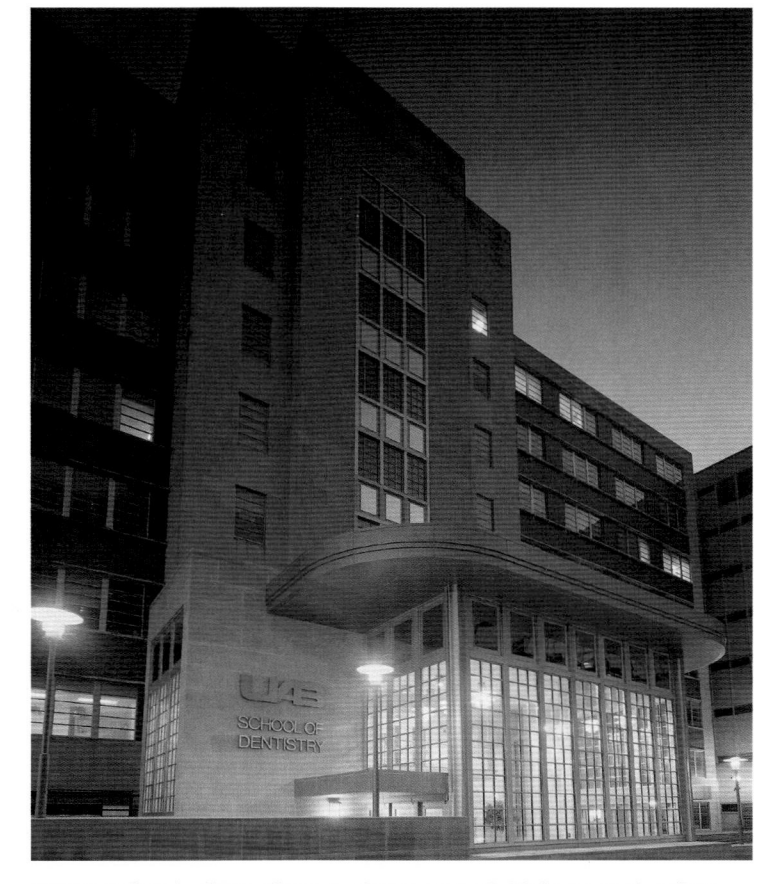

UAB's School of Dentistry trains many of Alabama's dentists, dental assistants, and hygienists.

Strength Through Education

One of the strengths of the UAB Health System is its ability to draw upon the experience, research, and training of professionals within all six of UAB's health schools. In addition to the School of

At UAB, world-class physicians are in your neighborhood.

Medicine, the schools of Dentistry, Health Related Professions, Nursing, Public Health, and Optometry fill vital roles in research, education, and training.

Researchers in the School of Dentistry were among the first to test the Periochip, an implantable chip that protects patients from gingivitis and periodontitis.

The explosion in the nation's demand for allied health professionals has helped fuel the expansion of UAB's School of Health Related Professions, ranked by *U.S. News & World Report* as among the best in the country. Today, more than 120 SHRP graduates work as CEOs, CFOs, or COOs at hospitals and other health care organizations around the U.S.

UAB's School of Nursing remains one of the nation's elite. Throughout the 1990s, *U.S. News & World Report* has ranked the school among the top 25 in the nation. The school recently became the first in Alabama to offer a Ph.D. program in nursing.

Community Outreach

The practice of medicine is more than the administration of drugs and the development of new surgical procedures. Community outreach programs are an integral part of the UAB Health System and its close relationship with the greater Birmingham area.

One project offers free breast cancer screenings and trains women as health advisors who promote breast self-exams and mammograms in their communities. Professionals from UAB's Burn Center and Trauma Program regularly visit schools and civic organizations to promote safety and preparedness. UAB Hospital even sponsors an Explorer's Post to acquaint young people with professions in the healthcare industry.

UAB's community health outreach efforts benefit Birmingham's citizens in countless ways. The UAB Health System promotes and administers a number of anti-smoking programs, as well as programs to stop teenage drinking and driving. UAB sponsors the "Think First" program, sending speakers into local schools to remind children to "think first" before indulging in hazardous behaviors. UAB also works with the Birmingham Junior League to provide car seats to new mothers who can't afford them.

The UAB Health System's public outreach extends throughout Alabama, including its rural counties. The School of Public Health is home to one of 24 federally funded Centers for Health Promotion, involving more than 100 faculty who tackle myriad rural health issues. Researchers in UAB's Injury Control Research Center hope to install a smoke detector in every home in Alabama by 2005.

UAB is also helping meet the need for primary care physicians in Alabama by encouraging and equipping medical students to pursue careers in primary care medicine. Some 56 percent of UAB medical school graduates choose primary care fields for residency training. UAB is also an important resource for physicians throughout the state, who have instant access to the expertise of UAB specialists through the Medical Information Service via Telephone (MIST). Using MIST, physicians can obtain immediate medical consultations or discuss new patient care techniques.

The Kirklin Clinic treats more than 450,000 patients per year.

The UAB Health Care Team

The innovations and accomplishments that emerge from the Health System result from its most vital resource—its people. From world-renowned physicians and research scientists to nationally recognized leaders in nursing, nutrition, rehabilitation, and health care administration, the health care team is the force that drives and sustains the UAB Health System. The names of UAB physicians regularly appear in a variety of "best doctors" lists, including more than 140 in the most recent edition of The Best Doctors in America. And, members of the UAB Health System team serve on national advisory boards, editorial boards, and accrediting boards and hold ranking positions in professional organizations.

These accolades and positions of leadership in research and patient care are no accident. They result from the work and dedication of highly motivated individuals who anticipate tomorrow's health care needs and strive to fill them today. Taking action to help make people's lives better is the sum and purpose of the UAB Health System. Because its future promise is as bright as its remarkable past, the health of Alabamians is in good hands. ■

UAB's Critical Care Transport service includes a physician, nurse, and respiratory therapist—the same staffing found in a hospital intensive care unit.

Methodist Homes for the Aging

Elizabeth Johnson and Kylie Berryman enjoy fellowship time and the companionship of one another, two qualities that Methodist Homes stresses to its residents.

I t is no secret that America is aging. An increasingly large portion of the population is retired, and individuals within this group are searching for the best way to spend their later years—when they may stay active for decades.

Methodist Homes for the Aging has been serving Alabama's seniors for more than 39 years, providing affordable, high quality housing, health care, and community services throughout the state and in northwest Florida.

Founded in 1956, Methodist Homes opened its first facility in Birmingham in 1961. Fair Haven Retirement Center, near the corner of Montclair and Oporto-Madrid Boulevard, has since developed from its original 140 domiciliary units to a multilevel facility providing cottages, apartments, assisted living, 115 health care accommodations, and a state-of-the art Alzheimer's Center known as Fair Haven North. During these same years, Methodist Homes opened facilities in Dothan, Decatur, Auburn, Montgomery, Selma, and Anniston. The nonprofit corporation now employs more than 1,000. Seventy percent of this staff is actively involved in providing personal, hands-on care to the residents.

Wray Tomlin has been president and CEO of Methodist Homes since 1978 and has overseen a good part of the corporation's growth. He says Methodist Homes serves a diverse population in its many facilities.

"We have all types of people here—those with sufficient income and those without as well as people in differing health situations. Our homes are designed to follow the changing needs of each individual over time." The mission of Methodist Homes is to serve all persons, regardless of religion, race, creed, or national origin.

Tomlin began his career as a Methodist minister, serving in

middle Tennessee for 19 years. After his many years in the pulpit, he says he began to feel that God was calling him to do something more specific with the elderly.

"I felt our country spent an enormous amount of energy and time providing for children and young people. But we must also plan carefully for those facing their senior years—God's older children."

Tomlin came to Birmingham to study health administration at UAB. He joined Methodist Homes for the Aging soon after earning his degree in the program. "I come to work every morning just as excited as I was when I started," Tomlin says with a genuine smile. "You really feel working here that you are making a difference in the lives of the residents we serve."

Methodist Homes provide high quality housing, health care when necessary, and a full program of activities and life enrichment opportunities so that seniors can continue to live significant and meaningful lives. Wray Tomlin describes a few of the activities:

"We have regular special events throughout the year—Independence Day, Labor Day, Oktoberfest, Valentine's Day—all the holidays. Around Veteran's Day, our residents that were veterans share their experiences. We have travel presentations, cooking classes, book reviews, high teas. A lot of residents like to participate in our political forums." Tomlin says that it is very important to residents that they stay informed about, and engaged in, the political process. Many local churches provide transportation to and from their services.

Residents at Methodist Homes participate in fashion shows, talent contests, and related activities. Some take advantage of in-state and

Doris Holladay enjoys playing croquet with Hermon C. Arneson. Recreational activities as well as exercise programs are provided at Methodist Home on a regular basis and are an important aspect of a senior citizen's life.

out-of-state travel opportunities. Tomlin says the corporation is developing computer laboratories for residents to use for e-mail, surfing the web, and other applications. "The senior market is the fastest growing segment for the computer industry these days," he notes.

Exercise and physical fitness are obviously important to seniors, just as they are to the younger population. Methodist Homes provide various athletic facilities for residents at its different locations. Stationary bicycles are common. Auburn has a swimming pool. Montgomery has a putting green. The new facility in Panama City has a pool, tennis court, and putting green.

"We have some exercise programs that are led by residents," Tomlin says. One woman led an aerobics class until she was 106 years old. Another taught ballroom dancing.

"As a general rule," Tomlin says, "the more active people are, the less medicine they take and the happier they seem to be."

Each of the facilities run by Methodist Homes offers a different combination of services. In Dothan, Wesley Manor Retirement Center provides apartments, assisted living, skilled nursing, and a state-of-the art Alzheimer's care unit. Wesley Terrace in Auburn has 99 apartments, 21 assisted living units, and 75 health care beds. This facility is developing an Alzheimer's care unit. In Montgomery, Wesley Gardens provides 72 assisted living units. Wesley Acres Retirement Center in Decatur, The Epworth House in Selma, and Wesley Apartments in Anniston all offer apartment units for the low-income elderly through the Housing and Urban Development (HUD) program. Wesley Glen, an affordable housing program for the elderly in Decatur was completed in 1998. The facilities in Birmingham and Dothan are certified for Medicaid and Medicare.

Reverend A. Wray Tomlin, President, CEO; Methodist Home for the Aging Corporation

In Florida, Methodist Homes' Mathison Center offers apartments in Panama City. The corporation is working on three centers in Pensacola: Wesley Scott Place, Wesley Haven Villa, and The Haven—a joint venture with Sacred Heart Hospital of Pensacola.

"Our varied facilities are designed to meet the needs in particular parts of the two states," Tomlin says. "Most people move into a facility near where they have lived before, but they can transfer to other sites as their needs dictate."

The growth of Methodist Homes has hardly kept pace with the increase in Alabama's senior population during the last four decades. Nationwide, more than 5,000 individuals are turning 65 each day. According to Tomlin, the fastest growing segment of the elderly population is people over 85.

"We see more and more people living well beyond 100—possibly up to 130. Individuals could be spending more time in retirement than they did working. As we help people to live longer, we have to find ways to help them live better."

Methodist Homes for the Aging is constantly raising money to support its care of individuals that do not have the resources needed for their lodging and health care. The corporation's fund-raising is divided into two basic programs. The "Fountain of Love" is an ongoing program to fund immediate financial assistance for individuals. Each spring around Valentine's Day, Methodist churches across Alabama and northwest Florida are asked for contributions. Additionally, the Aldersgate Foundation was established in 1992 as a nonprofit public foundation to raise funds to support Methodist Homes. The funds are used for endowment purposes to support residents who have depleted their resources and to allow for development and modernization of facilities. Each year, the amount generated to provide assistance to individuals exceeds a million dollars.

"We are facing a big job in the coming years," Tomlin says. "Right now we have long range plans for another six facilities in Alabama and northwest Florida. We are adding programs and making improvements at our current facilities all the time. I hope we can spread the word about what we're doing here a little more—to help in our fund-raising and, more important, to let people who are facing their senior years know what we have to offer. We're here to help people make the most of life." ■

Each facility is unique in its setting at Methodist Homes. Eloise Ragland spends a relaxing afternoon picking wildflowers on the grounds of Wesley Gardens in Montgomery, Alabama.

Southeast Alabama Medical Center

· ·

Situated in the southeast corner of Alabama, Southeast Alabama Medical Center serves as a regional referral center for the neighboring communities and counties of Southeast Alabama, Southwest Georgia, and the Florida Panhandle.

With a medical staff of over 250 physicians—representing virtually every specialty—and 2,000 support personnel, the Medical Center is the largest employer in the region.

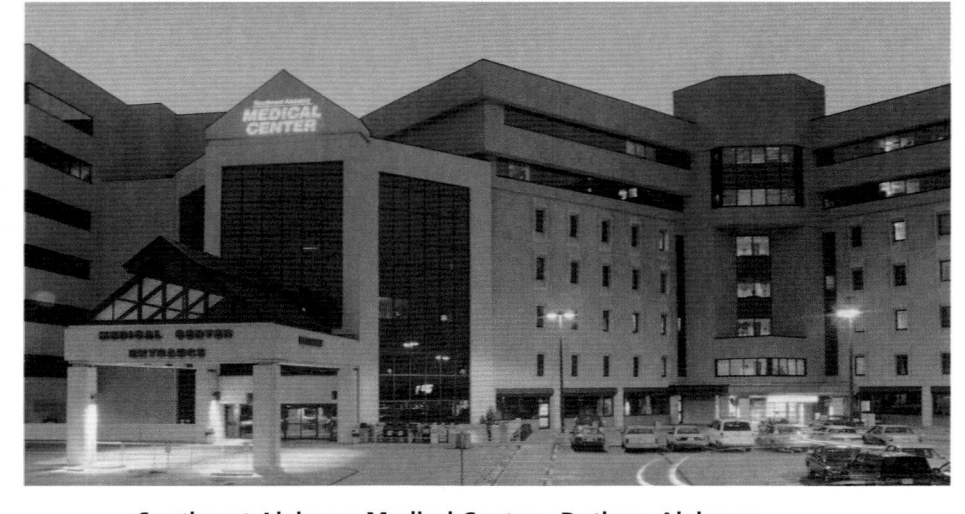

Southeast Alabama Medical Center—Dothan, Alabama.

CARDIAC CARE

Southeast Alabama Medical Center has earned a distinguished reputation for the level of cardiology services available to residents of the Wiregrass area.

Offering the full range of preventive treatment, surgical procedures, and rehabilitation, including two cardiac catheterization labs, an electrophysiology lab, invasive and noninvasive cardiovascular testing, open-heart surgery facilities, cardiovascular intensive care units, and monitored cardiac rehabilitation, their technologically advanced diagnostic and surgical techniques are on the leading edge of heart care.

CANCER CARE—*SOUTHEAST REGIONAL RADIATION ONCOLOGY CENTER*

The region's most modern cancer treatment center houses three treatment rooms, which feature a 2100-C Series Linear Accelerator. The Center's Tumor Registry is accredited by the American College of Surgeons' Commission on Cancer as a Community Hospital Cancer Program.

Other oncology services include a 42-bed oncology unit which provides inpatient and outpatient physician-directed chemotherapy administration. Registered nurses staffing the unit are chemotherapy-certified.

BIRTHING PAVILION

The Birthing Pavilion is dedicated to meeting the special needs of women and their babies. Mothers labor, deliver, and recover in the same private room that has been designed to ensure optimum comfort for the new family while keeping the latest in medical technology at hand.

The Medical Center's commitment to care for the family extends from the LDR suites to the nearby nursery where a skilled nursing and medical staff care for newborns in comfortable, nurturing surroundings.

EMERGENCY CENTER

Recognized as one of the busiest Emergency Centers in the State of Alabama, annual visits exceed 40,000. A newly constructed 27,000 square foot Emergency Center, opened in 1999, features completely equipped trauma rooms and an eight-bed diagnostic and treatment unit. There is also a rapid-treatment area for minor illnesses and injuries, as well as 13 additional emergency treatment rooms. Able to seat 70 people, the waiting area for family members and friends of the patients, also has a family/prayer room.

DIABETES TREATMENT CENTER

Through a cooperative agreement with Diabetes Treatment Centers of America, the Medical Center offers acute inpatient and comprehensive outpatient maintenance programs for diabetics.

PAIN MANAGEMENT CENTER

The only hospital-based chronic pain management center in the region, the center utilizes a comprehensive medical, physical, and psychological evaluation and treatment regimen which is tailored to each patient's needs.

SLEEP DISORDERS CENTER

The four-bed Center is accredited by the Association of Sleep Disorders Centers as a comprehensive medical facility specifically designed to diagnose and treat patients with sleep disorders. ∎

OTHER SERVICES

Behavioral Medicine	Breast Care Center
Endoscopy Suite	Home Health Care
Home Medical Equipment	Industrial and Occupational Medicine
Laboratory Medicine	Lithotripsy
Maternal & Infant Care	Medical Call Center
Neurodiagnostics	Orthopedics
Outpatient Diagnostics	Primary Care Network
Pulmonary Medicine	Radiology
Rehab Services	Same Day Surgery
Social Services	Surgical Services

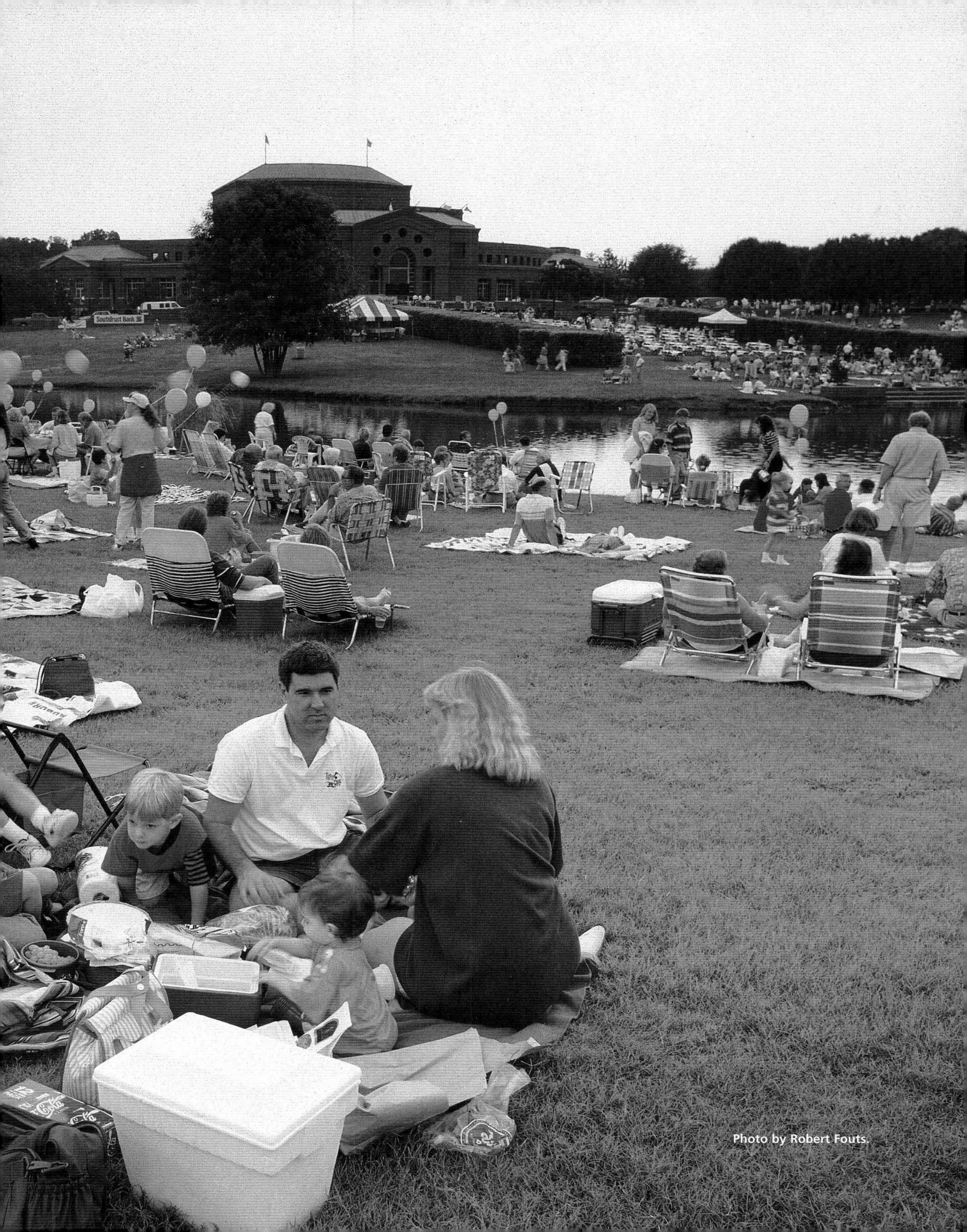

Photo by Robert Fouts.

C H A P T E R   1 7

The Marketplace & Hospitality

Photo by Scott Wiseman.

Saks Incorporated

The 1998 merger of Birmingham-based Proffit's, Inc. with Saks Holdings, Inc. combined two of the most compelling growth companies in department store retailing today. The result—Saks Incorporated, a powerful force as a style leader in fashion retailing with global recognition. With corporate headquarters located in Birmingham, Alabama, Saks Incorporated adds a distinctive element of style to the city.

Today, it operates over 35 million square feet of premium real estate across the country, with over 350 stores and nearly 60,000 associates. Merchandising, sales promotion, and store operating support functions are conducted in multiple locations. Its store nameplates include Saks Fifth Avenue, Parisian, Proffitt's, McRae's, Younkers, Herberger's, Carson Pirie Scott, Boston Store, Bergner's and Off 5th. Out-of-store, it markets through the Folio and Bullock & Jones catalogs. Each name has a valuable identity as a style leader in its individual trade areas. Its customers count on the stores of Saks Incorporated for early indications of fashion trends. There they find fashion-forward styles, exceptional quality, attractive pricing, and the legendary service on which Saks Incorporated's reputation is built.

With Customers, Details Make the Difference

Saks Incorporated fosters a culture of superior customer service. Each store thoughtfully builds and nurtures long-term relationships. Purchasing patterns and lifestyle requirements of customers are analyzed. Merchandise assortments are tailored to meet the needs of each customer group and marketplace. Preferences are tracked. Store encounters are personalized. Customers are greeted and thanked by name. Sales are followed by notes of appreciation. Saks Incorporated's detailed process of intense customer attention has become key to growing millions of valuable and lasting relationships.

Another important aspect of customer attention at Saks Incorporated is the in-store experience. Throughout its stores, unique design elements are tastefully combined to create environments that beautifully enhance the merchandise assortments. Lighting, fixtures, aisle width, and special amenities are carefully chosen to provide an extraordinary and exciting shopping experience.

Strategy for Growth

Saks Incorporated stock trades on the New York Stock Exchange under the symbol SKS. It holds a top-tier position in one of the most attractive and fastest growing segments in retailing, with a number of brand extension opportunities.

With a solid financial base and a strong operating infrastructure, it has grown according to its well defined strategy. Saks Incorporated has acquired several companies with strong franchises and customer loyalty, quality real estate in attractive markets, solid financial performance, and meaningful synergy opportunities. These companies have been successfully integrated into the Saks Incorporated family through a systematic process which includes maintaining and rewarding key personnel, maintaining the store identity and store-level associates to assure the acquisition is transparent to customers, and maintaining the distinctive merchandise assortments its customers have come to expect. Careful handling of the identity which acquired companies have built with its customers is key to the success of this strategy and sets Saks Incorporated apart from other large retailing organizations.

One lucrative area for growth of the company is private brands. Through the development and introduction of high quality proprietary brands, it can deliver exceptional value to its customers in a style that is only found through Saks Incorporated.

These exclusive labels are a perfect fit with the distinctive merchandise assortment customers look for in Saks Incorporated stores.

With the distinguished reputation as a unique fashion authority and global appeal of the Saks Incorporated brand name, the fast changing out-of-store arena, including catalogs and Internet strategy and applications, provides incredible potential for the future. As R. Brad Martin, chairman and CEO, remarks, "This is a fascinating time to be in the retail business."

Putting Values into Action

Saks Incorporated is a values-driven company. Its philosophy is founded on the four cornerstones of style, quality, service, and integrity. Its goals are to find better ways to serve its customers, to create a good work environment for associates, to increase shareholder value, and to maintain a culture that fosters a sense of purpose. While promoting individual achievement, Saks

Incorporated celebrates success as a team. And everyone shares in the rewards. Associates of Saks Incorporated can take advantage of qualified savings and stock purchase plans. By participating in the employee stock purchase plan, associates can acquire the company's common stock at a significant discount without incurring any broker fees.

By combining the strength of the Saks Fifth Avenue brand with the geographical diversification and operating infrastructure of Proffit's, the new company, Saks Incorporated, is well positioned to bring growth, not only to the company, but to the economy of Alabama as well. Saks Incorporated's name recognition is key to attracting premier retail talent to the Birmingham area and providing jobs for all levels of employees. The growth prospects of its future are proving to be highly valued by investors, customers, employees, and the communities Saks Incorporated serves throughout the state. ■

Natural Decorations, Inc.

. . . .

Nothing can change the atmosphere of a room as completely as the addition of plants and flowers. A floral arrangement can pull together the colors and textures of an interior space and even serve as the focal point of a room. Natural Decorations, Inc. has been helping people across the nation bring the beauty of the outdoors into their homes for more than 35 years.

Natural Decorations supplies the furniture and decorative industry with the finest quality fabric foliages and flowers on the market. Every NDI design is handcrafted by a dedicated staff in Brewton, Alabama, from a variety of materials, including cotton, paper, polyester, pongee, rayon, and taffeta to achieve a variety of realistic textures and designs. Realism is something of paramount importance to NDI's owners, Joe and Carol Gordy.

"When we bought the business we had decided we wanted to have a very natural looking, high-end product," says Carol Gordy, chairwoman and CEO of the company. NDI is well known for its exclusive use of natural flower forms and natural flower colors.

Natural Decorations' president and product developer, Joe Gordy, took an interest in floral design at a very early age.

"I grew up on a farm in Forest, Mississippi," Gordy explains.

Joe and Carol Gordy / Owners of NDI.

"My folks grew a little cotton and some vegetables. I was outdoors quite a lot, helping my mom and dad with the planting and harvesting. I wasn't interested in the mechanics of farming so much as the aesthetics of it."

Gordy says that he had a very practical father who didn't completely appreciate his son's perspective or priorities when it came to yard work. When Gordy went out to prune the shrubbery in the yard, his father asked why he didn't just let it grow.

Joe Gordy persisted in his interest, however, and entered Mississippi State University to pursue a degree in horticulture. He went to work in the floral retail business after graduation and began developing his skills as a designer.

"I guess I have worked with real flowers and shrubs and trees so long that it just doesn't feel right to create 'fantasy' plants. Our job is to create arrangements that take advantage of nature's own magic."

Carol's background was always in the floral industry as well. Her first job at 15 was in a flower shop in Albuquerque, and by the age of 28 she, along with her sister, Jan, owned three flourishing shops of their own. Carol's work was seen in print regularly in professional floral design magazines, and she designed and commentated numerous shows across the Unites States and Canada. She was inducted into the American Institute of Floral Designers in 1980.

Regina Waters—Customer Service Key Accounts, Bill Doyle—Customer Service, Elizabeth Wiley—Customer Service, and Ginger Jordan—Customer Service.

She and Joe met through an industry function and married in 1983.

Joe Gordy became involved with Natural Decorations, Inc. in 1978, when the company was a sister company of Knud Nielsen, Inc., in which he served as director of product development. Carol Gordy became national sales and marketing director in 1986, and they purchased Natural Decorations, Inc. from the Nielsens in 1991.

Natural Decorations, Inc. has expanded tremendously during the past 10 years. Its original facility was a former cotton warehouse in Evergreen.

With the tremendous growth of its business, the Gordys decided to move the company 25 miles south to Brewton, Alabama. After designing and building a new 95,000-square-foot-facility. NDI moved in April 1999.

Joe Gordy's office at NDI is decorated with photographs of some of the prominent people he has met over the years. Gordy may be proudest of his association with The White House. There are several pictures of Joe in front of the Christmas trees at the White House. Gordy was invited to help decorate three years while Reagan was in office.

Floral arrangements created at NDI have appeared on television soap operas, the Country Music Awards, and in a number of

Carol Gordy talks with Ramona Ward—Office Manager/Advertising Director, Mabry Cook—National Sales and Marketing Manager, and Sharon Smith—Customer Service Manager.

home decorating magazines. You'll also see them in upscale department stores such as Nieman Marcus and Gumps in San Francisco. NDI's designs color the homes of actors Eddie Murphy and Nick Nolte, author Sydney Sheldon, and a royal palace in Saudi Arabia, among others.

Perhaps even more impressive than NDI's list of clientele is the number of awards the company has received within the industry. It is the only company in the country that has received five "manufacturer of the year" Arts Awards given by the Dallas Market Center and Arts Council.

Joe Gordy has taken a leadership role in the floral industry during the past two decades. He has served as president of the American Institute of Floral Designers and was named a Friend of the Industry by Roses International. He has represented the United States in design shows around the world, including Australia, China, Germany, Holland, and Thailand, for which he has won several international awards. Gordy has served as a judge for a number of contests as well.

"I think the hardest job I ever had in my life was judging the Rose Parade in Pasadena, California," Gordy says. He had the honor of being one of three judges for the pageant in 1982.

Carol Gordy's leadership and Joe Gordy's creativity are at the heart of NDI's success in the floral industry. The company offers a broad selection of designs representing the natural habitat in different parts of the country. Customers can choose from arrangements native to their own region or any other. Each design reflects a combination of elements that would be found together in nature.

Don Grosso—Operations Manager and Minnie Fantroy— in the NDI Warehouse.

"Arrangements should never look contrived. I think people sense it when a design isn't realistic, and that spoils the effect you are looking for when you decorate."

Natural Decorations has participated in a number of special licensing programs as well, such as the "New Orleans" collection spearheaded by Councill Furniture. The "New Orleans" collection celebrated the culture and history of the romantic city with furnishings modeled after eighteenth and nineteenth-century pieces from the city's French and English colonial periods, as well as more traditional forms. Coordinated accessories included NDI's floral arrangements.

Arrangements were carefully researched to include foliage and flowers indigenous to the New Orleans area. NDI utilized brass containers and antiqued silver to complement some of the hardware on the Councill case pieces.

Further, NDI was licensed to develop a selection of floral arrangements for the Conner Prairie Collection. This collection reflects the early nineteenth-century style of furniture design and

Richie Hines—Designer, Tristan Robinson—Designer, and Steve Massingill—Designer.

motifs found at Conner Prairie, a living history museum depicting life in 1836 Indiana.

"We created designs from flowers that would have been found naturally in the 1830s," Joe Gordy says. His arrangements included hydrangeas, wild flowers, and grasses as their primary elements. Currently NDI is working with the Winterthur Museum, home of Henry Francis DuPont, to create floral designs to mirror the beauty of the grand gardens of Winterthur in Delaware.

NDI is represented in showrooms across the country in New York, Chicago, Dallas, Los Angeles, Denver, and in their own manufacturing showrooms in Atlanta and in High Point, North Carolina, at the International Home Furnishing Center. NDI believes strongly in trade and consumer advertising and regularly advertises in many major United States shelter publications such as *Veranda, Southern Accents, House & Garden*, and *House Beautiful*.

The popularity of NDI's product is seen in stores all across the country. A North Carolina retailer that serves an upper-end clientele has found that customers who voice an aversion to permanent flowers quickly change their minds when the see NDI's line.

"People see how natural these pieces look and realize it's really worth the investment," she says. The retailer says she has looked at the possibility of adding other lines of permanent botanicals to her inventory, but that any product she places next to an NDI arrangement looks "tawdry" in comparison.

Across the country in Palm Desert, California, NDI's arrangements are just as popular. Located 15 miles outside of Palm Springs, the area is famous for its exclusive homes belonging to the rich and famous. The owner of Martha's Gifts won't buy fabric

Popular rose bowl design in *Southern Accents* and *Veranda*.

Simple geometry advertised in *Veranda* and *Southern Accents*.

flowers from any other company.

"The business I get is primarily by word of mouth," Martha Bailey says. "Friends will visit a home that has an arrangement that I carry, and they will want the same thing or something similar." Bailey says the demand is high for designs by NDI.

To keep up with demand across the country, NDI has representatives for each region and works on a first-name basis with its customers and works to know the special needs of businesses it serves.

Each NDI employee is on an incentive bonus plan that has been so successful it was written up in *Inc.* magazine and adopted into its book *101 Best Management Tips.*

"We are very happy with what we've accomplished in the last 10 years," Carol Gordy says. "This is a business we both love."

Her husband couldn't agree more. Joe Gordy says that his work feels more like an enjoyable hobby than a job.

"This is what I've always wanted to do with my life. I've been blessed with the opportunity to do it."

Currently, Joe's creativity is showcased in the recently published *World Flower Artists 2*. The stunning design book was published in Japan and includes work of thirty of the cutting edge designers in the world. Only eight floral designers from The Americas were selected for inclusion in this publication. Each designer is a trendsetter who has made a significant impact on the flower arranging styles within his or her home countries.

Haskell Eargle, a famous designer in his own right, and a great friend of Carol and Joe's is a perennial guest designer for the NDI catalog. He will be joining Joe in May for a design show to benefit the Jefferson Davis Community College in Brewton. The Joe and Haskell design team is not only fun but also educational and has

headlined numerous charitable events across the nation.

When the Gordys aren't in their Brewton offices or traveling the world for the company, they retire to their Norman-style home in Brewton. Joe Gordy's home project is an English perennial garden—or his version thereof.

"I am out in the garden every chance I get," he says. He compares it to a laboratory. "I've always got my eye open to see what's growing and how things look together. That's where I get my best ideas for arrangements. That's where I see new flowers that we can replicate for people's homes."

As long as Joe Gordy continues his gardening and continues to develop new ideas for floral design, Natural Decorations, Inc. will keep sharing nature's beauty with customers around the world. The company will go on winning awards, and the company's reputation and reach will keep on growing. That sounds good to everyone at NDI—naturally. ■

The Lily is the newest consumer ad for the Winterthur licensing program and Henry DuPont's favorite flower.

Long-Lewis, Inc.

The fires of the Civil War had only started to cool when a young man named William J. Long became apprenticed to a tinsmith in his hometown of Xenia, Ohio. Long, the son of Irish and Dutch immigrants, was a journeyman in his trade by the time he was 15. He began selling farm implements for an Ohio hardware company to supplement his wages as a tinsmith, and also did work for the Pennsylvania Railroad.

Searching for new adventure at the age of 26, Long decided to join the American effort to build the Panama Canal in 1885. On his way to Panama, he passed through the newly emerging Alabama boomtown called Birmingham. Long was impressed with the area, and sensed tremendous opportunity in this part of the country. Less than a year later, after a short stint working in Panama, William J. Long returned to the Birmingham area to seek his fortune.

Long first found work putting a metal roof and cornice on a school. Various tinsmithing assignments took him to different parts of the city and the surrounding area, and in 1887, Long chose the newly incorporated town of Bessemer to open a business.

Named for Sir Henry Bessemer, the British inventor of the Bessemer steelmaking process, the new town seemed to provide abundant opportunities for a metalworker such as Long. He built himself a shop—the Bessemer Cornice Works—at First Alley and Second Avenue, and began producing highly ornate cornice and

From a 1915 newspaper.

In June 1906 Bessemer Cornice Works became Long-Lewis Hardware.

The new service department on Bessemer Highway, 1965.

For many years, hardware and cars were sold under the same
roof at Long-Lewis.

decorative metalwork. His red corrugated
metal shop was the source of work that
graced the McDonald Block, the I. Rosen
Store, the Kartus Korner Building, and the
First National Bank.

With profits from the success of his business, Long purchased additional property on
Second Avenue North to build a hardware
store. In a corrugated iron building he
stocked a mercantile line of tinware, nails,
stoves, ranges, screens, and padlocks. Long
was soon offering buggies, wagons, and harnesses as well.

A devastating fire struck Long's thriving
business in 1899 and destroyed the entire
building and all of his stock. Only a small
part of the loss was covered by insurance,
but the company was soon back in business
in a temporary location under the direction
of Long's stepson, John C. Perry. The economy in Bessemer remained strong in the
next years, and Perry helped Long build a
new brick store on the site of the original.

Bessemer Cornice Works was reborn in January 1901 with a two-story facility housing hardware, stoves, and ranges on the first floor and stock storage on the second. Long again added to his building as soon as he had sufficient resources, and began offering buggies and harnesses to supplement the hardware line.

William Long entered into a partnership with Issac Arthur Lewis in June 1906,

In 1998, Long-Lewis was awarded a Sterling heavy truck franchise. The Sterling truck operations are located on the Bessemer Super Highway.

and Bessemer Cornice Works became Long-Lewis Hardware. Long served as president and Lewis as vice president. Lewis left the company just two years later to form another business in Bessemer, but his name stayed behind.

In addition to his tinworking and hardware company, William Long entered the plumbing and general contracting business in the late 1800s. Long's son and stepson both went to work for the company eventually known as Sullivan, Long & Hagerty, which developed a tremendous reputation throughout the South for municipal improvement work, including waterworks and sewage construction, and for road building and paving work. Sullivan, Long & Hagerty split off from Long-Lewis in 1939.

Long lived in an era of tremendous change, and he energetically pursued new opportunities. When automobiles began to rumble across the American landscape, Long-Lewis gave up buggies in favor of the horseless carriage. The two-cylinder International built by International Harvester was the first vehicle Long-Lewis sold to customers in Bessemer.

William Long was introduced to Ford motorcars in 1911, when a fellow Bessemer merchant won one of these automobiles. The man was apparently afraid to drive the car and he sold it to Long. Four years later, Long-Lewis became an official Ford dealership.

For many years, hardware and cars were sold under the same roof at Long-Lewis. Salesmen had to be prepared to explain the inner workings of Ford automobiles as well as the utility of various

household building materials, depending on who walked in the door. Automobiles could be purchased on "open account" like hardware items, as long as the customer had good credit.

William J. Long passed away in 1920, leaving behind a thriving business with plenty of room to grow. John T. Hagerty became president of the company for a few short years, followed by John Perry, Long's stepson, in 1924.

William's own son, Charles A. Long, was elected a director of the organization in 1922. Charles had worked for the company during high school, but left to earn a degree in mechanical engineering from the University of Alabama in 1914. He returned to the company, then left again a few years later to join the American Expeditionary Force in Europe during World War I. Charles returned to Long-Lewis after the war, and eventually served in the positions of secretary, second vice president, and first vice president. He succeeded John Perry as president in 1938.

It was under Perry's leadership that Long-Lewis began to expand its wholesale and retail business outside of Bessemer. The company opened a store at Fifth Avenue and Ninth Street North in Birmingham in 1929, and the new outlet became a great success. The Bessemer store remained retail and continued to sell automobiles. The Birmingham location became a wholesale operation in 1946, and its salesmen covered the entire state, working with hardware dealers and contractors.

Long-Lewis Ford moved out of the Bessemer hardware store in

After over a century of business in Alabama, Long-Lewis continues to thrive at the beginning of the new millennium.

1965 to the Bessemer Super Highway near the Brighton turnoff. The dealership thrived, becoming the largest volume car operation in Alabama. Vaughn Burrell managed the Ford division for 22 years and eventually purchased the entire company from the Long family on December 29, 1986.

Long-Lewis expanded its automobile business by purchasing a Ford and Lincoln Mercury dealership in Cullman in 1990. In 1998, Long-Lewis was not only the largest volume Ford dealership in Alabama, but it was also the fifth largest in Ford's southeastern region. That same year, Long-Lewis was awarded a Sterling heavy truck franchise. Long-Lewis Ford relocated its car and light truck sales and service division to a new state-of-the-art, 82,000-square-foot facility in Hoover in 1999. The Sterling truck operation remains at the Bessemer Super Highway location. Long-Lewis sold the Cullman dealership in 1999.

After over a century of business in Alabama, Long-Lewis continues to thrive at the beginning of the new millennium. The company is still guided by the families that gave it birth and nurtured its growth. Dwight N. Burrell succeeded his father, Vaughn Burrell, as president of Long-Lewis in 1996.

Vaughn Burrell, who remains active in the company, says "Long-Lewis will be a force in the community for years to come." ■

Long-Lewis Ford relocated its car and light truck sales and service division to a new state-of-the-art, 82,000-square-foot facility in Hoover in 1999.

Jack's

After opening 40 years ago as a walk-up hamburger stand, Alabama's first fast-food restaurant chain, Jack's, is still in the minds of many Alabamians. The original store opened in 1960 in Homewood. The menu was simple, 15-cent hamburgers and fries and 20-cent shakes. The legacy of Jack's began. Due to its popularity, restaurants opened throughout the southeastern part of the country. Jack's grand openings were a big hit with parents and kids, with special appearances from local celebrities.

In the early years, children received 100 percent of Jack's marketing. Jack's sponsored Cousin Cliff, Bozo the Clown, and Sergeant Jack, who was named after the hamburger chain. Many Birmingham residents remember growing up with Cousin Cliff, enjoying hamburgers and singing the original Jack's jingle on the *Cousin Cliff Show*.

The jingle "Jack's Hamburgers for 15 cents are so good… good… good, you'll go back, back, back to Jack's, Jack's, Jack's for more… more… more." This jingle is still remembered by Alabama natives today. The jingle was composed by Henry Kimbrell and produced by Ed Boutwell.

Benny LaRussa, president and owner, started a relationship with Jack's by purchasing a single franchise in the '60s. In 1979, LaRussa decided to devote all of his attention toward his new hobby. After 27 years in the grocery business, he formed Big B Food Systems, Ltd. and bought a franchise territory of 13 units. Between 1979 and 1988 the franchise was expanded from 13 to 33 units.

The original Jack's opened in 1960 in Homewood. The menu was simple, 15-cent hamburgers and fries and 20-cent shakes.

In 1989, Big B Food Systems purchased total franchise rights to the Jack's concept. From 1989 to 1993, 15 Jack's locations opened.

In 1994, Big B Food Systems, Ltd. changed its name to Jack's Family Restaurants, Inc. Presently Jack's operates 63 locations throughout North Alabama, one in Mississippi, and one in Tennessee.

"Customer service has made Jack's the successful company it is," says LaRussa. "We've been able to grow and thrive in a highly competitive business by treating our customers right. If you come into Jack's to order a meal, you're going to be greeted with a smile and a friendly attitude. People tell us they notice the difference."

Jack's takes a very active role in the communities it serves. "We sponsor youth activities and festivals. We're active with muscular dystrophy and juvenile diabetes campaigns. People see us active in their community, and when they want to go out to eat, they think of Jack's," LaRussa said.

Jack's is one of the few homegrown, home-operated businesses in Alabama. Currently new locations are opening at a rate of four per year with locations chosen very selectively.

"We look forward to each new day as an opportunity to serve families and help our communities," LaRussa says. It is this attitude that will continue to make Jack's a success during its next 40 years. ▪

Benny LaRussa, president and owner, started a relationship with Jack's by purchasing a single franchise in the '60s. Photo by Randal Crow.

Parkman Cattle Co., Inc.

Richard Dean Parkman came to Montgomery from Seale, Alabama, in 1964 with $20 he had borrowed from his mother and his saddle. That's all he had in worldly goods, but he had a strong heart, will, and backbone to achieve his goals in life.

After being in the army for two years with time in Vietnam, he married Brenda Shipp Parkman in 1968. They have two sons, James Brendon Parkman and Richard Brent Parkman.

With Brenda by his side, they incorporated their business, Parkman Cattle Co., Inc. in 1977 and leased a pasture and an old wooden barn. Dean would go to the stockyards and buy cattle while Brenda kept the books. They both worked in the barn, sorting, shaping, and shipping cattle.

As Parkman Cattle continued to grow, the old wooden barn was too small to hold the inventory. Opportunities began to arise and there was no holding back on a long-imagined dream. Dean and Brenda bought 1,000 acres of land located in Bullock County. Later they were fortunate enough to purchase 3,000 acres located on Highway 231 South in Montgomery County. There they built a state-of-the-art livestock facility where they could process cattle with ease. They buy cattle throughout the Southeast and bring them into the barn, where they sort the different classes of cattle by quality, age, weight, and color for shipping. The trucks are loaded with approximately 50,000 pounds of cattle each. They are shipped to customers and to feedlots in the Midwest and up North. The Parkmans also graze cattle on their land and place thousands of cattle on contract grazing every year across the country from the peanut farmers in south Georgia to the wheat farmers in the Midwest. This gives the farmers an opportunity to receive an additional income after their crops have been harvested.

Dean and Brenda are especially fortunate because their sons take an active part in the company, along with their wives Kadra Guy Parkman and Dana Russell Parkman. The support and teamwork of all the employees are what makes the Parkman's business enjoyable and successful.

Parkman Cattle's success comes from the loyalty of the customers that they have had since the beginning of the company. These customers continue to order on a weekly basis because they are pleased with the class, health, and quality of cattle they receive. Although many changes have taken place throughout the years, Parkman Cattle's main goal is to meet the needs of its customers.

Although the future is uncertain regarding the cattle industry, as long as there are cattle there will be "Parkman Cattle."

Dana, Brent, Brenda, Dean, Kadra, and Brendon.

Enterprise Index

●●

McDowell Knight Roedder &
Sledge, L.L.C.
63 South Royal Street, Suite 900
PO Box 350
Mobile, Alabama 36601
Phone: 334-432-5300
Fax: 334-432-5303
www.mcdowellknight.com
Page 213

Mercedes-Benz U.S. International
Inc.
1 Mercedes Drive
Vance, Alabama 35403
Phone: 205-507-3300
Fax: 205-507-3700
www.mbusi.com
Pages 172-173

Methodist Homes for the Aging
1520 Cooper Hill Road
Birmingham, Alabama 35210
Phone: 205-951-2442
Fax: 205-956-5001
Pages 248-249

Mitsubishi Polysilicon
7800 Mitsubishi Lane
Theodore, Alabama 36582
Phone: 334-443-6440
Fax: 334-443-6406
www.mpsac.com
Page 186

Natural Decorations, Inc.
PO Box 847
Brewton, Alabama 36427
777 Industrial Park Drive
Brewton, Alabama 36426
Phone: 334-867-7077
        800-522-2627
Fax: 334-867-2525
        877-578-5101
E-mail: ndi@ndihq.com
www.ndihq.com
Pages 258-261

Noland Health Services
PO Box 925
Fairfield, Alabama 35064
Phone: 205-783-8440
Fax: 205-783-8441
E-mail:
pnichols@nolandhealth.com
Pages 240-241

Parkman Cattle Co., Inc.
PO Box 240129
Montgomery, Alabama 36124
Phone: 334-281-3522
Fax: 334-288-3727
Page 267

Personnel Resources
PO Box 8186
Dothan, Alabama 36304
Phone: 334-794-8722
Fax: 334-671-2785
Page 210

Protective Industrial Insurance
Company of Alabama, Inc.
2300 11th Avenue North
Birmingham, Alabama 35234
Phone: 205-323-5256
Fax: 205-251-7614
E-mail: piicoins@aol.com
Page 199

Quality Research
4901 D Corporate Drive
Huntsville, Alabama 35805-6201
Phone: 256-722-0190
Fax: 256-864-8200
E-mail: quality@qr.com
www.qr.com
Page 182

Rhecm Manufacturing
PO Box 244020
Montgomery, Alabama 36124-4020
Phone: 334-260-1500
www.rheem.com
Pages 174-175

Robinson Foundry, Inc.
PO Box 1235
505 Robinson Court
Alexander City, Alabama 35011
Phone: 256-329-8481
Fax: 256-329-0503
E-mail: sales@robinsonfoundry.com
www.robinsonfoundry.com
Page 183

Saginaw Pipe Co., Inc.
PO Box 8
1980 Highway 31
Saginaw, Alabama 35137
Phone: 205-664-3670
Fax: 205-663-6632
E-mail: info@saginawpipe.com
www.saginawpipe.com
Page 185

Saks Incorporated
750 Lakeshore Parkway
Birmingham, Alabama 35211
Phone: 205-940-4000
www.saksincorporated.com
Pages 254-257

Sherlock, Smith & Adams, Inc.
3047 Carter Hill Road
Montgomery, Alabama 36111
Phone: 334-263-6481
Fax: 334-264-4509
E-mail: mcdurmont_d@ssainc.com
www.ssainc.com
Page 208

Southeast Alabama Medical Center
1108 Ross Clark Circle
Dothan, Alabama 36301
Phone: 334-793-8107
Fax: 334-793-8010
E-mail: lodierno@samc.org
www.samc.org
Page 250

Thompson Tractor Company, Inc.
PO Box 10367
Birmingham, Alabama 35202
Phone: 205-841-8601
Fax: 205-841-5028
Page 180

Touchstone Energy®
PO Box 550
Andalusia, Alabama 36420
Phone: 334-427-3000
Fax: 334-222-3778
www.powersouth.com
Pages 156-159

The Troy State University System
216 Adams Administration Building
Troy, Alabama 36082
Phone: 334-670-3196
Fax: 334-670-3274
E-mail: paffairs@trojan.troyst.edu
www.troyst.edu
Pages 234-235

The UAB Health System
500 Building, Suite 416
500 22nd Street South
Birmingham, Alabama 35294-0500
Phone: 205-934-9999
Fax: 205-975-6095
www.health.uab.edu
Pages 244-247

The University of Alabama
Box 870294
Tuscaloosa, Alabama 35487-0294
Phone: 205-348-6010
www.ua.edu
Pages 222-225

The University of Alabama at
Birmingham
AB 1320
1530 3rd Avenue South
Birmingham, Alabama 35294-0113
Phone: 205-934-3884
Fax: 205-975-6147
www.uab.edu
Pages 230-233

The University of Alabama in
Huntsville
301 Sparkman Drive
Huntsville, Alabama 35805
Phone: 256-824-6120
www.uah.edu
Pages 228-229

U.S. Pipe and Foundry Company
3300 First Avenue North
Birmingham, Alabama 35222
Phone: 205-254-7000
Fax: 205-254-7150
E-mail: meades@uspipe.com
www.uspipe.com
Page 181

Vulcan Materials Company
1200 Urban Center Drive
Birmingham, Alabama 35242
Phone: 205-298-3000
Fax: 205-298-2963
www.vulcanmaterials.com
Pages 176-177

●●●●●●●●●●●●●●●●●●●●●●

PATRONS:

Dunbarton Corp.

Smith Services of AL, Inc.

●●●●●●●●●●●●●●●●●●●●●●

Index

Acknowledgements

Information used in the creation of this book was contributed by
Air University Public Affairs, Maxwell Air Force Base;
and Herb Vanderberry, Alabama Agricultural Statistics Service.

The following web sites were used:
www.alfafarmers.org
www.marriotthotels.com

Contributing Photographers

Annette Bitto, Auburn Chamber of Commerce
Jimmy Carlisle, Alabama Farmers Federation
Peggy Collins, Alabama Bureau of Travel and Tourism
Chip Cooper
Elizabeth DeRamus
Barry Fikes

Robert Fouts
Steve Goraum
Jeff Helme, Alabama Farmers Federation
Pat McDonogh
Paul Sumners
Scott Wiseman

Bibliography

Atkins, Leah Rawls; Flynt, Wayne; Rogers, William Warren; Ward, Robert David. *Alabama: The History of a Deep South State.* Tuscaloosa, Alabama: The University of Alabama Press, 1994.

Bush, George S. *An American Harvest: The Story of Weil Brothers Cotton.* Englewood Cliffs, New Jersey: Prentice-Hall, 1982.

Donelson, Cathalynn. *Mobile: Sunbelt Center of Opportunity.* Northridge, California: Windsor Publications, 1986.

Flynt, Wayne. *Mine, Mill & Microchip: A Chronicle of Alabama Enterprise.* Northridge, California: Windsor Publications, 1987.

Ibid. *Montgomery: An Illustrated History.* Woodland Hills, California: Windsor Publications, 1980.

Greenhaw, Wayne and Holland, Kathy. *Montgomery: Center Stage in the South.* Chatsworth, California: Windsor Publications, 1990.

Greenhaw, Wayne. *Montgomery: The Biography of a City.* Montgomery, Alabama: Montgomery Advertiser, 1993.

Griffith, Lucille. *Alabama: A Documentary History to 1900.* Tuscaloosa, Alabama: The University of Alabama Press, 1968.

O'Donnell, Joe. *Birmingham: Magic City Renaissance.* Montgomery, Alabama: Community Communications, Inc., 1992.